THE MOUNT COOK WAY

By the same author
Ski-plane Adventure

THE
MOUNT COOK WAY

*The First Fifty Years
of the Mount Cook Company*

by
Harry Wigley

Collins

AUCKLAND SYDNEY LONDON

Dedicated to the Directors and Staff,
past and present, who have laboured so
hard and so loyally to make RLW's
vision come true.

First published 1979
William Collins Publishers Ltd
Box 1, Auckland

© 1979 The Mount Cook Group Limited
ISBN 0 00 216953 3

Typeset by Jacobson Typesetters Ltd. Auckland
Printed in Hong Kong

Contents

Illustrations

Author's Note

MUCH OF THE MATERIAL in this book has been gleaned from newspaper cuttings, from old correspondence files and from advertising and publicity material.

The history of transport is the history of the pioneering development of the provinces of Canterbury and Otago. The Hocken and other libraries have material which is available to people for research today and in the future. It will always be there as the bones of the subject, but the meat — the tales told by drivers, guides and others round the fires of wayside inns, or in the staffrooms and bars of The Hermitage and in Queenstown is not recorded, and will be lost as the raconteurs and the men of action die out. For sixty years I have listened with rapt attention to these tales, some tall, some factual, some line-shooting, and some secondhand which have lost nothing in the retelling. Thus in many ways I provide a bridge which links today's generation with the pioneers.

Nearly all the people involved in the company for its first fifty years are gone, so I am concerned to get as much as possible recorded before I join them.

Two people will always give two versions of the same incident, so do not blow me out if you find the odd mistake. Some facts I have been unable to check through one cause or another, but I have endeavoured to paint some meat on the bones of fact and I hope you will find the picture life size.

H.R.W.

THE MOUNT COOK WAY

1

Foundations

A FINAL MUFFLED EXPLOSION rattled in their exhausts, and the engines of the two little motor-cars died, as if tired out by their long journey.

This had begun in Timaru twenty-two hours earlier. They had traversed 210 kilometres of rough country, unformed roads, and unbridged streams; it was the first time ever that one of these new horseless carriages had travelled to The Hermitage, Mt Cook.

Although it was four o'clock in the morning, the two drivers and their passengers were rather expecting a rousing welcome from the management and guests of the hotel. After all, they had made an epic trip which was destined — and indeed intended — to speed the development of the area and put it on the maps of the world in a way that no other single incident could have done.

The noise of the engines ceased, the smell of oil and petrol fumes hung in the still atmosphere, and the four men awaited the arrival of the manager, his staff, or even the guests, who would surely have been wakened by the arrival of two rowdy motor-cars at this untimely hour of the morning.

But no one showed up. They tramped round the building, knocking on sundry doors, and at last a drowsy member of the staff poked his head out of one of the side doors, told them the hotel was full, and went back to bed.

Dog-tired, they pulled the two small cars together, covered them over with a tarpaulin and dozed off to sleep in their seats.

This first trip from Timaru to Mt Cook by motor-car had proved that it was possible to cut the journey down from three days to one day. The journey had begun at 6am the previous day, when the two single-cylinder two-seater De Dion cars, one driven by RLW with F. M. Marchant, engineer for the Mackenzie County Council as passenger, and the other by John Rutherford of Opawa station accompanied by his son John, drove out of Timaru. John Rutherford had bought a De Dion about the same time as RLW and, as he had driven the first horse-drawn coach to The Hermitage, he was anxious to drive the first motor-car there as well. He suggested to RLW that they should do the trip together with the two cars, and so the end of the era of the horse-drawn coaches began to close.

They had foregathered in Timaru on 5 February 1906, checked their vehicles over thoroughly, loaded up supplies of petrol, oil and spare tyres, and prepared themselves for a six o'clock start the next morning.

Away sharp on time, it was not long before they were in trouble, and RLW used to recall, with a rather wicked grin on his face, that they had run over two dogs and mended three punctures before they arrived at Washdyke, only six kilometres out. (It is not surprising that the carnage among the dogs was fairly heavy, for cars were few and far between in those days, and the dogs would be infuriated by the noise, chasing the beast along the road for some distance, snapping at the tyres and barking.)

The first part of the journey went reasonably well, and as they chuffed through Fairlie, fifty-nine kilometres out, the locals were lining the main streets to cheer them on their way. Soon after leaving Fairlie, the Wigley car ran a big-end bearing and the other was sent back to Fairlie for spare parts. All through that day they bounced and jolted along the rough track, stopping frequently to examine the fords over creeks, to mend punctures and to refuel, and late in the afternoon they left Tekapo for Pukaki, which they reached after nearly twelve hours on the road, having covered 154 kilometres.

There were not many hours of daylight left when they launched themselves at 6pm to cover the final fifty-nine kilometres to The Hermitage. Fording unbridged streams, negotiating steep cuttings on to terraces, bogging down in swampy waterlogged stretches of the road — all these had made the going quite tough enough in daylight, but it must have been verging on the impossible when the sun went down and they had to rely on feeble acetylene headlights.

It was drizzling when they left Pukaki and with the failing daylight and no distant views of the magnificent Aorangi to inspire them, it must have appeared to be really a trip into the unknown.

The final stage of fifty-nine kilometres took them ten hours at an average speed of less than 6 km/h, a pace which the horse-drawn coaches could have equalled with ease.

Rodolph Wigley was the son of the Hon. T. H. Wigley, an enterprising pioneer who had successfully run cattle on the Murray River in Australia for a number of years before coming to New Zealand and taking up Balmoral station of North Canterbury and, later, Opua station in South Canterbury. He married a sister of William Sefton Moorhouse, a Superintendent of Canterbury and, many years after her death, Caroline Lysaght, who was RLW's mother.

RLW was educated at Christ's College, Christchurch where, apart from being in the First XV, he had an undistinguished career. His well-thumbed and pencilled textbooks show that his main interests were in things mechanical and electrical. On leaving school he returned to Opua, where he established a well-equipped workshop which held his interest a lot more than the farm did.

He had a lathe and various other tools, and from a kitset he bought from England he built a steam-engine which he used to power a crude sort of tractor made up from old reaper-and-binder wheels and other junk picked up around the farm. There is no record of how successful it was, or what became of it. He also dabbled in electricity and built a spark-coil which could throw a hefty spark of nearly three centimetres — and he satisfied his impish sense of humour by connecting it to doorknobs and other places where he could give unsuspecting people a jolt.

RLW was a big man in every way. He stood 193 centimetres tall in his stockinged feet and hung, in his prime, over 90 kilos on a fairly gangling frame. He had large, practical-looking but sensitive hands, and a long reach, as we kids learned to our cost on many occasions! His brown curly hair turned prematurely grey and then pure white as he got older, and this was matched by a large fierce-looking moustache, which diminished in size over the years until it disappeared completely when he was about fifty. Dark brown eyes, often sparkling with fun, were set in a ruddy complexion, and when telling one of his many stories, they would light up and the tears would roll down his cheeks.

He was a good hater, and when he got his knife into someone it was no temporary thing. He kept it in and would give it an occasional stir, but as a rule he liked people and got on well and was very popular with most of them. He never asked his staff to do anything that he was not prepared to do himself, and he inspired outstanding loyalty and enthusiasm amongst them. Many of them stayed with him for many years. Everywhere he went, his strong personality stood out, and his multitude of visionary and ambitious schemes were helped along by his charm and persuasiveness with cabinet ministers and other people in authority.

Money he tended to treat with disdain. The success of any venture, so far as he was concerned, was to get it operating to his satisfaction; whether it was profitable or not was of secondary importance. This attitude, and his unorthodox methods of raising finance for his various projects, were termed financial irresponsibility by some bank managers and members of the Company board, but they no doubt had their own skins to look after. The fact remains that a lot of the pioneering successes that RLW achieved would never have got off the ground if profitability had been an essential requirement.

A letter I received recently from Joe Malcolm gives a glimpse of RLW as seen in the 1920s by a young official in the Government Tourist Bureau. Joe had made his first trip through Milford, Queenstown and Mt Cook in 1927, and fifty years or later, after a long and successful career in the Department, and on the Meat Board, he had travelled through the area again on one of the Company's tours.

He wrote: 'My mind goes back to the legendary R. L. Wigley who, when I was a cadet, used to come into the Dunedin office, a greatly loved pioneer of the tourist industry with dreams and ideas that in those days seemed impossible of achievement. Facilities just didn't exist, and there was no money for their expansion, yet he talked of the future with faith and enthusiasm even though at the time he was struggling to find the rent for The Hermitage. In some hard times that followed, I know that the pay-packets of some of his staff were lean and even sometimes empty; yet they stayed on because they too had been infected by the bug of Tourism and fully believed that RLW's dreams were bound to come true.'

Over the years, with two wars and an economic depression, he had some real worries, financial and otherwise, in keeping the firm going; but he had tremendous courage, and nothing ever seemed to get him down, although my mother has said in her memoirs that he did have occasional moments of doubt and discouragement.

RLW's first road vehicle was a Stanley steam car, and by the hilarious tales he used to tell about it, he must have spent more time chugging around South Canterbury than working on the family farm. It was badly underpowered, could not maintain an adequate steam pressure for long, and had to be halted every few kilometres to allow the steam-pressure to build up again. He finally disposed of it and bought his first petrol motor-car. This was the little two-seater De Dion, which had a single-cylinder four-stroke engine of 6 hp, and a differential and gearbox very similar in principle to those used today. It would bowl along at 40-50 km/h under favourable conditions, and must have been reasonably reliable, for RLW did some quite long journeys in it, including the Mt Cook trip already described.

It was railed from Christchurch to Timaru and he took delivery of it at the railway station where, although he had never driven a car before, he succeeded in starting and driving it away in a fairly erratic fashion. With his enquiring turn of mind and mechanical knowledge, it would not have been long before he had taken it to pieces to examine its innards and to find out what made it work.

Mechanically, it must have been reasonably reliable for its vintage, but its tyres suffered frequent damage from sharp stones, horseshoe nails and debris shaken off other vehicles by the rough state of the roads. Occasionally it would encounter a hill too steep for its limited horsepower to climb, and this was overcome by turning it around and going up in reverse, which had a lower gear-ratio than the lowest forward gear.

The car was known as 'The Beetle' and served RLW faithfully for many years for his own personal business, taking mechanics up to breakdowns, carrying mail and so on until it was finally lost in a fire which destroyed the firm's garage in about 1913.

Around about 1903-4 (the dates are a bit hazy), RLW sold out his interest in the family farm and went into engineering, at first in the form of steam traction-engines. He formed a partnership with a man named Sam Thornley, and the firm of Wigley & Thornley operated these engines in South Canterbury, threshing oats, wheat and barley, and carting wool and other produce in and out of the Mackenzie Country.

Traction-engines were at this period rapidly supplanting the wagons drawn by teams of fourteen to sixteen bullocks or horses in back-country transportation. They could pull far heavier loads and would average some 20 km/h as against the 3 or 4 km/h of the teams and their wagons. They were also in universal demand for threshing the farmers' grain crops; the engine would tow the threshing-mill, two or three trucks and the 'calaboose' — a sort of four-wheeled caravan in which the crew slept and ate — right up to the stack of grain. When the mill had done its job, the grain was loaded on to the trucks and towed off down to the railhead.

With the rich smoke from the funnel, the whirling dust from the mill, and the oil and coal-dust of the engine, it was a pretty grimy business, and the facilities for washing and bathing — if any — would be some small local pond or creek. The outfit might be away from base for many days on end, living in the same sweaty clothes, unshaven and dirty, and you could smell them upwind for all of fifty metres. RLW used to say that the smell in the calaboose got so fruity that he preferred to sleep on the ground underneath it.

For the next two or three years he travelled the engines continuously up and down the Mackenzie Country, through a landscape always dominated by distant Aorangi — Mt Cook — overlord of the high Alps. In one way and another it was to dominate his life.

His mother had made a camping trip to Mt Cook (see Appendix II) in 1877, several years before her marriage, and she may well have kindled his interest in the area. From the time that he left school onwards, RLW was a man of the mountains, and one who always wanted others to share his delight in them.

2

The First Hermitage and its Successor

THE EARLY HISTORY of the Southern Alps and of the Mackenzie Country is somewhat beyond the scope of this book, but a short account of it is to be found in Appendix I. From this we see that it was not until 1862 that Julius von Haast and Arthur Dudley Dobson made the first survey of the Mt Cook area and estimated the height of Aorangi.

Their work generated immediate interest and publicity, and it was not long before visitors, including some ambitious climbers, were setting up expeditions to explore the area and competing with each other for the honour of the first ascent of New Zealand's highest peak. The Governor, Sir George Bowen, visited the region in 1873 and, after being shown round by the local runholder, was so impressed by it that he wrote to the Royal Geographical Society in London about its beauties and its possibilities as a challenge to mountaineers and artists.

The glowing reports of Sir George and other distinguished visitors had given such publicity to the Mt Cook region that more and more people became interested in paying it a visit. No accommodation was provided, so people had to travel in on horseback and camp out in tents. It was nobody's business to provide permanent accommodation or a coach service, and the first Hermitage seems to have been built almost by accident.

Governor Bowen had been greatly concerned about the destruction of the vegetation of the area by the settlers, yet it is probable that much of the burning-off was done hundreds of years before by the Morioris or the earliest Polynesian settlers who set alight to the bush to flush out the moas. There is evidence that most of the hillsides were covered by bush hundreds of years before the arrival of the white man, and that the bush which has survived is mostly in the gullies where the early fires were unable to reach it.

There is further evidence of a more extensive bush covering the hillsides, in the form of old tree-trunks lying on the ground in the vicinity of the airfield. These trees might perhaps have grown there, yet there is no sign of any pockets left by the root systems, and it is unlikely that the bush would have grown there anyway, as the Hooker River must have spread over the area during the past two or three hundred years. It seems more likely that the logs were carried down by floodwaters, for the only trees growing in the Hooker Valley today are in the Governor's Bush, where it is unlikely that floodwaters would have reached them. It seems logical to believe then that many of the hillsides were covered in trees several hundred years ago and in times of high flood the trunks would topple into the Hooker River or Blackbirch Creek, or be carried into them by landslides or avalanches, to be carried down to where they are lying today.

There is evidence also that large trees grew alongside the Tasman Glacier. I can remember that famous alpine guide Mick Bowie telling me many years ago that he had discovered a large log lying on the clear ice of the glacier. The mystery of how it could have got there was for some time the subject of argument and conjecture among the guides and other staff of The Hermitage. Here again, the logical answer to this puzzle is that the hillsides were covered with large trees and that this log was carried on to the glacier by an avalanche or flooded stream some hundreds of years earlier. There is certainly no evidence of forests having grown on the other parts of the Tasman Glacier today, and in fact most of the terrain is above the highest level at which these New Zealand trees usually grow.

Although the main alpine area was and is so vast and rugged that it is unlikely to be extensively damaged by any human agency, in 1884 complaints were being made about the destruction of the native vegetation, particularly the bush and the native lilies and daisies, by grazing and burning. In that year a petition was forwarded to the Government through Captain Suther, the Parliamentary representative for Gladstone, as the Fairlie district was then known. As a result of this, M. C. (Frank) Huddleston of Timaru, a fine painter in watercolour and a surveyor, was appointed ranger for the Mt Cook area.

While acting as ranger he became interested in establishing some visitor-accommodation there, and bought freehold sections of about twelve hectares near the base of the Mueller Glacier. On this land the first Hermitage was built. It was apparently a small cob building, and the depression in the ground from which the clay for the sun-dried bricks was excavated was filled in with water to form a pond, a feature of all the photographs of the early Hermitage. In 1885 Huddleston sold his land to the Mount Cook-Hermitage Company, which was formed to create a Swiss-type alpine village.

The Mount Cook-Hermitage Co. ran its own coach service between Fairlie and The Hermitage. They bought the best available vehicles, which included a brake capable of carrying sixteen passengers, and two twelve-passenger coaches. Francis Hayter of the Rollesby run, who was the first secretary of the Company, reported in his diary of 1 December 1886: 'The first day of the regular coach to Mt Cook — one tourist went up.'

The first coach to reach The Hermitage was a six-in-hand driven by John Rutherford, the same John Rutherford who drove one of the first two motor-cars to reach Mt Cook with RLW in 1906, twenty years later.

Some of the regular coach drivers included Mortimer Davey, Jack Summerville, and Billie Barry, a hunchback. In 1892 financial losses caused the Mount Cook-Hermitage Company to suspend its coaching service, but it was reopened at the end of the year. An opposition firm entered the field in January 1888; the new coach put on the road by McLeod & Rossiter was 'large and commodious', according to the newspapers, and it was driven by Frank Rossiter, one of the best four-in-hand drivers in New Zealand and a man of great nerve and experience. A few years ago, when the Burkes Pass Hotel was being rebuilt, an advertising card was found in the old woodwork, and this is reproduced among the illustrations of this book.

The new company increased its equipment to include four covered-in coaches, four wagonettes, and a number of buggies and gigs. Before long they had built up a reputation for conducting one of the most up-to-date coaching services in New Zealand, and drivers such as Charlie Wheeler enjoyed a national reputation for his handling of the horses.

When the horse-drawn coach service was in operation, it took a passenger three days to travel between Timaru and Mt Cook. The first day was by train from Timaru to Fairlie, where the night was spent at the Gladstone Grand or the other hotel. The second day the coach travelled from Fairlie to Pukaki, with lunch and a change of horses at the Tekapo Hotel, and the third day was spent travelling from Pukaki to The Hermitage, with a stop at The Rest.

In the old records The Rest is referred to as Kuri Tapu. It was halfway between Pukaki and The Hermitage, and here the passengers rested and ate lunch before continuing the journey with a change of horses. Later this place became the head-quarters of the Ministry of Works gang that maintained the road between Pukaki and The Hermitage, but it was not for this reason, as many people seemed to think, that Kuri Tapu was renamed The Rest.

The land between Fairlie and Burkes Pass was snugly developed in those days, with the fields fenced and cultivated for the growing of crops such as oats or barley, or sown down in grass for the grazing of stock. The holdings were relatively small, and houses dotted the landscape with comparatively young trees around them to give shelter. The township of Fairlie Creek, or Gladstone, where the railway ended, was a sizeable village with a couple of pubs and a few shops — and, until he reached Burkes Pass, a tourist was in a reasonably developed rural landscape. The road, with wire or gorse fences on either side, was passably formed and was probably metalled as far as the village of Burkes Pass, then the headquarters of the Mackenzie County Council.

On the far side of Burkes Pass the character of the landscape changed dramatically. Instead of the trim green fields, and the trees, houses and hedges, the flat brown featureless Mackenzie Plains stretched endlessly on and on to the foot of the Southern Alps, which then rose steeply to their rugged, ice-covered peaks. In the twenty-six kilometres between the top of Burkes Pass and Lake Tekapo there were no dwellings at all, while on the forty-two kilometres from Tekapo to Pukaki there were only four — Balmoral, The Wolds, The Irishman, and Simons Pass. Between Pukaki and Mt Cook, fifty-eight kilometres, there were only two, Glentanner and Birch Hill stations.

The Mackenzie Plains were wide open, with very few fences, and the bullocks hauling the wagons were free to zigzag their way over the plains in the general direction of the fords over the rivers. The coaches followed the erratic tracks made by the bullock wagons. The tracks were largely unformed and unmetalled and in the spring, when the ground was starting to thaw out after being icebound all winter, they became quag-mires. The ground would be frozen down to a depth of forty-five centimetres or more, and when the surface thawed there was nowhere for the water to go, so the road remained in a porridge-like state until the ground below had thawed right through to allow drainage to begin.

Once the frost was out of the ground, it would dry out very rapidly and soon be pulverised into dust by the traffic. Clouds of dust which could be seen for miles marked the passage of vehicles and, winter by winter, as the process was repeated, the roads got deeper and deeper, until they were over a metre below the level of the surrounding ground and very little wider than the tracks of the vehicles. For many kilometres it was impossible for vehicles to pass each other, and in other places it was possible only with great difficulty.

If two vehicles did inadvertently meet head-on, they had no option but for one of them to back-track until a passing place could be found; but such encounters did not happen often, as very few vehicles used the road — even in the early 1930s you might drive from Tekapo to Pukaki, for instance, without encountering anything more on the road than an occasional sheep or rabbit.

The road from Pukaki to The Hermitage did not suffer from frost-heave and mud as seriously as did the road from Burkes Pass to Pukaki, but it produced problems of a different kind. It threaded its way between the lake and the high Ben Ohau Range which, at certain times of the year, collected a considerable amount of precipitation in the form of rain and snow. This cascaded off the hillsides in streams of various sizes and, as they crossed the road in spate, they gouged it out. Frequently twenty or thirty eroded streambeds would have to be forded between Pukaki and The Hermitage, which made for rough and slow travelling whether by coach or motor-car.

Two days' journey by horse-drawn coach from Fairlie to Mt Cook over the flat, almost bare Mackenzie Plains, and then the almost endless weaving in and out of the gullies, along the terraces, down into the creeks and up the other sides between Pukaki and Mt Cook, with the incessant bumping and swaying of the coach, ought to have seemed dreary to those early travellers. Jolted every time the steel-tyred wheels struck a stone in the road, chilled by the bitter winds which so frequently sweep down the valley, or soaked by torrential rainstorms, travellers from overseas might have wondered where they were going and why they had undertaken such a journey. Yet they found it richly rewarding, judging by the many exciting accounts they wrote of the spectacle of mountains and glaciers.

The first Hermitage was a unique mountain hotel, with traditions all of its own. It had an air about it, an atmosphere, that set it apart from all others. Isolation had given it character, and it attracted in its day many celebrities from New Zealand and overseas, as well as internationally known climbers.

On an average summer's morning in the old days, guides would be seen carrying ice-axes, ropes and rucksacks, dressed in the riding strides and puttees of the day, and large hats with the smoked-glass goggles to protect the eyes from snow-glare, stretched round the headband. Wearing heavy nailed boots they strolled round the place chatting to the guests and giving the impression that this was a professionally-organised base for alpine expeditions — as indeed it was.

Frank Huddlestone, the first manager, made some interesting comments in his annual reports to The Hermitage Company. In 1886 there were 125 visitors to The Hermitage, and he notes: 'The actual number, although not large, was not, I venture to think, so bad in itself. The real mischief was in the extreme shortness of their stay, the average amounting only to about one clear day. This state of things may be accounted for principally by the disappointing (to use a mild term) action of the coach-proprietor. Needless delays expended on the road materially shortened the time at their disposal. Extra and, I might add, unexpected expenses were also incurred by tourists having to pay for the keep of the driver and the price of the conveyance while it was lying idle at The Hermitage. Washouts were always likely to maroon the visitors after heavy rain ... Another cause which ought to be mentioned was the uncertainty attending the return, because of the encroachment of the Tasman River in one place which, before the road was opened, caused people to hurry down at the slightest indication of a nor'west rain.'

Huddleston retired from the management of the Mount Cook-Hermitage Company in 1894, and soon afterwards it was in financial difficulties. It changed hands for the first time two years later in 1896, when the Government took it over. More and more people came as the roads improved and bridges were built, and when the new Mount Cook Motor Company began running cars on the old coach road in 1906 they chuffed up Burkes Pass from Fairlie and across the Mackenzie Country to The Hermitage in ten and a half hours at an average of less than 15 km/h. Increasing numbers of tourists were flocking to The Hermitage each season, and each year the demand for more accommodation became more acute. After forty years, the old building had been so battered by the weather and damaged by fire and flood that it was not considered worthwhile repairing it.

Sir John Findlay was asked to recommend an alternative site and the Government decided to build on the bluff overlooking the Hooker River, which was his choice. This was practically the same spot as that selected by Big Mick Raddock of Birch Hill station in 1873 when he set up a camp for Sir George Bowen. When Sir George was preparing to leave, he shook Big Mick by the hand and said, 'Take care of the bush where we camped. See that no harm comes to it.'

Big Mick is said to have replied 'By crikey I will, Your Excellency.' And so he did. He named the place Governor's Bush, and it has been preserved from that day to this by successive owners of Birch Hill station, by the owners and lessees of The Hermitage, and by the Mount Cook Parks Board.

The first Hermitage was further damaged by heavy floods as work began on the new building. Freda du Faur, an Australian, one of the most famous of the first generation of women climbers in New Zealand and the first woman to climb Mt Cook, was there when in January 1913, after sixteen days of rain, the Mueller broke its banks at Kea Point. She was talking to Peter Graham, then Chief Guide, when the manager rushed up with the news that the river was making for the building. As Miss du Faur recalled later:

When we reached the front of the hotel, the yellow flood was coming straight for us, sweeping everything before it. Shrubs, uprooted trees, boulders and ice were churned about in its raging waters. At the front gate the stream divided in two, one rushing down towards Pukaki and the smaller one making for The Hermitage. Soon the front of the building was surrounded by water.

In the dim hours of the morning I was awakened by a terrific crash, it sounded as if Mt Sefton was falling into the valley. The drawing-room was filled with a shivering white-faced crowd with their most cherished possessions. Water was flowing under the front door, and over the floor of the annex (twenty rooms added the year before).

The roar that awakened me was the grinding-together of great massive boulders swept down from the Mueller moraine by the river, and deposited not ten yards from the front door.

Two months later, at the end of March, the Mueller again

flooded the building, undermining the annex still further and carrying it away from the main building, leaving it to settle into the stream that now flowed beneath it. The old building was beyond repair.

The second Hermitage was opened in 1914. In spite of the war that was raging, it must have received reasonable patronage. When the war ended, traffic increased to such an extent that RLW was frequently quoted as complaining of the shortage of accommodation, but the Department of Tourist and Health Resorts controlled The Hermitage and was reluctant to spend money on providing additional rooms. In those days the economy of the country was dependent on the farming sector, and the infant tourist industry and its few entrepreneurs, such as RLW, were looked down on by the powers-that-be. Their requests for assistance were treated with apathy.

RLW's frequent trips to Wellington to get The Hermitage enlarged met with so little success that he apparently made an offer to the Government to provide finance to increase the accommodation. The Minister's reply, quoted by the *Lyttelton Times*, would be more expected today than on 4 November 1919: 'I have definitely turned it down,' declared the Hon. Nosworthy, Minister in Charge of Tourist Resorts, when Dr Thacker asked what he proposed to do with the offer of the Mount Cook Company to spend £20,000 to supplement the accommodation at Mt Cook. The Minister added that 'he would not have private individuals coming into the Tourist Department's business'.

Not only was there a shortage of accommodation; it was also the policy of the Department to close The Hermitage down during the winter, with most of the guides and other staff being paid off until the next season. Inevitably, staff found themselves jobs elsewhere, and so not many returned to The Hermitage, creating problems with recruiting and retraining.

This was bad enough, but RLW calculated that neither The Hermitage nor the motor services could operate economically if they could not be kept in operation for twelve months of the year. He tried to persuade the Government to keep The Hermitage open for the winter and to promote skiing and other winter sports, but his pleas fell on deaf ears. As he could not operate a motor service without controlling, or at least getting the co-operation of the hotel interests, he finally approached the Government for a lease of The Hermitage. After some delays and quite a bit of bickering through the newspapers, the lease was granted.

3

The Company Takes Over

THE MOUNT COOK COMPANY took over The Hermitage in 1921. A newspaper cutting of 1922 states:

The Mount Cook Hermitage is to pass from Government control, a lease over a period of five years having been granted to the Mount Cook Motor Company, which is confident not only of making it a payable proposition by private enterprise, but also of attracting much larger numbers of tourists annually by up-to-date methods of catering for their amusement and comfort.

This decision arrived at by Cabinet does not come as a great surprise, for The Hermitage has been run at a heavy loss for years. The difficulties and peculiarities of the Mt Cook tourist trade are known by none better than the lessees. Mr R. L. Wigley has been conveying tourists to The Hermitage since 1906, and first tried to obtain a lease of it from the Government in 1908. The Company's passenger service, which began in a very small way, has grown to embrace a fleet of thirty-five passenger charabancs, and the Mt Cook route is now the greater part of one of the finest motorist roads in the Dominion. . .

As a commencement, a large building will be erected at the back of The Hermitage with a passage down the centre and rooms on either side. A sufficiency of bathrooms will be provided, and it is hoped eventually to reach the point at which all applicants can be accommodated instead of, as in the past, hundreds of people being turned away annually. An electric plant will be installed for lighting, cooking and heating the buildings, and will be used for laundry work, drying-rooms etc.

The lessees rely on having transport and accommodation under one head so as to reduce many outlays, unavoidable in the past management of The Hermitage, but they have not entered upon such a financial risk on past tourist statistics.

Although the Government was happy to be rid of the responsibility and losses in running The Hermitage, and RLW was overjoyed at the challenges and opportunities which would occur with his taking it over, not everyone was happy about the deal. The Mackenzie County Council was concerned at the loss of rates it would receive through the Government reducing the capital value of The Hermitage, and the *Timaru Herald* reported:

At the monthly meeting of the Mackenzie County Council on Monday the loss with which the Council is threatened through the Government valuation having been reduced, was discussed with some concern. The Council formerly obtained £85 by way of rates from The Hermitage, this being based on the then rate of 13-16th of a penny in the pound. The capital value of The Hermitage was £25,235, but the Valuation Department has now reduced it to £4,000, the reduction being based on the fact that this is 5 per cent of the rent (£200 per annum), which the Mount Cook Motor Company pays to the Government.

Upon taking it over, RLW started to promote the place with his usual flair and enthusiasm, and got together at The Hermitage a large number of politicians, tourist agents, members of the press, and anyone else who might push the project along. The *Timaru Herald* of 15 October 1922 stated:

It was a happy thought on the part of the Mount Cook Motor Company which led it to organise a large weekend excursion to The Hermitage, which has been taken over by the Company from the Government, and the manager, Mr R. L. Wigley, intends to reduce accommodation charges and to provide improved facilities for the entertainment of guests, and in a variety of ways to make the resort, which possesses commanding scenic attractions, a lodestar and a veritable holidaymaker's paradise for tourists from New Zealand, as well as from other countries.

As a first step towards the attainment of this object, the weekend-excursion idea was put into operation, and last evening a widely representative gathering of about one hundred persons arrived at The Hermitage where they were entertained at dinner as guests of the Company. The major portion of this large party was transported to The Hermitage from Timaru in three of the company's big touring cars and ten or twelve private cars and taxis . . . As an instance of

Mr Wigley's thoroughness it may be mentioned that he had made special arrangements for the installation of a telegraph instrument at The Hermitage in order that the press matter might be despatched during the day.

In his speech on this occasion, RLW said the Company had a big hurdle to clear but he thought they could do it. The main object would be to please the public. His idea was that his company had not only to pay a dividend but also uphold one of New Zealand's best assets. They wanted to get everyone there, the poor man as well as the wealthy man. There would be differential rates from front rooms in The Hermitage to tents in the open. There would also be differential rates for families and concessions for those who stayed for a week or longer. The Company intended to keep The Hermitage open in the winter months because, while the weather was cold, the cold was not felt nearly as severely as it was on the coast by reason of the bracing air and rare atmosphere.

Camping parties would be catered for because there were people who could not afford the high tariff of a hotel. They could cater for those at £5 a head for a fortnight at The Hermitage, including the fare to and from Timaru, and the Company would carry the stores, blankets etc. for the campers. They also intended to run a store at The Hermitage at very reasonable prices. A party of ten or twenty would receive further concessions. He had still a little failing for the aeroplane (laughter) and he hoped yet to do something in that direction. In short he endeavoured to cater for the high climber or the low climber, and the verandah-sitter.

Now, fifty-four years later, it is possible to look back and assess what RLW's visionary approach to the area has achieved. He lived to see all classes of the community being catered for, large increases in all kinds of accommodation being built there, skiing being developed in a substantial way, and many alpine huts being completed.

Today The Hermitage is one of the main tourist and holidaymakers' resorts of New Zealand, with demand for accommodation far outstripping the supply for many months of the year. Two sizable hotels have been built, as well as motels, and large modern coaches and aeroplanes are arriving and departing all day long.

Right from the early days, the hotel people kept pressing for speedier services and for the trip from Timaru to be reduced from three days to two, and then from two days to one. (Today air services bring Mt Cook within 2¼ hours of the major North Island tourist resort of Rotorua.) But while the transport operator was steadily improving the efficiency of his services, he was complaining consistently that the hotel people were not doing enough to provide the enlarged accommodation that would make his speedier services economic.

The leasing of The Hermitage by the Company did a lot to overcome these problems and the Company set out forthwith to rectify deficiencies. A graduated scale of tariffs was introduced which would cater for almost every pocket, while at the same time the standards of service and cuisine were upgraded to equal those of similar hotels in other parts of the world. Overseas chefs were employed, and The Hermitage table and wine selection became recognised as one of the best in New Zealand.

To increase the medium-priced accommodation a large building was erected at the back of The Hermitage with a passage down the centre, bedrooms on either side, and a balanced number of bathrooms. A number of tents were erected in the vicinity with wooden floors, wardrobes, and eventually electric lighting, to provide accommodation for those seeking an economy tariff.

Tours combining accommodation, transport and railway travel from all parts of New Zealand were packaged and advertised extensively. (This was probably the first time this was done, and some of the early advertisements make amusing reading today.) They had the effect of building up the traffic to Mt Cook, and through Mt Cook to the Southern Lakes in the summer.

Today many people can afford an overseas holiday of only a limited duration, so the trend has developed for them to whizz through a country like a whirlwind, seeing and doing the points of major interest, and then speeding on to the next country. 'This is Tuesday, so it must be Rotorua' sort of thing, and it cannot be denied that many people would not undertake an overseas trip if they could not do it in this fashion. It was quite different in the 1920s, when people went to Mount Cook for a holiday in the full sense of the term and stayed there for a week, two weeks or more, relaxing, mixing socially with the other guests of the house, and doing the things people enjoyed doing in that more leisurely age.

Unless a person was confined to a wheelchair he would take one of the guided walking trips of varying durations to the glaciers, mountains, and points of interest in the area. These trips would be led by one of the professional guides employed for this purpose. Usually tall, lithe, handsome, burned a deep brown by the snow, they carried an ice-axe at all times, even on gentle walks across the flat. They were the lords of their own domain with personalities as rugged as the mountains themselves. It was the fashion of the day, and half the fun of the trip, to get dressed up to look like a mountaineer, and all men and women appeared at the appropriate meeting place suitably attired in riding-strides, boots and all. Some provided their own, but others hired them at the equipment shop which, for many years, was presided over by a character by the name of Gus Gauhan, whose philosophising and instructions on procedures on climbing to his customers caused considerable amusement and created just the right atmosphere for the beginning of the day.

The sun beats fiercely down from smog-free skies on many days of the year in this area; the glare is reflected off rocks and snow and ice, and can in a very short time give people, even those with dark skins, very serious doses of sunburn and snowblindness; and so large hats and dark goggles to protect the eyes were worn while the face and the backs of the hands were liberally smeared with a white zinc ointment, all of which made the walkers look like the reincarnation of escapees from the nether regions. The party assembled at the take-off point where they met their guide, who gave them brief instructions on the trip ahead and then led them off down the track, carrying a rucksack stuffed with the lunches for the whole party.

Frequently the guides were great raconteurs and had a wealth of knowledge of the glaciers and their movements and behaviour, the peaks, the birdlife, and the vegetation of the area. As well, they were prone to do a little leg-pulling and to tell a few tall stories on the side, and as the party strolled on, stopping from time to time to revel in the mountain scene, listen to the guide, and take photographs, they would settle down as a group to enjoy the day.

At lunchtime the guide would build a fire and boil a billy of tea, while dispensing sandwiches and other items from the packed lunches. He would give the names of the peaks and glaciers in the vicinity, and tell of climbs that he had done and personalities that he had met. Or perhaps, if it was springtime, he would interest his party in the display of alpine flowers which in those days grew in profusion almost everywhere — not only the large spectacular white Mt Cook lilies, the big double daisies, the celmisias, the veronicas and hebes, but the equally attractive rock plants of many species — or he would attract a kea by waving a handkerchief on the end of his ice-axe.

Such a day would be packed full of interest, and the party would return to The Hermitage pleasantly tired and thoroughly satisfied with their excursion into the world of the mountaineer, the glorious mountain landscape of black-and-white, and the beauty of our alpine flora.

The most popular day trips from The Hermitage were to the Stocking Glacier under the Footstool, to the Red Lake on Mt Sebastopol, to the Sealey lakes on the Sealey Range. Popular longer trips, where a night would be spent in an alpine hut, were to the Mueller Hut, the Hooker Hut, the Ball or the Malte Brun Hut, and those who got enjoyment out of the day trips enjoyed these overnight trips even more.

Conditions at the huts were very primitive, as everything had to be carried in by manpower alone. Most of the huts consisted of two rooms, one for men, where the cooking was done, and one for women, and the only lavatory would be fifty metres or more away, a tall austere-looking building of about two metres square built over a hole in the ground — if in fact the whole edifice had not been blown away by the wind.

People were expected to bring only the small amount of clothing they could carry on their backs, and on arrival most were cheerfully tired and prepared to dive fully-dressed into the sleeping-bags provided.

The guide could carry only a limited amount of fresh food, so he prepared meals from the stock of canned goods which had been carted in by manpower in the spring. The mouth-watering smells that came from the heating of haricot beans and other foods linger in one's memory to this day!

Typical of the day trips, and one of the most popular, was the walk to the Stocking Glacier. The party leaves The Hermitage and threads its way across the tussocks of the Hooker Flat to the dead moraine of the Mueller Glacier, where matagouri, mountain ribbonwood, speargrass, and other alpine shrubs grow sparsely among the rocks and debris left behind by the retreating glacier. Soon the track dips steeply down to the river terraces, where a suspension bridge crosses the Hooker River, often a beautiful chalky blue caused by the very fine rock-powder in suspension, flowing turbulently over the large rocks in its course. From there they travel under the flank of Mt Wakefield, which is covered there in subalpine scrub and in places gouged up to a great height by tremendous shingle screes — channels of continuously downward-moving shingle.

Several species of veronica with variously coloured flowers grow along the track and, for those interested, the many species of small alpine plants — the snowberries, wild strawberries, aniseed and native edelweiss — make a search among the rocks and stones most rewarding. Numbers of small moths and large red-and-green grasshoppers move off in alarm when disturbed. Looking up from the fascinating world at one's feet, one's eyes scan the stark jumbled mass of ice and rock of the Mueller moraine and up through the clear atmosphere to the massive ice-covered face of the Moorhouse Range, rising nearly 2500 metres from the valley floor. Whichever way you look, there is something new and fascinating to observe.

The track follows the river as far as a huge glacier-worn rock to which a second suspension bridge is attached. The party threads its way round a narrow goat-track with a wire-rope handrail on one side, and a drop of twenty metres into the river below, and then come shrieks of mock-alarm as one by one they file across the wobbling bridge. From there on the track winds through large tussocks of snowgrass and spaniards which protect masses of Mt Cook lilies and celmisias growing in every cleared space.

At the bridge over the Stocking Glacier Stream the guide unburdens himself of his rucksack and goes through the routine of lighting a fire and boiling the billy for tea. Sandwiches are distributed, and in half an hour or so, when everyone is refreshed and rested, the party moves onwards and up to the glacier. The climbing gets steeper and steeper. Snow tussock gives way to the smaller alpine species of plant. The climb gets steeper and rougher, and the chatter dies away as the party concentrates its energies on reaching the target ahead, the white ice of the glacier.

When this is reached they take a breather and revel in the views spread out below them — the Hooker and Mueller Glaciers hemmed in by high mountain ranges and with Mt Cook towering over all, eleven or twelve kilometres away. The guide cuts easy steps in the clear ice and cautiously shepherds his party for a short distance over icy ridges and valleys to give them an idea of the high climber's exertions. To many it is their first experience of snow and ice, an unforgettable moment.

Returning to The Hermitage in the late afternoon, they bath, dress, do repairs to the occasional blistered heel, and then adjourn to the bar for a pre-dinner drink and to review the day's experiences with kindred spirits. It has been an exciting day of exploring a terrain astonishingly different in every way from anything they have ever known before, an experience identical with that enjoyed by the first man ever to walk up that valley.

In that era the dinner following the day's exertions would be a formal affair. The ladies would dress specially for it, many of the men would change into dinner-suits, and the tables would sparkle with white damask, gay flowers, shining silver and glittering glasses.

The Company organised alpine holidays of this kind, catered for them and encouraged people to spend a long enough period at The Hermitage to enjoy a wide variety of day-trips. It is a pity that our present-day tourist industry has to use the limited amount of accommodation to cater principally for people wishing to rush through the country in a great hurry, and that there is no encouragement for the average city person to spend his or her days exploring it with or without a guide. Even camping in the National Park is prohibited, and this excludes a very big sector of the New Zealand population, the family groups who love camping and would prefer not to live in a motel or hotel.

The opening of The Hermitage during the winter and the publicising of winter sports to support it, and increased overseas promotion by the Tourist Department, the shipping companies and the Mount Cook Motor Company all caused summer usage to increase to the extent that accommodation was always overtaxed.

The Company's transport service was capable of feeding a much larger number of hotel rooms. Also, an increase in the bedroom-capacity of The Hermitage would make it a much more economic proposition. The Company went ahead with plans to build a new wing, and this was completed in about 1924. It extended from the old part of the two-storey Hermitage to the west, and was the last word in luxury: every room had its own wash hand-basin with hot and cold water, and some of the suites even had a complete bathroom attached! This was in the days when it was routine to have to trudge down a draughty corridor to bathroom and toilet, and years before every bedroom had its own facilities.

Central heating was also installed throughout the building, with hot-water radiators in every room, and this made it a cosy place to live in, even in the depths of winter. Lighting was by acetylene gas when the building opened, but this was never very satisfactory. The lights were poor, and a lot of labour was required to maintain the system; every day heavy weights had to be winched up to the ceiling of the generating room to provide the necessary pressure, and human fallibility caused this system to be somewhat erratic.

Electricity was coming into general use and small plants operated by water-power were becoming available, so it was decided by the company to change over to electricity for lighting and heating, and to erect a hydro-electric power plant on Sawyers Creek, three or four kilometres below The Hermitage. Pipes about fifty centimetres in diameter were erected from the powerhouse near the main road to a dam 200 metres higher up in Sawyers Creek, and although the system suffered damage from floods from time to time it gave reasonably good service until The Hermitage was linked to the national grid soon after World War II.

The erection of the plant was under the control of a man who was apparently a brilliant electrical engineer but who, unknown to the Company, had never obtained (or had lost) his licences, with the result that the Company got into serious trouble with the powers-that-be for employing an unlicensed engineer. They not only got into trouble with the authorities, but had difficulty in getting the installation certified, as no one would put his signature to another man's work.

The story is told that when this engineer was excluded from his profession, he took up dairyfarming in Southland. The local power board found it was losing a considerable amount of power, and suspected leakages on one of its transmission lines. They checked and double-checked every possibility, but could never detect the leakage. This went on for something like fourteen years, when it was discovered that the ex-Hermitage electrician had run a fenceline under and parallel to the high-tension lines and had insulated a section and, with his knowledge of electricity, had been able to induce off enough power to run his cowsheds and all the heating, cooking and lighting for his private house. The power board gave him full marks for ingenuity, but prosecuted him just the same. They had some difficulty in making an assessment of what he owed them for power.

Sawyers Creek, which provided the water for the power

plant, is in a beautiful steep-sided little valley. Over its boulder-strewn bed the water cascades in a series of waterfalls and pools, and for much of its distance it runs through stands of beech forest. Where there is no forest it rises steeply into rocky bluffs and shingle screes right up to the peaks 1000 metres or more higher up.

As kids, we used to enjoy the daily walk up the pipeline with Doug Elms, who was in charge of the plant, to inspect it for damage and to clear the intake of stones and other debris. Doug wore gumboots and walked straight up the pipe itself, even where it occasionally crossed the stream on trestles seven or eight metres or so above its rocky bed. But we lacked the nerve to walk on the pipe over the big drops, and would leave it and laboriously scramble down to the stream, boulder-hop across it and climb up the other side while Doug, who used to keep a fatherly eye on us, would get rather impatient at the delay.

One day when my brother Sandy and I were about to leave the pipeline and clamber down to the stream bed, Doug turned round quickly, gathered us up, one under each arm, and lugged us across to the other side. I must have been about fourteen at the time and quite a big enough weight for one man strong and all as Doug was, to carry under one arm. I could feel myself slipping all the way across, and with nothing but fresh air between us and the creek below, Sandy and I were quite relieved to reach the other side. The fact that Doug never offered to carry us again spoke volumes!

Right from the early days of the first Hermitage, horses had been used to transport climbers and others to the Ball Hut. The horses had a limited capacity, and with their harness always wearing out, and the need for constant shoeing, and saddle-sores and other ailments, they needed a lot of costly care and attention. As well, they had to be kept on over the winter, and fed for a lot of the time when the ground was under snow and they could not work for their living.

Supplies for the huts and also wood, corrugated iron and other building materials were carried by trains of packhorses to the Ball Hut, a slow and cumbersome means of transport. Occasionally a horse would slide off a narrow track and injure itself and its load, and occasionally something would frighten the lead horses and the whole packtrain would bolt, strewing their loads over four or five kilometres. It became obvious that with the growing popularity of the area, some sort of a road had to be constructed to the Ball Hut to allow motor vehicles to replace the horses.

Between twenty-five and thirty-five horses were carried as a rule. The man who looked after them with loving care and shod them later became well known as one of New Zealand's best alpine painters, Duncan Darroch. Duncan, a rather taciturn New Zealander who was very close to his Scottish ancestors, arrived at The Hermitage to work as a blacksmith. He was extremely good at his trade, tailoring the shoes beautifully to fit the varying sizes of hooves of the horses, and each fitted shoe was a work of art. Duncan would also do expert smithy work for other departments of The Hermitage.

He had a great affection for his horses. He knew them all by name and what their temperaments were, and could quieten down even the most high-spirited and fit it with new shoes without getting kicked to pieces in the process. During the three months that we spent at Mt Cook during the polio epidemic of 1925 I was fascinated by the work of the smithy and spent a lot of time there, helping Duncan in small ways and learning quite a lot about the trade. During this time I got to know him very well, and watched him graduate from the anvil to become one of New Zealand's foremost landscape painters.

Right from the time that he arrived at Mt Cook, he developed a tremendous love for the alpine scene, the mountains, glaciers, trees, shrubs, and wild birds. He had a great desire to record and express and paint things he saw around him, but he had had no training whatsoever in painting and started, as with so many other things that he did so well, in a most unorthodox way. He bought tubes of oil paints and, as he did not have the money (or so he said) to buy drawing paper and brushes, he started daubing on pieces of flattened-out corrugated iron with his finger.

There were sheets and odd pieces of old iron scattered all round the Hooker Flat after the old Hermitage and some of its outbuildings had been torn about by explosive winds, so Duncan had plenty of 'canvas' on which to paint. Inevitably, his first efforts were crude, and he would paint them out and start again; but gradually the bold contours and the harsh clear colours of the mountains began to emerge in a style of painting which was unique at that time and has since been copied by other painters of the alpine scene.

Duncan was painting very well and had sold a quantity of his work to guests at The Hermitage before he took any form of tuition, and then he was helped by Cecil Kelly, director of the School of Fine Arts in Christchurch, and several others, to improve his technique and to make greater use of brushes and conventional materials, but he continued to make some use of his fingers when painting.

He became part of the Hermitage landscape, and his small house on the hillside was a jumble of paintings in various stages of completion, with keas and other wild birds perched all around about the place waiting for his daily handouts. He was certainly one of the most colourful characters living at The Hermitage during the period the Company had the lease, and for many years afterwards.

4

The Guides

AORANGI — Mt Cook itself — was a magnet for overseas climbers from the very early days, and the Rev. W. S. Green and a number of others made annual excursions there in an effort to be the first to conquer the peak. These early climbers passed their knowledge on to the local guides, and it was finally a party of New Zealanders that first reached the summit.

From about 1880 until the beginning of the war in 1939, practically all climbers in the Mt Cook district used professional guides, and a number of tremendous personalities in this field emerged. Guiding achieved a professionalism unlikely to be seen again; a guide not only developed his skills to get his clients to the top of the mountain and back safely, but also acted as philosopher and friend, regaled them with amusing stories of the mountains, and undertook most if not all of the menial chores around the camp.

Celebrated guides included the Graham brothers, Alex and Peter; Frank Milne; Harry Ayers; Mick Bowie; Vic Williams; Frank Alack; Joe Fluerty; Jack Pope; Alf Brusted: and many others became known internationally for their skill on ice and rock and for their records of always bringing their charges safely home.

Frank Milne was probably the first really scientific climber to guide in the area. He was wounded and gassed in World War I, developed tuberculosis, and went into the Mt Cook country seeking a job as a guide. A quiet, slight, lithe man, he took naturally to climbing, but the basic skills were not enough for him: he studied every aspect of climbing, from the use of rhythm in order to conserve energy when walking over rough ground, to strengthening each one of his fingers and toes for the most hazardous moments of rock climbing.

As a kid, enthusiastically trying to emulate the guides, and scrambling all over the place and getting into trouble, I once had a lecture from Frank on walking. He explained that everyone can and does develop a rhythm while walking over a flat paddock or track, but for alpine climbing it was absolutely necessary to develop a rhythm that would conserve energy by taking so many steps to the minute, and so many steps to the breath. When he moved from flat ground to the hills a climber should continue to take the same number of steps per minute, but making them shorter as the gradient increased, thus maintaining the rhythm which would allow him with a heavy pack on his back to go on for hour after hour without tiring.

This sounded a good theory to me, but I asked him how he managed to maintain his rhythm while walking over a stony riverbed, or a glacial moraine, or rough ice, where every step had to be different. His method was to balance completely on each foot with each step and so maintain the rhythm which, of course, cannot be done if one is merely stumbling from rock to rock.

He had an extraordinary strength in his fingers and toes, and he did some quite incredible things in the staff lounge of The Hermitage. This room had a high ceiling, and about seventy centimetres below it a picture-rail ran right round the walls, protruding by about three centimetres. Frank would jump up and grip the picture-rail by his fingertips only, and then go right round the room, hand over hand. Then he would jump up on top of the old upright piano, put his hands on the ceiling and his toes on the picture-rail, and so work his way right round the room again.

Another exercise of his was to take off his boots and socks and, with his hands and feet pressed against the opposite sides of a narrow corridor wall, climb up until his head was against the ceiling and then proceed to manoeuvre his way down the length of the corridor.

These exhibitions of skill and strength were a challenge to the younger guides, and competitions used to take place almost nightly to see who could put up the best performance. These methods of training for alpine climbing are fairly well known today, but Frank Milne must have been been one of the pioneers in developing them. In addition to his skills in balancing and climbing, he had a tremendous eye for country and an unerring ability to select the best routes through icefields and up rock faces. He was a legend in his day, and with good reason.

If Frank Milne was outstanding, his pupil Vic Williams was no less so, but with a different personality. Vic started climbing at Mt Cook in 1922, and was Chief Guide until he retired about 1938-39; during this time he did many outstanding climbs with some of the best-known climbers of the period, including Miss K. D. Gardner and H. E. L. Porter.

While attempting to climb Mt Tasman they erected two tiny tents on the névé at the head of the Fox Glacier, but these were demolished by an unpredicted mountain storm of some severity which lasted for a number of days. They managed to re-erect the tents further down the névé in a crevasse which was partly filled with snow, and stayed there for eight days until the weather cleared enough to let them out. During this time they were continuously wet, and on occasions when the temperatures dropped, their clothes and sleeping-bags were frozen rock-hard.

Down at The Hermitage they had been given up for lost, for no one could believe that any human being could survive that hostile environment almost without food in a storm that raged for eight days. Everyone, from RLW down, was astounded and overjoyed to hear that they had walked out safely. There is no doubt that Vic's unfailing cheerfulness under all conditions, the amusing stories that would light up his face as he told them, and his example and advice on how to get exercise to keep warm, were responsible for the survival of his party.

Vic was a climber at heart, and though he tolerated RLW's development of the sport of skiing, he showed little enthusiasm for it. Typically, he spent more time laughing at his own shortcomings on skis than in trying to master the technique. Strong as a horse, he always took his fair share of work, whether it was kicking steps in the snow or backpacking supplies to the huts.

In the mid 1930s, when the winter traffic to the Ball Hut was building up rapidly, manager Charlie Elms thought that Vic ought to learn to drive a car instead of having to rely on others to drive him about. Vic drove just as he did everything else — slowly, cautiously, and in a calculated way. On one trip to the Ball Hut, with my brother Sandy as passenger, he was driving a seven-seater Studebaker car which had oversize tyres and was rather difficult to handle on bumpy roads. Vic, resplendent in a brand-new white sweater with an elaborate cable pattern and stockings to match which his loving wife Hilda had knitted, had navigated his way over the snowpacked road to a point where it travelled on the crest of the lateral moraine with an almost vertical drop on either side. The wheels started bounding on some big rocks poking through the snow, the car did a Waltzing Matilda act, dropped over the side for five or six metres and finished up on its roof. In no time they were out; Sandy said it was the first time in his life that he'd ever seen Vic really agitated. He kept groaning 'What will Hilda say! What will Hilda say!' His lovely new sweater was covered with black gearbox oil, and he was much more concerned about this than any damage to the car or the narrow escape from mortal disaster.

When Vic retired in about 1936 he handed over the reins of Chief Guide to one of his pupils, Mick Bowie, another outstanding personality, but quite different in character from Vic or Frank Milne. Mick was as strong as a horse, and his slow steady gait would carry him over moraine, snow or mountainside for hour after hour, pipe stuck in his mouth, without any apparent fatigue. Being younger than Vic he was ready to make some concession to RLW's skiing developments, and learned to ski reasonably well and safely enough to do a considerable amount of ski touring, as I have related elsewhere in this book and in *Ski-plane Adventure*.

In the 1920s many people travelled to The Hermitage every summer to spend a climbing holiday. With few exceptions they employed the professional guides when they attacked their chosen peaks, and with the time required to climb out to the huts used as bases, waiting for the weather to clear, and/or for the rocks and ice to improve in condition, several days might be needed for each climb.

If a climber had set his sights on several high peaks he might require the services of two guides for three weeks or more and, as the climbing season was relatively short — no more than some three months and often much less — it was hard to get enough experienced guides to cater for the demand. While the guides were away on climbing expeditions there was no one to guide the parties on the easier day-excursions, and as these parties provided more of the bread-and-butter than the high climbers, they had to be catered for too.

RLW overcame this problem by employing students as guides during the long university vacation. Their weekly pay was not high, and they were given a diversity of jobs to do — peeling spuds for the kitchen, keeping the walking tracks in repair, backpacking stores out of the alpine huts, guiding the day-trips to the Stocking Glacier and the lower huts. As they gained more experience, they were nominated as second guides on the high alpine climbs.

Although it was not very lucrative work, it was virtually a

paid holiday away from the normal grind, and in utterly different surroundings. In many of them it engendered a love of the mountains which has endured to this day. Many of them became expert climbers and guides, many have earned fine reputations overseas for their climbs in the Himalayas, the European Alps, in China and in South America. The names of Lud Mahon, Fred Chapman, Lynn Murray, Dan Bryant, Charlie Hilgendorf, spring to mind, and many others.

They did an excellent job for the Company, even though their differences of opinion with Charlie Elms would occasionally cause him to erupt with a stream of his own blunt type of vernacular. As was to be expected, the students had a lively sense of humour, and the tall stories they told to the tourists and the high-spirited antics they got up to from time to time were a constant source of amusement.

During the height of the climbing season the provisions at the mountain huts had to be replenished from time to time and eighteen-litre tins of kerosene for cooking and canned or dehydrated food were backpacked in loads of between eighteen and twenty kilos. There was always competition for the bulky but light goods, which made up into an impressive-looking load but one that was not too heavy.

One well-known guide had a reputation for being a slow starter when any work was in the offing and was always very fast off the mark when the splitting-up of packloads was being done. He would fill up his rucksack with bread, cereals, and all the bulky stuff that he could get his hands on, and finish up with his rucksack bulging out in all directions and stacked as high as his head. As they filed out, on their way to one of the mountain huts, the admiring guests would say: 'My, look at the load that Alf is carrying. What a tiger for hard work!' Little did they know that Alf was all show and was probably carrying far less than another guide who was carrying seventy-two litres of kerosene which weighed eighteen kilos but didn't even look like a load.

Sometimes they acted as porters for climbing expeditions going into one of the more remote huts. They would go to The Hermitage store and draw a list of supplies required by the expedition — so many loaves of bread, so many tins of meat, jam, cheese, butter, potatoes, and so on down the list. I was in the store one day casually watching the drawing of supplies and was amused to hear one guide calling out the tins of this and tins of that: when he came to tins of pineapple, the storeman said: 'But Mr Clark (or whatever the climber's name was) doesn't eat pineapple.' There was a chorus of 'But *we* do', and the pineapple was put in the pack.

At times the student guides' sense of humour ran away with them and their audience of tourists had difficulty in separating fact from fiction. All sorts of stories were told about fishing for frostfish on the Tasman Glacier, or chasing the Cycle Cougar (a mythical animal that always grazed from left to right round the mountain and whose top legs were therefore shorter than the bottom ones to keep him on the level).

Typical of such quips was one attributed to Lud Mahon. He was travelling with a busload of passengers from The Hermitage to the Ball Hut, and at one point the bus was stopped high up on the ridge of the lateral moraine. Below were thousands of hectares of huge rocks and assorted rubble brought down by the glacier which, acting as a conveyor belt, deposits masses of such moraine over its lower reaches. Very little ice is visible, and what there is is covered by wet sand and looks like anything but ice. Lud explained that the moraine had been brought down by the glacier, and when he had finished his explanation a woman tourist asked, 'And where is the glacier now?'

Quick as a flash Lud replied, 'It's gone back for another load.'

Long after their student days were over, many of these men kept coming back to climb in the Alps, and they were the forerunners of the present generations of guideless climbers. Many of these lads developed a high degree of skill and proficiency which allowed them to tackle the toughest climbs without the help of professional guides. Their development of icework to a standard higher than that seen in any other part of the world stemmed largely from the fact that the New Zealand Alps are built of rather rotten treacherous rock which defies the techniques developed overseas on hard and stable rock. It forced them to use the ice as much as possible. Also, the enormous ice accretion on the Southern Alps forced them to use the ice in order to get anywhere, and they had to develop techniques to cope with it. It is said that Sir Edmund Hillary's success in the first climb of Mt Everest was to a large extent due to his knowledge and experience of the alpine ice and snow of New Zealand.

Teams of these climbers started exploring new routes up the mountains and attempting climbs from angles which the more conservative professional guides, whose first responsibility had to be the safety of their charges, were prepared to leave alone in preference for the proven, safer routes. Lud Mahon and the late Dan Bryant were the first to climb the extremely difficult eastern arête of Mt Cook. Jacko Jackson and another climbed Mt Sefton for the first time by an extremely difficult eastern route, and there were many others, far too numerous to be detailed in this book.

In 1913 two Mount Cook guides and an English climber were overcome by a tremendous avalanche which swept down the Linda Glacier while they were returning from a climb of the traverse of Mt Cook. One body was recovered at the time, but the two others disappeared completely until, fourteen years later, they started to show up in the white ice of the Hochstetter Icefall not far from the Ball Hut. Fragmentary remains appeared on the surface of the glacier over a two- or three-year period: pieces of clothing, alpine rope, and some rather gruesome relics such as a crushed boot with the foot still inside it.

We came across these bits and pieces from time to time while guiding Ball Hut parties out on the two-hour trip over the Tasman Glacier, and on most occasions we threw them into the nearest crevasse; however, one party headed by Frank Drewitt and including others with a macabre sense of humour, came across a large part of a leg and parts of the trunk lying in the ice, and decided to take it back to the Ball Hut.

After much discussion among the local guides they decided they should take it down to The Hermitage, so phoned through and booked three rooms for the night under the names of Drewitt, McClymont, and King. After arrival they climbed out of the bus and reported to the reception desk, where the girl asked them to sign. Drewitt and McClymont signed, and she said, 'But where is Mr King?' Drewitt replied, 'He's in a sugarbag, hanging up in a tree.'

At The Hermitage no one seemed particularly interested in Mr King's remains so, after a fairly boisterous evening amongst their mates, they got a pick and shovel and carried Mr King up to the King Memorial on the Hooker Glacier moraine about three kilometres from The Hermitage, where they dug a hole under the memorial, placed Mr King in it, sat round singing 'For he's a jolly good fellow', then buried him and departed.

It seemed at the time a kindly thing to do for Mr King, but they were soon in serious trouble with the law, which arrived early next day in the form of the Fairlie representative of the constabulary. He soon tracked down Drewitt and his mates and impressed on them the seriousness of tampering with human remains before reporting them to the police.

This episode kept them involved with the law for far longer than they had ever bargained for, for enquiries had to be made into the circumstances of the finding of the leg, and later they had to attend a formal inquest.

There were many colourful characters amongst The Hermitage guides in the early days, but one became something of a legend because of his colourful use, or I should say misuse of the King's English.

His name was Jimmie Stout, and he worked at The Hermitage as a porter and a guide from the early 1920s to the early 1930s. He was a small wiry character, with two piercing blue eyes set in a wrinkled sunburnt face. He seldom smiled and appeared to treat everything in his vicinity, and particularly us kids, with hostility. An immigrant from Ireland, he never lost his brogue, which was so deep that he was very difficult to understand, and the twist that he gave to his comments and description of the countryside to parties he guided, kept them in fits of laughter. Along with other expressions he punctuated every comment with 'my bloody oath', which in Stout language was 'my bluddy oat'.

The story is told of Jimmie guiding one of the New Zealand Governors-General and his wife out on a trip to the Stocking Glacier. Jimmie had been told to treat his charges as VIPs and give them the utmost respect, to speak to them in English, and on no account to let these refined people hear his bad language. They stopped for lunch at the Stocking Stream and while the billy was boiling, they sat around. Jimmie's behaviour was exemplary. The Governor-General's wife listened to his description of the mountains and then told him some anecdotes of climbing in other parts of the world which impressed him so much that he came out with a 'my bluddy oat, Mrs'.

Another climber whom Jimmie escorted round the Alps was a man by the name of Dr Bikkersteath, but Jimmie had difficulty pronouncing his name and always addressed him as Bikkerstick. One day Professor Algie, who was later Speaker of the House and was a great climber, heard Jimmie talking about Dr 'Bikkerstick', and he said to him, 'Jimmie, you really will have to say his name properly, or you'll get the bikkerstick.' In spite of his fierce disposition, Jimmie had a heart of gold, and for a number of years after his departure from The Hermitage — which was apparently hastened by his fondness for the poteen — he worked with Jimmie Smith on the road gang on the Pukaki/Hermitage road and always seemed to be very pleased to see those of us whom he knew.

He made no contribution to the development of the company, but he was a character who will be remembered when many others are forgotten.

Jacko Jackson and Lud Mahon did a lot of climbing together and seemed to get on reasonably well in spite of the fact that their temperaments were poles apart. Lud was easy-going and casual, never owned a watch, and had a sense of humour which was lost on almost everyone but his colleagues. To keep themselves fit they would go for long weekend climbs on the mountain ranges behind Timaru and those surrounding Lake Tekapo at its northern end. Jacko was always out of bed early and raring to go, while Lud preferred to see the sun at a decent distance above the horizon before he stirred. Jacko would be booted and spurred and ready to go, while Lud would still be hunting around for bits of lost equipment.

On one excursion which entailed several hours of climbing up a long ridge, Jacko as usual took off like a rocket, with Lud tailing along behind. After half an hour or so Lud started complaining about feeling unwell and asked Jacko to stop for a spell, which he agreed to, fairly reluctantly, some time later.

Half an hour later Lud again called for a spell, and this went on right through the morning until finally Jacko too began to complain of not feeling well. Never had he known his pack to feel so heavy, he grumbled, and shortly afterwards he suggested to Lud that they sit down for lunch. They selected some reasonably comfortable rocks to sit on, put their rucksacks down close by and proceeded to open them up to extract their lunches. Jacko got red in the comb, his eyes stuck out like crayfish behind his glasses and he exploded. Every time they had stopped for a spell, Lud had quietly slipped a hefty stone into Jacko's rucksack. . .

Several years later Jacko and another climber were lost in an avalanche in that area, and their bodies were not recovered until the spring. Lud was among the party who walked in to carry them out. He put himself at the head of Jacko's stretcher and started off downhill at a pace which the others in the party had difficulty in keeping up with: they kept yelling to Lud to ease up, for the pace was killing them. At last he did so, and they asked him why on earth he had refused to slow down. His reply was, 'Why should I? Jacko would never stop for me when I wanted him to.'

RLW introduced cheap skiing excursions to the Ball Hut for schoolchildren, and these were often in charge of a teacher who had been a student guide several years before. Sometimes the snow was well down on the Ball Glacier, and at other times it was necessary to lug skis, lunches, and other gear up several hundred metres to get skiable snow early in May. All the streams would be frozen up, and it was necessary to carry water, tea, or some sort of cordial to drink. One gets extremely thirsty after several hours climbing in the heat of the sun.

We often took along one or two bottles of beer, taking turns at carrying them. One day Lud and two or three of the other teachers had lagged behind, and we were already seated on some rocks and eating our lunches when they arrived. We were very thirsty and were looking forward to enjoying a sip of the beer which Lud was carrying. He pulled out a bottle, knocked the top off, and passed it over to me. I took a good long swig and for a moment could hardly believe my tastebuds, but it quickly occurred to me that those lousy practical jokers had downed the beer themselves, had located some water some-where, maybe by melting snow, had filled the bottle up with it and replaced the top.

They waited for me to explode, but I said 'Good!', wiped my mouth with the back of my hand, and passed the bottle to a newcomer who was spending his first day on the glacier. A rather surprised look crossed his face but, as I had said nothing, he obviously thought that his tastebuds must be at fault and, after a good swig, passed it to the next man. The bottle was passed round and no one said a word, but later in the day, someone mused, 'It's astonishing how one's ability to taste things disappears in the mountains!'

Student guides did a lot for the Company and the experience did a lot for the students. They helped to show thousands of people the beauties of our alpine regions, and in their later professional life as schoolteachers or members of other pro-fessions they persuaded many more to look to the hills and mountains for the rest and zest always to be found 'above worry-level'.

5

Ball Hut or Tasman Chalet

THE ORIGINAL BALL HUT was built near the Rev. W. S. Green's camp between the lateral moraine and the mountain, and about three kilometres below the site of the present hut. It consisted of one and later two small tin sheds with bunks and accommodation for about a dozen people, and it was destroyed by an avalanche in the spring of 1927. No one knows exactly when it was destroyed but, so far as I can see, my mother, one or two other members of the family, some other skiers and myself were the last to use it in late August of that year.

The new hut built to replace it consisted of two bunkrooms with twelve bunks in each and a central livingroom for cooking and eating. Rainwater was collected from the roof and stored in large tanks, but no running water was laid on to the building and there were no facilities for washing. In those days, of course, one slept in one's clothes, so no wonder the chamois and thar were so frightened of human beings — they probably smelled us from three kilometres away!

With more and more interest in downhill skiing, the poor slopes and the lack of snow in the vicinity of The Hermitage, caused the second Ball Hut to be used more and more by skiers. It was twenty-three kilometres from The Hermitage and it was necessary to walk there or go on horseback until the road was completed. From then onwards practically all the downhill skiing activities were concentrated there, and it was improved year by year to cater for them.

RLW could see the need for a motor road to the Ball Hut and had been pushing for it for a number of years. At last the Government decided to go ahead with it. It was built in stages over three years or so, and was completed and opened to motor traffic in 1927 and 1928. From then on, buses replaced the horses, which disappeared from the scene, and Duncan Darroch then divided his time between painting, and guiding the glacier parties on day trips.

Three phases of transport to the old Hermitage. *Top*, bullock team at rest, about 1895 (*Alexander Turnbull Library*). *Middle*, horsedrawn coach of the era immediately preceding the motor service (*Alexander Turnbull Library*). *Bottom*, the motor service in the ascendancy, 1906.

The Hermitage, about 1910. Note the height of the Mueller Glacier in the background.
Floods in 1910 spelt the doom of the original buildings.

RLW at three ages. *Top left*, the painfully contrived studio backdrop fore-shadows the schoolboy's lifelong love of outdoor life. *Top right*, taken about 1909 — the successful young businessman with a vision of tourism. *Bottom*, to RLW (holding gun), an office chair was merely a springboard to outdoor fun and adventure.

Top Ball Hut 'packhorses', 1898. *Left*, first winter ascent of Mt Cook, 12 August 1923. RLW and Frank Milne on the summit, photographed by Norman Murrell. *Bottom*, two famous Hermitage guides, Frank Alack (*left*) and Vic Williams, with renowned English climber Kate Gardner.

Booming in the 1930s despite the Depression. *Top left*, The Hermitage with new wing added, 1935. *Top right*, a typical advertisement of the 1930s. *Bottom*, Mount Cook executives and associates, 1934, *Back row*, J. Leggott, J. Ambler, F. Findlayson, W.H. Amos, H. Coxhead, S. Gilkison, H.R. Wigley, W. McIndoe, RLW. *Front*, Miss N. Naggitt, Charlie Elms, Norrie Coxhead, Lena Leslie, Tui Elms.

In 1976, a staff farewell to Keith McGowan. *Left to right*, Bill Adams, Squib McWhirter, Bill Hocking, Jack Ballinger, Ian Brodie, Keith Robertson, Jim Simmers, Ted Tank, Geoff Maslin, Noel Cochrane, Horton Hill. In front are Harry and Isla Wigley, Zelda and Keith McGowan

RLW with an elderly Hermitage visitor and two fashionably-dressed young ladies of the 1920s.

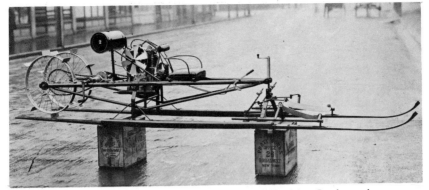

An unsuccessful bid to solve over-snow transport difficulties. In the early 1920s Charlie Jones, the Company's engineer, designed and built this ingenious sledge.

Sledging stores to the Ball Hut, early 1930s. *From left*, Hughie Fergusson, Harry Wigley immediately behind him, Mick Bowie, Vic Williams, Doolie Coxhead (obscured) and two visitors.

Skiing on the Ball Glacier in the mid-1930s.

Prizewinners, about 1935. Harold Elworthy, Christina Guy, a lady whose name has not been recorded, Alan Kirk, president of the Aorangi Ski Club, and RLW.

The road did more than anything else to open up the Tasman Valley for, rough and all as it was, the twenty-three kilometre journey could now be done in an hour and a half or less, compared to a whole day's journey on horseback or three or four days on foot — the time taken by the early explorers such as Green, Mannering and Dixon.

The road and the increased accommodation at the hut stimulated the demand for accommodation at the small Malte Brun Hut about eighteen kilometres farther up the glacier. If the transport of materials for the Ball Hut had been a major problem, transport for the same quantities over this extra distance of moraine and the clear ice of the Tasman Glacier presented one which might have been insuperable. However, the first Byrd expedition was preparing to leave New Zealand for Antarctica, and two teams of sledge dogs were to be kept in New Zealand as reserves. On hearing of this RLW — always a quick-thinking opportunist — welcomed it as a heaven-sent opportunity to solve his transport problems and get some publicity for the area at the same time.

He got in touch with Innes Taylor, an experienced dog-handler from Canada who was in charge of the dogs and the equipment during their stay in New Zealand. The dogs were in quarantine at Quail Island in Lyttelton Harbour, and there is no doubt that Innes Taylor was just as delighted as RLW to get snow work and training for his dogs while they were in New Zealand. The dogs had already attracted considerable publicity, and when it was announced that they were to be based at Mt Cook it produced a sharp reaction from the Mackenzie Country farming community, who were concerned that the dogs would run loose and go wild, or cross with domestic dogs. A controversy soon broke out, and RLW had some difficulty in convincing the powers-that-be that it would be safe to take the dogs to Mt Cook. As it turned out, his confidence was justified.

Some of the newspaper articles of the times make interesting reading. One from the *Christchurch Press* dated 10 April 1929 states, in part: 'An unusual feature of the work of the erection of the hut will be in connection with the transport of materials up the Tasman Glacier for a distance of ten or twelve miles. For this work it is expected that the dogs of the Byrd Antarctic expedition at present in quarantine on Quail Island will be used. The material will be loaded on sledges, each sledge carrying 3,000 lbs. It is intended to get the materials as far along the road as possible before the winter. It will be stored at this point until such time as the ice on the glacier is in good condition for sledging.'

There was some fear from the Canterbury A & P Association, T. D. Burnett of Mount Cook station, and other landowners that if these dogs should escape they would constitute a danger to the high-country flocks:

'We have got enough pests at large as it is,' said Mr Nicholson. He explained that the dogs had been bred by crossing wolves with Alaskan sledge dogs and they could only be handled by being kept in a state of semi-starvation. It took the owner of a team all his time to keep the dogs in subjection, even under these conditions. The only way that they can be kept in subjection is for them to be worked so strenuously that they are heartily worn out at the end of the day. 'If the Government will give me permission I'm willing to take charge of that team and, at running the risk of being dog-handled, I'd drown the lot in the pool at Sumner,' said Mr Nicholson.

Mr Innes Taylor, the man in charge of the fifteen dogs, replied: 'There is not the slightest possibility of dogs annoying human beings or stock; they are not half-starved.' Mr Innes Taylor, an ex-member of the Royal North-West Mounted Police, has had considerable experience in the handling of this type of dog, which is of the Husky breed evolved by crossing the Newfoundland or St Bernard with a wolf. He stated: 'The dogs may fight amongst themselves, but a stranger can go amongst them with impunity. At Banff and other Canadian resorts we have dog derbies, and thousands attend to see the dogs race with sledges. Never yet has the question of danger cropped up. In all my years with them I've never known a case of danger to human beings or to stock as long as teams are properly handled.'

Mr Wigley promised to give all possible assistance in the way of providing a good training locality for the teams. The new Malte Brun Hut will have twenty-eight bunks, of structured timber like the Ball Hut, covered with corrugated iron. A similar building in Christchurch would cost no more than £300-£400, but the cost to the Government of the Malte Brun hut will be £1,550, this being the amount of the successful tender by the Mount Cook Company. If the dogs were allowed to be used, it would mean a saving of about £500 in the construction of the Malte Brun hut.

In spite of the objections voiced by the farming community,

approval was granted to use the huskies at Mt Cook and they were reported as starting work on 17 July 1929. From *The Press* of this date: 'Mr Wigley stated that on Sunday two sledges were yoked up and tried out on the snow in the vicinity of The Hermitage. A large number of visitors enjoyed rides. The strength of the dogs was marvellous, and their presence at The Hermitage had aroused much interest. They are nothing like the wild animals they are credited with being, said Mr Wigley. They were patted and petted by the visitors and even small children enjoyed making friends with them.'

Two dog sledges presented to RLW by Sir Ernest Shackleton were used to transport most of the materials. They were light in weight and built to a design proven over many years in Canada. No nails, screws or steel were used in their construction, and they were held together with thongs of rawhide, which would stretch and give them flexibility without members becoming fractured.

A cutting from the *Timaru Herald* of 21 August 1929 states: '15 Alaskan dogs at Mt Cook had done 537 miles of sledging up till 14 August. They have hauled 20,300 lbs of materials and supplies, and as the snowfall has been heavier than for several years, the dogs have been particularly useful.'

The completion of the Malte Brun Hut stimulated interest in the area for people who, while not classified as high climbers, were fit enough to walk or ski up the glaciers and climb the easy snow slopes to the Lindenfeldt and Tasman Saddles and even some of the lower peaks. Many of these parties were under the charge of student guides who had received enough instruction and had had enough experience to make them competent to carry this relatively simple responsibility.

Over many years thousands of people enjoyed these mountain excursions in perfect safety, and it was a tremendous blow to RLW and all the Company staff when a party of five under the competent leadership of a popular student guide, Teddy Blomfield, died on the Tasman Glacier while descending from the Malte Brun to the Ball Hut.

The news of the tragedy shocked everyone, for as well as the fact that the victims included some popular young people from Christchurch, there was an air of mystery as to its cause. Weather conditions had not been particularly severe and the party were certainly not killed by the cold, as many of them still had spare clothing in their rucksacks. Neither could they have fallen, as they were found lying on the surface of the glacier nowhere near deep crevasses or ice faces. It was concluded that they had been killed by a strike of lightning, and this verdict has been substantiated by evidence of similar accidents which have since occurred in other parts of the world.

The sort of work in which the Company has been involved over the past seventy-plus years must be, by its very nature, hazardous. Air and road transport, despite Governmental regulations and the most stringent care taken by Company management, still have their risks; and skifield work and mountaineering have inherent dangers, no matter how carefully supervised and managed. RLW, his staff and their successors, have had to live with constant thought and worry over these hazards.

RLW's success in building up the Mount Cook Company was due in no small way to the quality of the people whom he selected as executives and the loyalty and enthusiasm that he inspired in them. C. D. Elms, or Charlie as he was known to all and sundry, was one of the stalwarts who served the Company faithfully and well for nearly all his working life.

Born in Pareora district in 1873, he joined the Company in Fairlie in 1905. For many years he drove the horse-drawn coaches and later the cars between Fairlie and The Hermitage. Buggies were used in the winter months to carry on the mail service, and on one occasion when Charlie was driving there was a heavy frost on the ground and his foot slipped on the iron steps when he was getting back into the vehicle after delivering the mail at one of the stations. The horses moved on as he fell, and he was dragged. Though concussed and suffering from a badly fractured jaw he managed to clamber up on to his seat and — with characteristic determination — to drive back to Fairlie to complete his mail run. On arrival, he was found to be badly injured and had to spend several weeks in bed.

Charlie drove the Darracqs to The Hermitage for many years and he had many interesting stories to tell about the early days. When the long telephone line was first put through in 1909 the linesman could not possibly maintain its whole length, so he solved the problem by paying Charlie and other drivers five shillings every time they saw the line was down and retied it to the insulators.

Charlie was the manager of the Fairlie branch of the Company for a period, and when the Depression was at its height in the early 1930s, and RLW wanted someone at The Hermitage who could take a tough line on costs and keep them reasonably relative to revenue, he sent Charlie there as manager. It was during his eight or ten Hermitage years that he became so well known to climbers, skiers, overseas tourists, and New Zealanders on holiday.

He was short, squat and, in his latter years, fairly rotund; below his curly brown and later greying hair shone a couple of piercing blue eyes, and he sported a fierce moustache. Charlie could turn on a charming smile which would disarm the most hostile guests — or he might stand there with his hands on his hips and his thumbs stuck into the tops of his trousers, his moustache bristling and his face as fierce as any Corsican bandit, roaring out a torrent of vernacular abuse. Although his formal education was limited, he had a tremendous flow of invective with which he could wither some poor unfortunate member of the staff. His loyalty to the Company was such that he was not above giving his house guests a sample of his quaint vernacular if he felt the Company was being unfairly criticised. Rough diamond and all that he was, Charlie gave the Company good service for most of his working life. RLW relied on him completely to keep The Hermitage going over those difficult times, and Charlie never let him down.

Most of us had received the rough end of Charlie's tongue on occasions, and we were all a little bit scared of him. One day he was on the phone talking to the garage-boy, and halfway through the conversation he realised he was talking to himself. He yelled down the phone 'Hello there! *Can you hear me?*' a few times, but to no effect.

Suspecting that the boy had become a little too independent and had walked away from the phone, he jumped into his car and drove down to the garage — to find the boy lying dead on the floor under the telephone. This gave Charlie a hell of a shock, but apparently the poor lad had had some heart condition, and his time was up. Charlie stopped a lot of snide remarks for months afterwards to the effect that he had better moderate his language or there'd be staff dying all over the place.

Lud Mahon, a one-time student guide, had a keen sense of humour and was very clever at cartoons. One of these, done in about 1938, shows RLW and Charlie Elms admiring a grandiose new Ball Hotel in the far distant year of 1960. Charlie's favourite expression to cap any conversation with emphasis — 'Obsolutely!' is expressive.

Unfortunately the magnificent Ball Hotel envisaged by Lud was never built, partly because the skiing development at Coronet Peak had begun to attract skiers away from Mt Cook,

and partly because the lateral moraine on which Lud showed
the imaginary hotel has been carried away by the glacier. The
original Ball Hut is now (1979) right on the edge of the drop of
over a hundred metres and will probably fall into the glacier
during the next year or so.

Charlie was certainly one of the most colourful employees of
the Company, and he is remembered with affection by all the
oldtimers. His four sons, Tui, Doug, Percy and Charlie, all
worked for the Company for long periods and gave good loyal
service right up until the Company began to fall apart during
the latter part of World War II.

The Ball Hut at 1128 metres above sea level is 500 metres
higher than the hotel and also higher than the level at which
the snowline settles at the end of winter, consequently it has a
more assured and a deeper supply of snow in its vicinity than
The Hermitage. The mild slopes in front of the hut are splendid for beginners and intermediate skiers, while the chutes and
alpine meadows on the ridge above the hut are steeper and
more suitable for the better skiers and for racing. Behind the
hut the glacier led gently up to the bottom of the Caroline
Icefall, which provided gentle undulating slopes of no great
difficulty, and at the end of the day four or five kilometres of
gentle running back to the hut could be enjoyed. Plentiful
snow, a wide variety of sunny slopes, and magnificent alpine
scenery encouraged people to use the Ball Hut more and more
and The Hermitage less and less, until the latter became almost a transit hotel in winter.

The demand for accommodation at the Ball Hut during the
latter part of July, August and September far exceeded the
supply, and early in the 1930s a decision was made to enlarge
it. The building was enlarged to provide accommodation for
ninety-nine people as well as a number of staff. But although
the accommodation was increased so considerably, it was no
more luxurious than before, as people still had to sleep in
bunkrooms with two tiers of bunks round the walls. Lighting of
a kind was provided by kerosene lamps, and when the hut was
filled to capacity the confusion was indescribable. There were
no wardrobes, drawers, or facilities for parking clothes and
gear, and when getting dressed in the morning (if one had
troubled to undress the night before) one never knew whose
pants or socks you were jumping into. It really was a case of
'first up best dressed'.

A special drying-room and a bath-house were provided, but

there was no running water either hot or cold, and the only way
to have a hot bath was to heat buckets or water over the coke
stove, which was a very slow business. The bath-house
seconded as the drying-room, or perhaps it was the other way
about, and several clotheslines were strung from one end of the
room to the other to dry sodden clothing, socks and boots.
While taking a bath one always had a number of visitors, male
and female, but in the dimly-lit room they were, as often or not,
unaware of the body in the bath.

The kitchen was enlarged considerably to cater for over a
hundred people and running water supplied to it from large
concrete storage tanks that collected rainwater from the roof as
there is no water running naturally in the vicinity. This rather
precarious water supply became almost nonexistent during the
hard cold winter when everything was frozen up. At the end of
one winter complaints were being made about the quality of
the water, and it was decided to clean the tanks out in the
spring. Fourteen very dead keas were pulled out — these in-
quisitive birds had been investigating the vents into the tanks
and had been unable to get out.

The lack of water was probably the greatest obstacle in the
way of developing a large accommodation facility in that area,
but finance was also a problem because the country was in the
middle of a major recession. Bankers and other financial insti-
tutions had no faith at all in the tourist industry, let alone
commercial activities based on the whims of a handful of
lunatics who strapped barrel-staves on to their feet to slide
down slopes of snow.

Not only was finance a problem, but there was a definite
limitation on the amount of money which could reasonably be
spent on a facility which would be used for only three months
of the year. The building was erected in the cheapest possible
way with corrugated iron nailed over a wooden framework. On
its northern end it was two storeys high with large faces exposed to the full force of the northerly and westerly winds. It
was flexible when it was built and became even more flexible
with every gale, so much so that it was possible to open or close
many of the doors only between gusts. How it survived as long
as it did without being blown away is hard to understand, yet it
is still there today. But its days are limited — not because of the
wind, but because the ground is subsiding underneath it.

The building was completely unheated, although the kerosene stoves in the open kitchen did generate some warmth.
There was no insulating material in the ceiling and the walls

so, as might be imagined, when only a few people were in residence, it was like sleeping in a refrigerated container. On the other hand, when it was fully occupied and all the windows were closed to stop the cold air getting in, the atmosphere could have been cut with a very blunt knife.

The building could not have been described as imposing or as anything but a bigger version of the old primitive Ball Hut, but to bring it into line with the home of the downhill skiing which was gaining so much popularity, someone decided it should be given the grandiose name of the Tasman Chalet. This name raised a great horse-laugh from the skiers and the staff, but the publicity men persevered with it in all advertisements for a year or so afterwards. The new name never stuck, and to everyone it was still the old Ball Hut.

In spite of all its shortcomings the hut served an extremely useful purpose and probably did more than anything else to popularise skiing amongst young people. Rough and ready as it was, it provided a base for many people for happy cheap holidays on the snow, and even today I keep running across people who did their first skiing from there during their school holidays.

The lack of water made it impossible to install flush toilets, and the rocky ground and the difficulty of digging holes created problems with the outside ones. Two-holers were built for men and women, fifty or sixty metres away from the hut, and people had to wade through the snow and the storms to get to them. These buildings had a fairly narrow base and, because of the rocky ground, were difficult to anchor; after a time the guy-wires would go slack and the little buildings would rock all round the place in a gale.

One night during the August school holidays of 1936 or thereabouts, the hut was buffeted by a gale-force wind, and driving sleet and drifting snow soon obliterated all tracks to the outhouses. About ten o'clock at night someone came into the hut and reported that the women's toilet, known as the Angel's Rest, had been blown away. This posed quite a problem, for no one knew whether or not it had been occupied at the time. A number of guides and others were organised to do a search of the area downwind from the site of the toilet, but this was inconclusive as the drifting snow could already have covered anyone lying there. Everyone was then turned out of bed so that a tally could be taken; fortunately no one was missing.

The buildings had to be shifted from time to time and new holes dug, and in the process of one of these shifts a not very observant girl visited the building and then retreated to the Ball Hut in great distress to tell her friends, 'There's a *man* down the hole!' The building had just been moved, and a workman was down at the bottom, tidying up and finishing the excavation.

Lack of inside facilities were a serious problem, not only for the skiers, but also for the Company, for many men were reluctant to venture far into the freezing night along the snowy track to the toilet, but would urinate in the snow outside the hut, which became fairly unsightly between snowfalls.

One evening a bit of a party was going on and one or two of the lads were getting a little the worse for wear. One of the occupants of the hut warned them that they would suffer almighty hangovers in the morning, and kindly offered them some pills that would relieve the pain. They accepted these gratefully, and at last retired to their bunks.

The first one outside in the morning walked about ten metres from the door of the hut and let go, and was perfectly horrified when he stained the snow bright green! He rushed in to see the resident doctor, convinced that he had contracted some appalling kidney complaint, and demanded to be taken down to Timaru immediately. It was not long before the second lad was also calling on the doctor in a similarly frantic condition, and the matter was not cleared up to their satisfaction until a little later when the doctor, who was in the know, broke the glad news to them that they had been sucking De Witt's pills and not Aspros.

If the shortage of water created occasional problems, the transport of supplies to feed a hundred or more hungry mouths was an everyday one, and a constant pain in the neck for management and staff. Tinned and dried foods as well as non-perishable items were used to the maximum extent and were taken up to the hut in the autumn before there was any danger of the road being closed by snow. The road was seldom closed before the end of May and, for reasons of finance as well as the possible deterioration of the goods, the transport of stores was usually left until the last possible day. One autumn, about 1935 or 1936, an unseasonable early snowfall occurred in the middle of April, and although there was a metre or more round the hut, we were not unduly concerned about it, expecting it to be followed by the usual nor'west winds and rain which would reduce it to negotiable limits. However, a further snowfall, again of about one metre, occurred three days later, and it was now deep enough to withstand considerable thawing and block the road all winter.

All means at the Company's disposal were hastily brought to bear, and these ranged from the use of primitive snowploughs, the use of buses as battering rams, and manpower with the shovels. All ablebodied staff who could be spared were sent from The Hermitage to help, and after some four or five days of bashing and digging our way through, we finally opened the road to the hut. Several truckloads of supplies were transported to the road terminal and manpowered up to the storerooms of the hut, and then everyone sat back to relax, exhausted, but satisfied with the good job that had been done.

Next day the glass started to drop. A gale-force wind developed, followed by torrential rain, and this went on for another three days or so. By the time it cleared, there wasn't enough snow to put together one average-sized snowflake in the whole length of the road. To make matters worse, it didn't snow again for another six weeks.

Conditions at the hut may have been ruggedly primitive, but the atmosphere was outstandingly happy and informal. All hands willingly helped with setting tables, serving the food and washing up, and, when that was over, the crowd would spend a couple of hours, tired but happy, bawling out all the old favourite songs and choruses. The daily transport of fresh supplies of food and passengers with their luggage and skis was also a major problem. The road was often passable right to the hut, but the area is subject to violent storms, and heavy falls of snow can close the road overnight. Equipment for clearing the roads of snow was in its early stages of development in the United States, Canada and Switzerland. RLW had received some information on this from overseas sources and decided to get some built locally.

A Case crawler-tractor was purchased and a manually-operated bulldozer-blade was designed and manufactured by Parr & Co. of Timaru. The blade could be moved up or down and angled from side to side, and it was tested by bulldozing the shingle on the beach at Timaru, where it performed quite satisfactorily. It was put on a truck and sent up to The Hermitage to do its job of snowclearing, arriving there about a year after the 'Tasman Chalet' was built.

It did a reasonably good job on light snowfalls but was quite incapable of handling the heavy falls which occurred at the top end of the Ball Hut road. Its system of steering was unsuitable for snowclearing as it was done by brakes on the rear driving-wheels. To counteract the tendency of the blade to pull the tractor into the snow at the side of the road, the brake had to be applied on the opposite side, but the tractor did not have enough power to overcome the drag of the snow on the one side and the drag of the brake on the other.

Another major problem was the inability of the tracks to keep themselves clear of snow, which would become compacted into hard ice by the driving sprockets and stress the tracks to their limit until they would jam. The driver then had to get out with a hammer and cold chisel and chip the ice away to allow the tracks to turn again, but after a few hundred metres it would grind to a halt again. Modern designers have overcome these problems, and today bulldozers can clear snow off roads extremely efficiently, but our old Case tractor was one of the first, if not the first, of the bulldozers to be used in New Zealand.

Hughie Fergusson was the main driver on the Ball Hut road for many years and he also drove the Case tractor and in spite of its deficiencies he persevered and succeeded in getting quite a lot of useful work out of it. But even Hughie, with his determination and resourcefulness, could not succeed in clearing the snow much further than Husky Camp, about six kilometres below the Ball Hut, during an average winter, so with some reluctance RLW decided to abandon the thing.

It finally disappeared over the edge of the lateral moraine one day when its brakes failed, and it fell 100 metres down to the glacier below. No one but the vintage vehicle boys mourned its passing.

From then on, the routine was that the buses would take passengers and stores for as far as the road had been cleared. They then travelled on a sledge or a four-wheeled trailer pulled over the surface of the snow by a tractor, and this system worked reasonably well. The tractor would compact the snow and beat out its own track but, even so, the road was far from being a main highway and the dips and hollows pitched the trailer up and down and sometimes violently sideways towards the almost vertical drop down to the bottom of the lateral moraine, scaring the very daylights out of nervous passengers. Once was enough for many of them, and they preferred to get out and walk the remaining distance.

When it was operating, the tractor was satisfactory, but it broke down frequently and then the perishable stores had to be carted in by manpower. When the snow was hard, the stores were carried on a sledge pulled by six or eight people, but when it was soft, after a new fall of snow, it was necessary to use skis and backpack the loads. All surplus staff from The Hermitage and our Timaru office capable of carrying a pack on their backs were sent up to help out and, as most of us were reasonably fit, it was no great hardship and we enjoyed getting up into the snow for a few days.

6

Some Climbing Firsts

THE SHORTNESS of the climbing season and the high demand for guides over this period made it difficult for RLW to achieve some of his own personal climbing ambitions, particularly the ascent of Mt Cook. He did quite a number of the lower climbs, such as Sebastopol, Sealey, Wakefield and others, and must have built up a reasonable amount of technical skill and knowledge from conversations and excursions with the guides. He enjoyed taking parties out on the lower climbs, and he was as hard as nails and physically very fit indeed.

He could not take the guides away from the lucrative high-climbing work and so deprive the Company of revenue during the climbing season, but he started talking in a casual way to Frank Milne and other guides about climbing in the winter off-season. They believed it was feasible, and started planning an attack on Mt Cook itself. RLW no doubt reasoned that if he could succeed in climbing Mt Cook during the winter, it would not only allow him to fulfil a cherished personal ambition, but would further his efforts to show the world that the Mount Cook region was one to be enjoyed at all seasons of the year, and was not just an Arctic wilderness to be deserted with the arrival of the first winter snows.

Looking back, the attempt seems to have been extremely foolhardy. Skiing had not developed to the extent where the guides had any great knowledge of snowcraft, and they had no knowledge whatsoever of the depths of winter snow they would encounter — whether it would be stable or subject to very frequent avalanching, even on relatively flat slopes; whether it would be dense enough to carry the climbers' skis; what wind velocities they were likely to encounter; and, finally, how low the temperatures were likely to be. It was known that the midwinter temperatures could drop to very low levels at altitude, so was their clothing adequate to protect them from such sudden drops? Could they survive these low temperatures in the event of an accident? Could they camp in the unheated Haast Hut at over 2000 metres without getting frostbite?

The insulated clothing designed for today's polar and high alpine expeditions had not even been thought of, and all they could do was to wear heavy woollen socks, underwear, sweaters and windbreakers as used by Shackleton's Antarctic expedition. The windproof parkas, regarded as essential today, had not then been developed, and the best they could get were open-fronted tweed jackets. With so many unknown factors ahead of them, it was a bold move to challenge New Zealand's highest mountain in the middle of winter. It had taken many years, and many attempts had been made to conquer it during the summer. Some of the world's best climbers had tried it and failed — yet here was RLW tackling it in the depth of winter. But he had always shown abounding courage, and this foray into the unknown was exactly the sort of challenge which really roused him.

The planning, the physical fitness, and the courage of RLW and his two guides, Frank Milne and Norman Murrell, paid off, and the first winter ascent of Mt Cook was achieved on 12 August 1923. They were away from The Hermitage for five days, and in the absence of telephones and mountain radios there was no way of the outside world knowing what had become of them until they returned — or were found by a search party. My mother recalls that the suspense of awaiting the outcome of this very hazardous venture was one of the most tense and worrying experiences of her long life, and I can remember the heartfelt relief shared by everyone when the party returned triumphant to The Hermitage on 14 August. In the *Christchurch Press* dated 17 August 1923, RLW described the climb in detail:

> 'The success of the whole trip was due to Frank Milne, who is an absolute marvel on ice and rock, and has a wonderfully fine judgment of snow conditions.' In these words did Mr R. L. Wigley express his opinion of Guide Milne, who pioneered the steps of an intrepid trio to the summit of Mt Cook last Sunday. 'It has always been generally considered that Mt Cook was not climbable in winter time, but we have thought for some time that it might be possible; so, on Thursday morning last, in perfect weather, we set out to see what we could do, intending to go as far as possible and learn at first hand what the winter conditions actually were.
>
> 'Arriving in due course at the Blue Lakes we discovered

that the snow was too deep for the horses so, donning skis, we continued our journey to the Ball Hut, at which we arrived at 4.30am on Friday. From this point to the foot of the Haast Range was successfully negotiated, and we were hopeful of skiing most of the way to the Haast Hut, but snow conditions were against us. We finally arrived at the Haast Hut too late to make any preparations in the way of kicking steps over Glacier Dome in readiness for climbing Mt Cook the next day. Saturday, however, was spent in kicking steps over the Dome and round Silberhorn Corner, and on Saturday night swags were prepared in full readiness for the great climb on the morrow, the alarm being set for 3.45am on Sunday.

'At last the hour dawned, and sharp at 4am, with swags and skis, we started off and tramped to the top of Glacier Dome. From here we skied to the Silberhorn Corner, and found skiing in the dark a most novel experience. Leaving our skis at the foot of Silberhorn we again started off in the steps kicked on the Saturday, and by daylight we were well up the Linda Glacier. From this point on, conditions were fairly good, the snow being very soft, and the prospects of reaching the top looked good. Several recent avalanches were crossed, and for two hours or more our nerves were on edge as we trusted to luck that one would not catch us. Some of the crevasses on the Linda Glacier are of great size, and absolutely magnificent, and in some instances we could see no bottom. The summit rocks we found in good condition, which luckily made climbing good.

'At this point we halted a few minutes for a bite of bread and cheese, and a drink from our water bottles, which we had previously filled with cold tea. It was now very cold, and one of the bottles was frozen so hard at the neck that the ice had to be broken before the owner could drink out of it. Resuming the climb, we found the summit rocks were ice-glazed and very steep, but otherwise conditions were good right to the summit, which we attained at 1.30pm. Hands were shaken and mutual congratulations were exchanged on having accomplished what had been considered hitherto an almost impossible feat. It was a glorious day, giving great visibility; both our coastlines were clearly seen, as were also thousands of peaks both north and south, Mt Aspiring being particularly noticeable and easily distinguishable.

'At 1.50pm, after taking several photographs, we left on

the return journey to the Haast Hut, carefully negotiating several schrunds which we had crossed on the way up, and where the ice steps don't give you much of a hold on New Zealand. If one of us had slipped here, it would have been fatal to the three of us. Crossing schrunds is rather ticklish work: two of us did the best we could with ice-axes stuck into the snow as an anchor while the third person was crossing. In one instance the leader partially broke through the ice bridge, but got safely across and anchored on the other side. The middle man [this was RLW], however, broke the bridge completely, and was dangling in mid-air while the other two were anchored on either side; but after careful handling he was safely landed on the other side. The difficulty then was to get the last man over. The first two anchored as best they could while the third man cut convenient steps to enable him to get a small run and to jump the crevasse.

'This he eventually did while being held by the other two, but it was a most anxious moment for all concerned. The rest of the journey was accomplished without incident, and we finally arrived at the Haast Hut at 8pm, very very tired but very pleased with ourselves.

'Next morning we glissaded from the Haast Hut right down to the glacier and skied from there to the Ball Hut and thence to the Blue Lakes, where we were very thankful to find the horses waiting for us. We were away from The Hermitage for five days, and had glorious weather the whole time.

'We had, however, to put up with very intense cold, so much so that we were not able to remove our clothes the whole time we were away. It may give you some idea of the temperature when I state that, on getting back to the Haast Hut, one of the party had to leave his socks in his boots, as they were frozen solid through the leather. We were very lucky in having such a glorious day. With a wind, it would no doubt have been so cold that we would have had to abandon the climb.

'I was blessed with two fine companions for such a trip, in Messrs Milne and Murrell, but the success of the whole trip was due to Frank Milne, who is an absolute marvel on ice and rock and has a wonderfully fine judgment for snow conditions.'

It is worth noting that this climb was not repeated until some fifty years later, when it was done in September, considerably later in the winter.

Although it was fairly well known that my brothers, my sisters and I were closely associated with skiing in New Zealand, most people imagined we had no interest in climbing and had done very little of it. We were debarred from doing high alpine climbing in the summer for the same reason that RLW was, but over the years we covered a tremendous amount of the Park climbing, ski-touring, shooting, or just generally exploring.

Soon after the Company took over the lease of The Hermitage our parents took us there for the school holidays. We became imbued with the spirit of the Alps, and we tramped and climbed more and more extensively through the area. We would listen to the stories of the guides, and learned a lot of the techniques they used with ice-axe and rope. With crude ice-axes knocked together in the smithy forge, we would cut steps up every clay bank in the vicinity, and frequently came home covered in clay and bruises after having fallen out of our steps and crashed a dizzy four or five metres to the bottom.

One of my first climbs of any magnitude was to the top of Sebastopol. With the son of the manager of The Hermitage we started off for a climb up through Governor's Bush, down to the Blackbirch Stream on the other side and then up to the Red Lakes, halfway to the top of Sebastopol. The day was sunny and calm, and in spite of our parents' instructions to go no further than the Red Lakes, we boxed on up to the top. We were no more than nine or ten years old at the time, and were so thrilled with our exploit that we naively told our parents about it. Fortunately we did not incur the full vent of their wrath as they did not think we were capable of such a climb and simply didn't believe us! However, it was later confirmed by another party in the area that we had been right to the top.

One of our earliest trips was to the old Mueller Hut. RLW took us up to Kea Point, up the Mueller Glacier, past the Green Rock and round to the hut, where we spent the night. Next day we returned over the Sealey Range to The Hermitage. He also took us to the Hooker Hut and, with Vic Williams, we made a memorable climb of Mt Wakefield.

This climb could have put us off climbing for life and in more ways than one. Immediately below the peak a long icy snow slope dropped away 150 to 200 metres to a mass of large angular rocks at the bottom. We were roped, and were moving one by one across this slope in steps cut by Vic Williams. One of us slipped out of the steps, Vic made a dive to grab him and fell out of his steps, pulling the other two of us down. We soon picked up a tremendous speed while tumbling and sliding down over the frozen snow. Fortunately for us, the slope eased out and the snow had become softened by the sun a short distance from the rocks. This saved us. However, it taught us a very sharp lesson and curbed our more venturesome activities for some time afterwards.

During the polio epidemic of 1924-25 all schools were closed, and we were taken as a family to The Hermitage, where we were ensconced in one of the cottages, complete with school-teacher, for about three months. In theory we were supposed to spend so many hours a day in school, but in practice we were off to the hills, tagging along with some of the parties, scrounging rides on the trucks and buses, or helping Duncan Darroch at the smithy, shoeing the horses. We became as fit as fleas, and I can remember on one occasion my brother Sandy and I running all the way from the Hooker Hut back to The Hermitage, about eleven kilometres, in under an hour.

In 1927, RLW was keen to get us on some of the high climbs, and when Sandy was twelve and I was fourteen, he took us with guides Jack Pope and Jack Crombie up the Footstool, just over 2740 metres. We spent the first night at the Sefton bivouac, and next day after an early start we climbed up in perfect weather through the broken ice on the face of the Moorhouse Range and then up the rock ridges to the top of the Footstool, where we stood and enjoyed fantastic views of the forests, ranges and valleys stretching away to the west coast, and the series of ranges, the Mackenzie Plains and Lake Pukaki to the east.

Sandy and I got a great kick out of this, our first high climb, and it stimulated our enthusiasm to do higher and some difficult ones until we were able to tackle Mt Cook. A shortage of guides during the summer and various other factors stopped us doing this, and it is one of the regrets that I have today that I did not get to the top of Mt Cook on foot. However, I did do one or two quite interesting firsts in the area.

Alf Brustad, a Norwegian, was always very keen on the traditional Norwegian approach to skiing. In Norway skis were developed as a practical means of travelling over the snow during the long winter, and the sports side and competitive side sprang from this. The high-speed downhill skiing which is so popular today was unknown in Norway until quite recently.

Alf's ambition was to traverse all the glaciers, cross all the alpine passes possible, and also to climb peaks in the winter, and with other skiers he achieved some notable feats in his time.

A trip which he was very keen to do was from the Ball Hut up the Caroline Glacier, over the Ball Pass and down the Hooker Valley to The Hermitage. He persuaded RLW to allow me to accompany him, even though at that date my knowledge of skiing was fairly elementary. Late in the August school holidays in 1929 Alf and I set out from the Ball Hut a couple of hours before daylight. We attached strips of sealskin to the skis in such a way that they would slide forward but would not slide back, thus enabling us to walk straight up relatively steep slopes.

We donned the skis low down on the Ball Glacier, and Alf, carrying the one and only torch, took off as if he was starting on a world championship cross-country race. I had some difficulty in following him, and while he could see the dips and hollows in the snow ahead, all I could see was the bobbing glare of the torch and Alf's black outline against the snow. For the first kilometre or two the track was reasonably well defined — it had been used by skiers over the previous few days — and I managed to pant and grunt along behind him. But then we got into the dips and hollows and the more rugged going at the head of the glacier, and here Alf had to twist and turn to keep to the flattest snow, to dodge the hummocks and the exposed ice faces and crevasses. All I could do was to take a straight line across country, following the general direction of the torch ahead.

Everything underfoot looked a flat unbroken white. It was impossible to see what was uphill and what was downhill, and I was wasting a prodigious amount of energy in simply keeping on my feet. Suddenly I found myself flying through space, hoping that the crevasse I was falling into was not more than fifteen metres deep and had some soft snow at the bottom, rather than hard rocks and ice.

I landed on snow about three metres below and it just about knocked the stuffing out of me. It was some time before I could get my skis, rucksack, arms and legs sorted out and my hat back on my head, and was able to stand up on a patch of sloping snow. A while afterwards Alf came back looking for me, and I gave that Norwegian a dollop of good New Zealand vernacular for tearing ahead and leaving me without any light.

Slowly we worked our way over the broken uneven ice of the Caroline Glacier and then across a long traverse of the eastern side of the valley. Although the hillside was steep the slope was smooth, the going was very much easier, and I had no difficulty in following Alf's tracks. As we left the traverse and turned to the right and up the long snow slope later known as Elworthy's Run, the first light was showing as a yellow tinge on the top of Mt Cook, the best part of 3000 metres above us. With every step we climbed upwards this yellow glow brought out more features of the mountain, its outline against the dark sky, black rock faces surrounded by snow slopes and ice hundreds of metres in thickness. This ice flowing down at three, four or five metres a day was torn and twisted into all sorts of fantastic shapes, some like skyscraper buildings, others like cathedral spires, others like anvils, and between them tremendous black crevasses descending far down to the hard rock below.

As the light increased, showing minute by minute more details of the mountain face, it changed from yellow to a light pink which grew in intensity until it was bright red. Soon the whole top of the mountain was painted red and black as the light threw everything into relief. We stopped climbing and gazed in sheer wonder as the colours built up to a climax and then faded.

Some time later the sun came over the eastern horizon of jagged peaks and shone fully on the slopes we were climbing, creating a warmer and much more benign atmosphere. Above us was the rugged, ever-changing view of the Mt Cook eastern face, and round to the right we looked down on the Tasman Glacier, sliding its way down its five-kilometre-wide bed, hemmed in on either side by steeply-rising mountain ranges. The sun, now beating down mercilessly, was reflected back from the north-facing snow slopes, and although it was mid-winter we were soon peeling off our outer clothing. The top of the pass, 2195 metres, was reached later in the morning and we sat back on our rucksacks eating lunch and enjoying the view before starting on the descent.

Twenty-seven years later, when I landed the first ski-plane on the Ball Pass and then skied down to the Ball Hut with my son Brian, I couldn't help thinking of that first trip so many years before. The distances which had taken us so long to cover on skis were dwarfed by the aeroplane, and it was hard to believe that the laborious climb which had taken us some four hours had been reduced to about fifteen minutes. To have made the first winter crossing of the Ball Pass on skis, and years later to have landed the first aeroplane there, was something I couldn't help reflecting on with not a little pride.

Many kilometres of rough untracked country lay ahead of us and, tempting though it was to relax in the sunshine for a while longer, we stripped the sealskins off the skis and skied off downhill. The first part of the descent was over a narrow snow slope leading between rocky bluffs, and this soon opened up into a wide steep fan. Alf started off on a traverse, putting both sticks together and holding them one hand at the top and the other halfway down, with the tips brushing the snow. If he wanted to stop, he jammed them in a bit harder and swung the skis uphill, and if he wanted to turn, he did a sort of stem turn, swung the sticks over the other side, dug them into the snow and used them to drag him round on to the new traverse. It was very primitive but surprisingly effective, and it demonstrates how little we knew about skiing back in 1929. I am horrified that I too used this method of turning on this trip, but it was apparently accepted practice in Norway and, at that time, it seemed to be the only way to get down under control.

At the bottom of the snowfield a narrow canyon led two or three hundred metres down to the lateral moraine of the Hooker Glacier, and this was filled with rough lumpy snow left behind by avalanches. We stopped for a breather and Alf explained to me that we were about to take off the skis and climb down an avalanche chute, probably formed through thousands of years of avalanches pouring through it. He explained that avalanches were likely to come down at any time, particularly after the sun's rays had warmed the slopes, and that we now had to travel just as fast as we possibly could to get through before the next avalanche.

He then took off like a rocket, as if an avalanche was already crashing down behind him, but in fact the only thing crashing down behind him was myself, stumbling and falling over large lumps of snow, losing my skis and hat and having to pick them up again, and then charging on, not daring to look behind for fear of what I might see. Alf was almost running and kept increasing his lead on me, which put me into a state of near-panic; when I reached the bottom of the chute, some time after him, I was just about exhausted.

For the next few kilometres we skied along snow on the lateral moraine in and out of the mountain scrub and spear-grass until we hit the Hooker Track at the upper suspension bridge.

Chamois were very numerous at this stage, and so tame that they carried on their winter sport of glascading without paying much attention to us. They would climb up to the top of one of those snow-covered fans which had fairly hard snow on its southern side, gallop down a few metres and then lock their legs and glascade down to the bottom, closely following one another. Then they would gallop up to the top of the fan and do it all over again. It really was a most extraordinary performance, but there have been many reports of people witnessing it since then in New Zealand and overseas.

It was late when we reached The Hermitage and, if I remember rightly, the trip took us about thirteen hours, a very long day. We had done the first winter crossing of the Ball Pass from the Ball Hut to The Hermitage, and I don't imagine it has been done many times since.

Another trip which I think was a first, was a midsummer climb of Mt Sealey, mostly on skis. With my brother Sandy and Harold Elworthy, and with Mick Bowie as the guide, we carried our skis up on to the Sealey Range and donned them above the Sealey lakes as soon as there was enough snow. We climbed up to the crest of the range and then enjoyed some excellent downhill skiing to the Mueller Hut, where we spent the night. The most memorable part of the night at the hut was delicious-smelling oyster soup which Mick took some time to concoct while we sat around in a fairly ravenous state after all the day's exertions. The soup was duly served, but fell somewhat short of expectations as he had used sweetened instead of unsweetened condensed milk! We got through it just the same.

Early next morning, we put on the sealskins, climbed up over the Sealey Range, over the Annette Plateau and across to Mt Sealey, where the final ascent was made on rock. The return trip gave us some exciting downhill skiing. Another night was spent at the Mueller Hut and next day we used the skis again to climb over the Sealey Range and down to the Sealey lakes, then home on foot. It was a most enjoyable excursion, and as far as I can ascertain, the first time that skis were used for the greater part of the ascent of Mt Sealey. This would be about 1932.

In August 1934, Sandy, Mick Bowie and I made the first winter ascent of the Minarets on skis. We skied up the Tasman Glacier and spent the first night at the de la Beche Hut, which is at the confluence of the Tasman and Rudolph Glaciers. Next morning, an hour or so before daylight, we climbed up the ridge, skirted round Mt de la Beche and finally made the ascent of the Minarets, 3064 metres, removing skis only when it was necessary to cut steps, put on crampons and climb up over some of the icefalls. The view from the top was magnificent, but we did not spend much time there as the cold was intense; in spite of all our exertion, we were unable to keep our hands and feet, ears and noses, from becoming extremely cold. The run down on skis was exhilarating, but not as enjoyable as it might have been, as the snow was not in very good condition. However, we kept on traversing and turning, for about 1500 metres until we arrived back at the de la Beche Hut, cold, tired but well satisfied at having made the first winter ascent of the Minarets.

As well as these climbs, we made other excursions, ski-touring or on shooting trips which took us into most parts of the Park, and all this experience spread over a number of years has enabled me to gain a wide knowledge of almost every aspect of it.

It was this knowledge of skiing and the snowfields of the glaciers which encouraged me to develop retractable skis for aeroplanes to enable them to land on these huge snowfields, and it was this knowledge and love of the area which is behind our wish to share our enjoyment of it. Although we delight in showing it to other people we have no desire to see it despoiled or polluted in any way, and have for very sound reasons developed a much more protective attitude towards it than so many critics who, in fact, know a lot less about it.

There's no point in having these glorious assets kept in cottonwool, as it were, where no one can see them and enjoy them. But people must be allowed to enjoy them in an orderly way, so that the area is not polluted and other people's enjoyment is not impaired. To date, there has been no indication of such detrimental trends.

RLW had a great love and knowledge of the mountains, glaciers and flora of the area, and he made every endeavour to ensure that others enjoyed it as much as he did. Frequently he would gather up a few people sitting round the Hermitage lounge and, acting as their guide, would take them out walking through the bush or up one or other of the valleys. He always carried the ice-axe he used on the first winter ascent of Mt Cook, and usually a rucksack with the makings of lunch or morning or afternoon tea. His love and enthusiasm for the country were obvious and infectious, and people from all over New Zealand have told me of the happy times they enjoyed on those excursions.

Although he had no great botanical knowledge, he knew the

common names for a great number of the many species of trees and plants growing in the Park. His favourites were the Mt Cook lilies, the *Ranunculus lyallii* which used to grow in profusion throughout the Southern Alps. This plant has large green, fleshy, cupshaped leaves, the size of a soup-plate, and in spring it sends up a flower stem holding eight or ten flowers, ten to twelve centimetres in diameter, with pure white double petals and a brilliant yellow centre. Seen against its harsh natural background it is one of our most spectacular and beautiful alpine plants.

RLW used to delight in picking a dozen or so stems and taking them back to my mother in a bucket of water, and when she put them in vases they would brighten the house for many days. My mother, who was an accomplished painter, was also very keen on the lilies and did numerous paintings of them. One day round about 1913 RLW brought some lilies home and gave her instructions to paint one of them as he wanted it to use as a design for a luggage label. She sketched one out and was tentatively covering the stamens when RLW came home and said, 'That's *exactly* what I want!' and took it away without allowing her to finish it. That lily design, almost exactly as my mother designed it in 1913, is used as the Company's emblem today and thus has become known to thousands of people in New Zealand and all over the world.

However, very few people have seen the lily growing in its natural surroundings, although it can be seen growing in profusion only four or five kilometres from The Hermitage. Its large succulent leaves appeal to the chamois, thar and deer that were introduced after the turn of the century, and by the early 1930s the lilies had almost disappeared from the scene. It was amazing that so much havoc could be caused by the animals to this and other species in so short a space of time, but fortunately the Park Board's policy of extermination of the animals, which commenced soon after World War II, has given the lilies a reprieve, and they are now coming back in large numbers each year in their original habitat.

Trips up the Tasman Valley to the Ball Hut or the Malte Brun Hut were popular with many visitors. The trip was completely different from the walks to the Stocking Glacier; it called for a greater degree of physical fitness and three or four nights living in the alpine huts.

In the days before the road to the Ball Hut was built, the Company kept twenty or twenty-five riding horses to carry supplies and people over twenty kilometres to the Ball Hut. The horses were all very quiet and even non-riders could sit on them and be carried on for kilometre after kilometre enjoying the ever-changing scenery. The guide would lead off and take the party across the Hooker Flat, round the end of the Mt Cook Spur, and then up to the terminal face of the Tasman Glacier, where lunch would be served alongside the beautiful Blue Lakes Stream, which cascaded its way down in a series of ripples and pools through the overhanging alpine scrub — mountain totara, veronicas and speargrass, with mountain lilies on the water's edge. A stand of mountain ribbonwood, with its light green foliage and profusion of white flowers in the spring, provided shelter from the burning heat of the sun. After lunch the bridle track threaded its way between the lateral moraine and the hillside, becoming extremely rough in places, and almost as much as the horses could handle.

Avalanches crossed the road quite frequently during the winter and spring, and left behind them great ridges of packed snow and rocks of all shapes and sizes; although some work was done on the track, it was only just enough to allow the surefooted animals to pick their way across, often with a terrified passenger trembling in the saddle.

The Ball Hut would be reached in the late afternoon, and a rather tired party would relax, repair some of the damage done by the unaccustomed riding, and enjoy the glorious alpine views while waiting for the guide to prepare the meal on a kerosene stove. Next day the party would do the trip over the Ball moraine on to the clear ice of the Hochstetter Icefall before returning to The Hermitage, or else would travel the seventeen kilometres up the Tasman Glacier to the Malte Brun Hut.

The Tasman must be one of the most spectacular alpine valleys in the world, with the clear ice and moraine filling-in its four or five kilometre width, while from its sides Aorangi and the other peaks rise to tremendous heights. The eastern face of Mt Cook rises nearly 3000 metres sheer; it is plastered by hundreds of metres of thickness of ice which is continually moving down and fracturing into crevasses or crashing down in avalanches when the mountain becomes too steep for it to cling to.

7

Skiing at Mount Cook

THE THOUSANDS OF HECTARES of snowy slopes in the Mount Cook National Park in the summer, and the snow-covered country in the vicinity of The Hermitage during the winter, were an open invitation to early climbers and other alpine enthusiasts to make experimental use of skis. Skis have been used in Scandinavia for hundreds of years, and many of the early climbers had some experience of using them.

Skis were developed primarily to allow farmers, reindeer herders and others to travel over ground which was covered by several metres of soft snow during the winter, just as the North American Indians developed snowshoes for the same purpose. Skis were used by some of the early climbers in the Mt Cook region not for a sport but as an easier way of crossing the snowfields than floundering through the deep snow. For example, Mannering and Dixon used skis to cross the Grand Plateau on one of the early attempts to climb Mt Cook.

Three or four pairs of skis were presented to RLW by Sir Ernest Shackleton before his departure for Antarctica in 1913, and these historic skis were fixed to the wall of the Ball Hut for many years, until someone improvising a sledge to cart supplies to the Ball Hut in the mid-1930s rather stupidly used them as runners.

These skis were interesting in that they were made by the early miners at Kiandra, one of the Australian goldfields. The miners had heard about skis but had never seen them, and so developed their own to get over the snow-covered ground and to while away the time during the hard cold winters when the frozen ground brought mining activities to a standstill. The miners formed a club to organise races and other activities, and this is claimed to be the oldest ski club in the world. During a visit to Australia in 1937 with the New Zealand ski team I was presented with one of the original Kiandra Ski Club badges, dated 1871.

Apart from the historical aspect, the Shackleton skis were unusual in that instead of having a single groove to keep them straight, they had fifteen or twenty very small longitudinal ones, much like the old-fashioned butter-pat. The bindings consisted of a large leather loop into which the skier pushed the toe of his boot. There was nothing to hold the heel in place, and it must have been difficult for the skier to exercise any form of control. Single poles were used, and the early Kiandra pictures show skiers holding this in both hands while skiing down comparatively short flattish slopes. As with so many other things of historical interest in the Mt Cook area forty or fifty years ago, the historic interest of these skis was ignored and no effort was made to preserve them.

RLW had played round on skis at Fairlie and at The Hermitage at various times, and made good use of them on the first winter ascent of Mt Cook in August 1923. They donned skis at the Blue Lakes, eleven kilometres from The Hermitage, and skied the remainder of the way to the Ball Hut, and later from the Ball Hut to the bottom of the Haast Ridge. On the day of the great climb they skied from the top of the Glacier Dome to the Silverhorn Corner, and this helped them considerably.

Although skis had been used to facilitate travel over the snow, very little had been done in New Zealand to popularise skiing as a sport, and it appears that it was not until 1915 that a serious effort was made to attract people to Mt Cook to ski. The advertisements of the Company indicate the lack of co-operation between the Company and the Tourist Department, who owned The Hermitage: the Company advertised that skiing at Mt Cook opened on 1 October (which would be considered well past the height of the skiing season today), and emphasised the fact that the Department closed The Hermitage during the winter and did not reopen until 1 October.

In spite of this the Company persevered with its effort to establish skiing, but it was not until it took over the lease of The Hermitage about 1922 and kept it open through the winter that skiing had a reasonable chance of becoming popular. The advertisements of August 1915 are probably the earliest efforts made to popularise skiing in the South Island. From the *Timaru Herald*:

WINTER SPORT
THE WORLD-RENOWNED SPORT OF SKIING
TO THE SOUTHERN ALPS A GREAT AND NEW
ATTRACTION

The Hermitage will open on October 1 with full staff of guides and skiing experts etc.

The Tourist Department has a plentiful supply of skis and boots.

The Mount Cook district affords a splendid playground.

A twice-weekly motor service will be maintained between Fairlie and The Hermitage during October.

Write us for further particulars or enquire at the Government Tourist Offices.

MOUNT COOK MOTOR COMPANY LTD., FAIRLIE.

This was followed by some editorial comment a few days later:

Skiing bids fair to become as popular a form of recreation, so we are informed, in the South Island, as it is in some parts of the northern hemisphere. From a notice in another column it will be seen that The Hermitage will open on 1 October with a full staff of guides, ski experts etc. The management have a plentiful supply of skis and boots.

The Mount Cook district is specially adapted for skiing, and affords a splendid playground. The Tourist Department and the Mount Cook Motor Co. are sparing no effort to make this world-renowned sport popular, and consider that it will be one of the great pleasure attractions of New Zealand and a big drawcard for both local and overseas tourists.

On the Mueller Glacier is to be made the first start of skiing. One day's walk from The Hermitage to the Mueller Hut and a visitor is on what experts consider is one of the finest skiing grounds in the world. The hut is fitted with all the necessary beds, food etc. Separate compartments are being arranged for men and ladies.

The cost of the trip can be worked out by taking the rail fare to Fairlie and from there the motor-car fare, 96 miles, for £5 return. The Hermitage tariff is 10s per day and includes the use of huts etc., a small charge being made for boots and skis. Guide fees are on a sliding scale according to the number in the party extra.

Motor-cars will leave Fairlie for The Hermitage on Tuesdays and Saturdays, returning on Mondays and Wednesdays, the first trip leaving Fairlie on 2 October. The night coming and going will need to be spent at Fairlie.

No records are available as to the type of skiing indulged in by the people attracted by the advertisements, but it would seem that it was the *raison d'être* of the exercise and that the real enjoyment was in the journey to the Mueller Hut and from the Mueller Hut back to The Hermitage.

I do not know what happened in 1915, but I do know that in the early 1920s skiing parties would trudge up the five-kilometre track to Kea Point, descend down the lateral moraine to the Mueller Glacier, climb over the large glacial rocks and shingle of the Mueller moraine up to Green Rock, which was ascended precariously to the track which continued for another kilometre or two round to the Mueller Hut, all among magnificent scenery.

It was virtually a day's trip in dry conditions, and if snow had fallen it was tough going. When the Mueller Hut had been reached in the afternoon it was too late to do any skiing and, in fact, the terrain in the vicinity was so steep as to be unsuitable for the sort of skiers who would have made the trip. While the guide was getting the hut ready, the party would be enjoying the fabulous views up and down the Mueller Glacier, to the south towards the Barron Saddle with rock and ice peaks on either side, and to the west towards Mt Sefton, and to the precipitous rock and ice faces which extended in a semicircle from the west round to the south. The hut consisted of two rooms, one for women and one for men, with three or four double tiers of bunks for each room.

The men's room was the living and dining-room as well. It had a rough board table and forms in the centre, and at one end a bench and a couple of Perfection kerosene cooking stoves. There was no running water during the winter as the tanks were frozen, and all supplies for eating, drinking and washing had to come from snow, which was melted in large pots.

The lavatory consisted of a 1 x 1-metre building erected over a large hole in the rocky terrain about fifty metres away, and during the sojourn at the hut and during the trips further afield it was no place for the prim and the modest. When nature calls it is no respecter of persons, and if there was no shelter or visual protection, that was just too bad and the parties had to accept it. Conditions were cetainly crude, but it was exciting, and a completely different way of life from what most people had been used to.

The country in the vicinity of the Mueller Hut was too steep for the skiers of those days, so when breakfast was over and the hut tidied up, the party would follow the guide and climb for an hour or so up over ribs of rock and steep snow slopes to the crest of the range, where the skiing began. Here the country was much more suitable, with snow slopes descending steeply from outcrops of rock and gradually flattening out, ideal for beginners.

Skis and sticks were piled behind a large rock and it was the guide's job to issue these and fit the rather crude 'Huitfeldt' bindings to the skier's climbing boots. These bindings consisted of steel plates inserted through a slot in the centre of the ski and bent upwards on either side to hold the toe of the boot in place. The plates were bent to the shape of the boot by a few bashes from a hammer, and woe betide anyone unfortunate enough to be suffering from corns when being fitted by a guide whose aim was less than perfect.

The technique of skiing and turning on skis was almost unknown, so the day's exercise consisted of herringboning up the slope as far as one's courage and ability would allow, then schussing straight down until disaster or the flatness of the slope brought the skier to a standstill, when the whole business would start all over again. The rather fanciful advertisements of the day showed girls dressed up with long skirts, woolly sweaters and scarves and big wide-brimmed hats, sailing through the air above the snow with hair and clothing hanging straight down, as if the skier was suspended from a balloon.

Lunch carried by the guide from the Mueller Hut would be served out, and the party would sit round on the rocks, chewing away at doormat-size sandwiches and enjoying the fantastic views, some of the best anywhere in the Mt Cook National Park. Away to the north, Mt Cook rises clear and unobstructed from the Hooker Glacier and, to the west, Mt Sefton, and the Moorhouse Range with its tremendous glaciated face appears to be only a stone's throw away, though it must be all of three kilometres. Lumps of falling ice and rock make sharp reports like rifle shots, while avalanches sound thunderous. Away to the south, the head of the Mueller Glacier and the high peaks surrounding it are equally spectacular, but in a different way.

At the end of a day's skiing the party would either return to the Mueller Hut, half an hour or so away, or descend down the northern side of the Sealey Range, past the Sealey lakes and so down to The Hermitage.

The long snow slopes above the Sealey lakes lend themselves to glissading — sitting in the snow and lifting the legs up in the air and letting gravity take over — a form of descent which can be lots of fun, even though it often ends in some fairly violent tumbles, but I would not imagine that it would have been tackled with much enthusiasm by the more decorous females wearing long skirts.

Skiing was really an excuse for alpine excursions and was not an end in itself, as it is today. There are no records available to show how many parties made the trip to the Mueller Hut to ski, so it is not possible to estimate its effect on the long-term development of skiing in the area. Although the advertising was continued, skiing does not appear to have developed as a sport by itself until the Company took over the lease of The Hermitage in 1922, and kept it open during the winter to cater for skiers while the snow was on the lower slopes.

Throughout its history the Company has been forced into various new fields of activity in order to generate traffic for its bus and air services, and the development of skiing at Mt Cook was a case in point.

Until 1921 the Government, owners of The Hermitage, operated it during the summer to cater for visitors, but closed it down from March or April to the end of September. RLW believed that by keeping it open and developing winter sports, sufficient traffic could be built up to give a far better economic utilisation of his buses, it was just too wasteful for Government assets in The Hermitage and the Company's own cars and plant to be lying idle for six months of the year.

Despite his efforts to persuade them he could not get the heads of the Tourist Department to change their minds, and it was not until he succeeded in taking over the lease of The Hermitage from the Government that he could put his theories to the test.

To prepare for the winter sports, a natural ice-skating rink was built behind The Hermitage. This was kept clear of snow and serviced and planed for most of the winter; it played its part in publicising winter sports and no doubt attracted a number of enthusiasts to The Hermitage. But the main drive was in the development of skiing, and in the expectation that snow would be lying round The Hermitage for the greater part of the winter, trails were cut up through the matagouri scrub a few hundred metres to the west of the building. The larger rocks were shifted out of the way and a certain amount of grooming was done on the slopes, which are rather flat by today's standards but were quite adequate for those taking on the sport of skiing in the early 1920s. The matagouri, which is very slow growing, has not regenerated on these trails and they are still quite evident today.

Skis and sticks for hiring, and brightly coloured caps, scarves, sweaters and other items of skiers' clothing were imported from Switzerland for sale. Word got round that the Company was looking for ski experts, and a number of Norwegians, who had arrived in the country on whaling ships and left them in circumstances into which the Company preferred not to enquire, applied for the job. Whether they had any real knowledge of skiing is doubtful, but they had broken accents and a great deal of charm, and did as much as the sport itself to attract the ladies on to the snow.

Much had to be done to The Hermitage itself to cater for winter traffic, particularly in heating, and with all arrangements made, the advertising was released.

However, during the first winter, difficulties hit the Company from every direction. No firewood had been brought in earlier, and what was later gathered was damp and refused to make the roaring fires that people needed and expected. The roads were too soft to bring in much coal. There was no power, and the guests muttered about the 'Stone Age' when they found they had to have candles in their bedrooms. All these difficulties were overcome, but it all took time.

The response must have been encouraging, with skiers travelling from all over New Zealand, as the following newspaper clip of 1923 shows:

Auckland 3 September.
A party consisting of thirty-three Aucklanders who left on 12 August for a holiday at The Hermitage, Mount Cook, all expressed themselves in enthusiastic terms with regard to the general comfort and rapidity of travel and complete absence of any inconvenience from cold. In the early part of the holiday there were large falls of snow, thus giving facilities for all forms of winter sports in the immediate vicinity of The Hermitage. The popularity of this form of holiday was evidenced by the fact that during one weekend there were as many as seventy guests in the hotel while during another weekend there were sixty-two.

The majority of members of the party made good progress in the art of skiing, under the instruction received from the guides. A group of twelve travelled on skis from The Hermitage near the Mueller Glacier to the Mueller Hut, a total distance of fourteen miles, and involved a climb of over 3000 feet.

One outstanding feature of the journey was the shortness of the time occupied in covering the distance between Auckland and The Hermitage: the party left Auckland on

Stylist skier Barry Caulfield was brought out from Switzerland by the Company for several seasons to the Ball Hut to demonstrate and teach up-to-date techniques.

The Case tractor and trailer carting stores and passengers to the Ball Hut in the mid-1930s. RLW stands behind the tractor.

The Ball Hut, main base for Tasman Valley expeditions until the new hut was built, *circa* 1928.

Coronet Peak. The first rope-tow — a terrific innovation when installed.

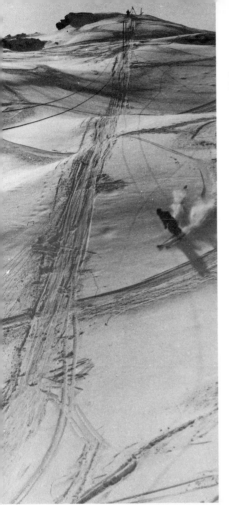

Another angle on the Coronet Peak rope-tow.

The chairlift at Coronet Peak is taking shape. Ray Robinson perches on top, Johnny Bell on the right.

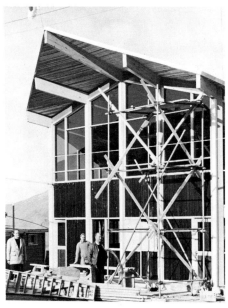

Coronet Peak restaurant under construction. Otto von Allmen on left, Jack Anderson on right.

Opening of the chairlift. *From left*, Geoff Maslin, Harry Wigley, Eric Chapman (of CWF Hamilton Ltd), Sir Leonard Wright, Sid Odell (general manager of Government Tourist Dept.), Aub Rollinson, Fred Walker.

Isla and Harry Wigley on the double chairlift.
The triple chairlift, with other lifts and facilities in the background.

Press cartoonist commemorates an unrehearsed chairlift incident. The lift stopped and two unauthorised passengers, tired of waiting for it to start again, removed their slacks and made a sort of rope ladder of them, then dropped on to the ground beneath. The lift started again before they had time to retrieve them . . .

Wigley & Thornley's tractor-engine train, the 'calaboose' at rear, outside the Dominion Hotel in Timaru, 1905. RLW is perched atop the second wagon-load of woolbales.

Petrol invasion. The two gallant little 6hp De Dions outside The Hermitage after their epic trip from Timaru. John Rutherford's car on left, RLW's on right.

'The Beetle', RLW at the helm, setting out to deliver His Majesty's mails.

Above, the Company's Queenstown office in the early 1920s. *Middle*, Tekapo House, 1922. *Bottom*, Pukaki, about 1922.

A splendid performer in its day. The 40hp Darracq that inaugurated the Fairlie-Mt Cook service.

Sunday evening and reached their destination in time for dinner on Tuesday evening.

Professor Ronald Algie, later Sir Ronald, Speaker of the House, brought parties of twenty or thirty from Auckland to The Hermitage each winter, while many other parties were organised from Wellington and other points not so far afield. The thought of a winter holiday, enjoying this exhilarating sport in the clear crisp air in a world of white, was appealing to more and more people, and traffic continued to build steadily, giving good off-season utilisation to the hotel and the Motor Company's fleet. This expansion continued until the world-wide depression brought everything nearly to a standstill in the late 1920s.

Contrary to his expectations, RLW found that the snow did not lie round The Hermitage all winter. There were frequent snowfalls that did, but there were also quite long periods when it was not possible to ski. To overcome this, day excursions were made to the bottom end of the Mueller Glacier, where a number of pairs of skis and sticks were cached. This entailed a walk of five kilometres to Kea Point and another kilometre or so over the rough moraine of the Glacier before reaching areas 300 metres or more above The Hermitage, which held more snow and provided better slopes. The broken state of the glacier made the runs very short and unsatisfactory. It did provide some skiing, but interest swung away from the Mueller to the Ball Hut.

The traditional form of skiing in Norway is cross-country travel, where light narrow skis are used for touring over quite long distances; in cross-country racing the skiers would lope along at high speeds over flat or undulating ground for forty or fifty kilometres. The Norwegians' influence on skiing at Mt Cook was naturally towards this type of sport, and they encouraged people to visit the outlying Malte Brun Hut at the head of the Tasman Glacier, and to use this as a base to make day-trips to the Tasman Saddle, the Lindenfeldt Saddle, the Hochstetter Dome, and other places where the slopes were ideal for this type of skiing.

Among the overseas people who enjoyed using skis as a means to an end rather than as an end in themselves and who toured extensively through the Park, was Captain Fox, the secretary of the British Ski Association. A newspaper cutting of 1923 gives his views on this subject:

Captain J. N. Fox, Secretary of the British Skiing Association, has just completed a three weeks visit to Mount Cook.

Interviewed yesterday by the Timaru representative of *The Press*, Captain Fox, who is an instructor of skiing in Switzerland and holds a first-class certificate, stated that people in New Zealand did not realise the great asset they had in Mount Cook ... Mount Cook compared very favourably with some of the finest alpine sports places in Switzerland.

The Hermitage provided exceptional accommodation for visitors, and there were unlimited opportunities at the mountain for winter sport, particularly skiing. He was greatly impressed by the grandeur of the scenery and the possibilities for development. Lovers of alpine sports, he said, would find at Mount Cook all the material of Switzerland in the way of sports grounds ready at hand, and all that was needed was the realisation on the part of the public of the opportunities available. Captain Fox intends taking a party of forty to the mountains next winter.

The telemark turn, devised for soft-snow skiing, was introduced by the Norwegians, and is done by sliding one ski forward until the boot on that ski is opposite the tip of the other ski, when it is turned inwards to turn the whole outfit round like the front wheel of a bike. The base is very narrow, and it is so difficult to get the weight evenly balanced between the two skis that the telemark has never become really popular in this country.

It was, however, the first step in the development of interest in the downhill skiing practised today, where nearly all the fun is derived from sliding downhill at slow, moderate or immoderate speeds, and controlling the descent by a series of turns. This type of skiing did not come into popularity at Mt Cook until the early 1930s, when people who had done it in Europe, such as Harold Elworthy, Tom Mitchell and a number of others, visited the Ball Hut and taught us the rudiments.

In the early 1930s many of us had been skiing enthusiastically for ten years or more. We had read overseas books of instruction on the subject and had gleaned what information we could from the Norwegians and others who had had some experience in Europe, but we knew very little about it. We could probably do some sort of a stem turn and attempt christies and telemarks, but were not capable of doing anything more advanced than this.

One of the reasons was that we had to climb uphill, a laborious process, for every metre we skied downhill; so, playing around on small slopes, we were expending an awful lot of energy to get, in a whole day, as much as a single run on a modern uphill lift would have given us.

Another reason was that we were generally limited to heavy soft unbroken snow, which is extremely difficult if not impossible to turn in. If we wished to pack the snow we had to do it by the laborious process of sidestepping uphill on the skis, tramping it down and making it smooth enough to turn on, but the amount we could pack in this way was so limited that it provided no scope for really worthwhile practice.

Although we had read the books, most of us had never seen a proficient skier in action, so when Harold Elworthy from Timaru and his friend Tom Mitchell from Victoria returned from Europe, where they had spent several winters in Switzerland learning the Arlberg technique, we were all excited to see how it was done by the experts. Harold and Tom were very good, showing us all they knew; and now, having someone to emulate, it was not long before we started making real progress.

RLW listened enthusiastically to all their stories of the skiing developments in Switzerland and Austria. He realised that we had to get away from the Scandinavian type of skiing and go almost completely over to the downhill style being developed in Central Europe. To do this, the services of a suitable overseas instructor must be obtained. He engaged for the job Barry Caulfield, who arrived out in time for the 1934 season. Barry, a tall suave blond Englishman who had spent most of his life in Switzerland, was an ideal man for the job. He was the son of Vivian Caulfield, one of the pioneers of the development of downhill skiing in Switzerland, who had written several books on the subject. Barry had started skiing at an early age, and after a number of years of successful racing he had become a professional ski teacher in Switzerland, teaching the technique which his father had developed and perfecting it.

As opposed to the Arlberg method of teaching, where the skier squatted down and was said to leave five tracks in the snow, Barry stood erect with slightly bent knees and skis held tightly together, executing his turns with a swinging motion which was effective and very graceful to watch. Although quietly spoken, he had a keen sense of humour and was popular with the guides, staff and skiers. He returned to the Ball Hut each year until the war put an end to his trips at the end of 1939.

Always progressive, RLW was prepared for the Company to carry considerable expense in acquiring such a fine instructor for the Ball Hut, and paid for Barry's fare from Europe to New

Zealand and back, and his salary for a number of months annually. This paid off, for many of our staff and other New Zealanders learned his technique and spread it, with the result that the standard of skiing in New Zealand improved rapidly in the years immediately before the war. Their teaching allowed others to make rapid progress, and they returned enthusiastically again and again. In later years many of them brought their children with them to Coronet Peak.

Right from the early days of skiing at Mt Cook, races of one kind or another were run and prizes given to stimulate interest. But there was no continuity, and the early standards were not very high. Early in the 1930s the Company organised a series of races at the end of July and the end of August, and induced business firms to support these with trophies and prizes. The Company also organised parties of schoolchildren to visit the Ball Hut in May to learn to ski, and here again races were run at the end of the holidays.

These meetings attracted quite a lot of interest, particularly in slalom racing where the skiers ran one by one down a timed zigzag course through pairs of flags, and they allowed the skiers to demonstrate to themselves and everyone else that they had learned something about the art of standing on the skis and turning. Every year the standard got higher as a result of Barry Caulfield's training and as more and more skiers, such as Dr Paul Wood, who had been trained overseas, took part in the competitions.

Earlier, a number of flat cross-country races were organised by Alf Brustad and other Norwegians, starting from near the Malte Brun Hut and finishing about fifteen kilometres further down the Tasman Glacier, but this was too strenuous and too uninteresting to appeal to the average skier and was eventually discontinued.

The New Zealand Championships, under the control of the New Zealand Ski Council, were first held at Mt Cook in 1935, and afterwards alternated between Mt Cook and Ruapehu. The slaloms were held on the slopes behind the Ball Hut, descending down through a fairly narrow gut and ending on the flatter slopes just below the hut. The courses, which had to be packed down laboriously by skis, were of a higher standard each year, and many of the better skiers from the North and South Islands became capable of more and more creditable performances. The downhill races were run from the Ball Pass at 2201 metres down to a point about 750 metres lower down at the head of the Ball Glacier. The long, even, snow slopes of the course lent themselves to high speeds rather than turning, and it was a question of who could stay on his skis the longest and take the fewest tumbles who won the race.

The course was a little over three kilometres long, and it was impossible to pack it, so skiers pointed their skis straight down the unbroken slopes and hoped that tricky conditions, breakable crust, sastrugi and other natural phenomenon would not tip them out! The better the skier, the more speed he developed — and the greater the crash when he finally baled out. Some of the crashes were really spectacular and it's amazing that these tremendous eggbeaters and cartwheels didn't fracture more limbs.

On occasions the snow would be reasonably hard over the full length of the course, and if the weather remained fine over several days it was possible for racers to put on sealskins, climb up to the Ball Pass each day, and ski down over the course, which became reasonably well marked and well packed and took some of the sporting hazard out of it.

In 1937 an official American team visited New Zealand, headed by one of its leading racers, Dick Durrance, and three other prominent skiers, Jim O'Loughlin and Steve and Dave Bradly. They were far ahead of the New Zealand skiers, who watched in amazement as they controlled their high speed through the flags of the slalom. But our chances of evening the score on the downhill seemed to be reasonable; not much turning was required, we knew the course, and we felt we could hold as high a speed as the Americans, so we spent many days practising and training over it. The conditions were good, with hard-packed snow which got better and better as more and more people trained over it every day. We must have been extraordinarily fit in those days, for we could fix the sealskins to our skis, climb over 1000 metres up to the Ball Pass and, after a very brief spell, ski down again at racing speed. On one occasion my brother Sandy and I did the return trip from the Ball Hut to the Ball Pass and back to the hut in a few minutes under the two hours. It probably took us an hour and three quarters to climb up and fifteen minutes to ski down again.

When the great day of the race arrived, the weather was perfect, the snow conditions on the course were as good as they had ever been, and we New Zealanders were out to show that we could compete with the Americans on equal terms. We raced at minute intervals, starting from the top of a very high steep slope which ran out a kilometre or so away on to flatter snow. All the skiers preceding me had skied off to the left and turned back to the right lower down to avoid a steep slope which they feared they could not hold, but during the preceding few days I had been going straight down the left-hand end where the drop was least, and had managed to hold it, although going really fast. The conditions on the day were really good, and I thought that if I could go over the steepest part and hold it, I would be well ahead of everyone else. So, when the starter gave the 5, 4, 3, 2, 1, 'Go' I pushed straight over the side of the slope, which kept curving away out of sight below me.

It felt like falling into space, and I had never gone so fast on skis before nor since. Although crouched down, I had to lean against the air as if it was solid, and after what seemed to be minutes, but which was only seconds of intense concentration, with the skis clattering on the snow and almost out of control, and my clothes rattling with the speed of the wind, I gradually rode out on to the flatter snow and relaxed for a few minutes before diving into the next and more difficult part of the course.

I was extremely lucky to have stayed on my feet, but I felt that if I continued to hold a straight line, Durrance would have no show of catching me. I took the straightest course possible, went through the finish and turned to a stop, feeling rather smug about the whole performance.

I was soon disillusioned. Dick Durrance had started after me and had watched me go over the top. He followed in my tracks and continued to follow them till he went through the finish. My time was 2 minutes 45 seconds and he knocked fifteen seconds off this, but how he did it I do not know, to this day.

After racing against the Americans at the Ball Hut, the New Zealand team travelled over to Mt Kosciusko in Australia and raced against them again as well as against an Australian team.

The standard of New Zealand skiing had improved enormously in the few years before the war, thanks to the efforts of Barry Caulfield and others, but progress was bound to be slow where the skiers had to climb laboriously up for every metre they had skied down, and it was only a matter of time before the Ball Hut, with its lack of facilities, had to give way to skifields such as Coronet Peak, which were designed in the modern idiom with road access to the snow, modern uphill lifts and public rooms and cafeterias.

In the days of the Ball Hut the skier of average standard

would probably get no more than 200 metres of downhill running in a day, whereas at Coronet Peak he could easily get 10,000, all on packed snow, which is much easier to ski on and requires the expenditure of less energy.

8

Queenstown and Coronet Peak

EVER SINCE THE GOLDRUSH DAYS the Southern Lakes — once known as the Cold Lakes to distinguish them from the thermal lakes of the North Island such as Rotorua — have attracted tourists and holidaymakers. As far back as 1870 the newspapers reported an influx of tourists. The hotels, built to handle large numbers of people in the days when the goldmining boom was at its height, were ready to welcome tourists and holiday makers when the gold was fading out.

An idea of the magnitude of the goldrush and its effect on the development of the population of Queenstown will be gained from notes made by Linton Mann in 1930: 'In the great goldrush of the early 1860s, the Shotover was the greatest attraction. In 1862 there were 120 claims operating, and four times in nine months the mines were flooded out. The miners mostly came from Bendigo, Victoria. The richest claims, owned by a man named Dwyer, were near Skippers. Commencing washing up, he got 48 ounces of gold in the first foot of the boxes, then a flood came and the river rose ten feet and washed away his boxes containing gold estimated to be about 300 ounces. Sew Hoy commenced dredging in the lower Shotover near Arthur's Point in 1865 and worked until 1872, collecting £32,406 worth of gold; this portion of the river is now known as Big Beach. Dwyer returned in 1872 and started lower down the river, diverted its course and drove shafts to a depth of 40 feet where he struck the old riverbed carrying very heavy gold, nuggets weighing up to 4 and 5 ounces being found. During the rush, the population of Queenstown was 12,000 and in the town itself there were twenty-six hotels and four stores.'

Other facilities which lent themselves to the development of the tourist industry were the Government paddlewheel steamers, the *Ben Lomond*, and the *Mountaineer*, and much later the twin-screw *Earnslaw*, supplemented by smaller motor-launches owned by such characters as Jock Edgar and Harold Tomkies. Roads had also been cut through some very rugged but spectacular mountain valleys and passes such as the Crown Range road, which links Wanaka to Queenstown, and from Queenstown up to the Shotover River to the mining town of Skippers, the so-called 'Cobb & Co' horse-drawn coaches ran from Queenstown to Skippers and over to Wanaka.

All the ingredients for a tourist industry was there, and as the miners moved out, the tourists moved in.

The Company promoted the area from the time it connected it by motorcoach service with Mt Cook; and the Railways, which ran from Invercargill to Kingston and operated the lake steamers, also promoted it. Early in the 1900s Queenstown had become well known as one of the main tourist areas in New Zealand.

Like The Hermitage at Mt Cook, it prospered during the summer but went to sleep in the winter, as it was extremely cold and had nothing to offer visitors. The hotels and other services would reduce staff drastically, and the total winter population of the town right up until the time of World War II would drop to probably fewer than 150 people.

The local tradesmen had virtually nothing to do for the greater part of six months, during much of which the ground was too frozen for even the normal winter chores in the garden. Most itinerant employees would leave the town and many of the shopkeepers and hoteliers would do the same, while those that remained would spend their days chatting away on street corners or lounging round the fires at one of the four pubs.

In 1938 my brother Sandy, a very competent skier, was sent to Queenstown to be branch manager for the Company, and it was not long before the depressing waste of tourist facilities lying idle caused him to do something about it by way of the development of skiing. Snow falls quite frequently around Queenstown, and he persuaded some of the local lads to try skiing for themselves. Soon he had a band of enthusiasts, keen to exploit the potential of the area.

The obvious places to start were the Crown Range, where the road ran up to over 1200 metres, and the Skippers Saddle at about 1000 metres, at which height the snow lay for a number of months each winter. Although no snow-clearing equipment was provided by the Lakes County Council, the Crown Range was selected as it seemed to hold more snow. A 4 x 5 metres hut, which had previously been Jock Edgar's office on the water-front, was transported up to a suitable site during the summer and used for storing skis and to provide shelter during skiing excursions in the winter.

Jock Edgar was one of the characters of the district. A confirmed bachelor, an inveterate gambler, he had no family ties and not many other responsibilities, and would periodically go on a bender for two or three days. Jock, who was never known to hurry, had a Southland drawl, and when he told one of his innumerable yarns, often against himself, his eyes and florid face would light up.

In his youth he was once lined up before the local magistrate — who happened to be his father — on a charge of being drunk and disorderly, and in due course he was fined 7s 6d. After listening to the magistrate make his pronouncement, Jock said in a loud voice: 'You'll have to pay it, Dad.' He went off to the South African War and gambled his way round that country with varying degrees of success, finally arriving on board the ship which was to take the contingent home with not a penny in his pocket, and only the clothes he stood up in. He claimed that when he stepped ashore in New Zealand he owned nearly all the loose cash on the ship, as well as a wide range of saddles and bridles, watches and other gear.

Returning to his hometown of Queenstown, he bought a graceful old launch — the *Thelma*, with a yacht-type counter stern and a slow-revving single-banger engine — and with this he ran trips for tourists to Bob's Cove and other places, as well as charter trips to the many parts of the lake not serviced by road. The old *Thelma* was later used on Lake Ohau for a number of years until she went ashore and was damaged beyond repair, and as far as I know she is still lying on the beach below the Lodge.

To cope with expanding traffic Jock had built a modern passenger launch, the *Kelvin*, and he also developed walking trips up the Routeburn Valley and down the Greenstone, using a series of mountain huts and packhorses to carry in supplies. He ran the business from a small building on a piece of land he owned on the waterfront across the road from Eichardts, and it was this building which was moved to the Crown Range and later on to Coronet Peak to establish skiing there.

In the mid 1920s the Company bought the whole of Jock Edgar's business, including the launches, the land on the waterfront, and his huts and horses. A modern building to replace Jock's hut was erected on the waterfront site to house the branch office and staff. Once a year Dooley Coxhead, who was then Company secretary, did a round of the Routeburn and Greenstone Valleys to check the huts and count the horses, but it was not until some years later we found that the ones that Jock had sold to us actually belonged to the Tourist Department! Jock owned property all round Queenstown, and in his latter years he lived in a house high up on the hills behind the town. His route home was steep, almost too steep for a motorcar. After one of his benders, he was seen making a determined but very erratic attack on the hill; finally, determined not to be beaten, he dropped to his hands and knees and proceeded, if not more rapidly, at least more steadily. A passer-by yelled out 'Hello Jock, you've sure got a skinful tonight!' Jock replied, 'Yes, and if I'd had any more I'd have to go back for a second load!'

A number of skiing excursions were made to the Crown Range and others to the Coronet Peak area, but after a season or two it became obvious that Coronet Peak held considerably more snow and for a longer period, so it received more and more attention as time went on.

Sandy's enthusiasm spread to more and more of the local people, and enthusiasts who had patronised Mt Ruapehu, Mt Egmont and Mt Cook, now heard about Coronet Peak and travelled down to see what it was all about. By the time World War II was declared, enough skiers were coming into the town to provide some winter business for the local tradesmen, hotels and road services, and it was clear this trend would continue to expand.

The first mechanised transport of skiers in Queenstown probably took place in the winter of 1938, when heavy snow blanketed the whole area. The Lakes County Council had cleared the road to the Skippers Saddle and beyond to provide access for the farmers and miners living in the Shotover Valley. The opportunity presented by this to get some downhill skiing without having to climb for it was too good to miss, so we fitted a car with chains and got RLW to drive us up to the Skippers Saddle. From there we skied upwards across the face towards the present chairlift site, and then 600 metres or more down to the flat, where we were picked up and taken back up to the Saddle again for another run.

In 1944 the lease of The Hermitage reverted to the control of the Tourist Department, who took little interest in continuing the development of skiing in the Mt Cook area. Without the skiing, the Company's bus fleet would revert to the position it had been in in 1920 before the development of skiing, when it was completely idle for the winter months. This was not only a backward step as far as the sport was concerned, but it was putting us back into the hopeless position of having staff and equipment lying idle for the winter months of the year.

It was obvious that we had to move urgently towards building up Coronet Peak to take the place of Mt Cook. It was a big job, but with the hard work and enthusiasm of so many of our staff and others who assisted us, Coronet Peak soon became established as a popular skifield, attracting skiers from all over New Zealand, as well as from Australia and further afield.

The oldtimers told us that heavy snow lay on the Skippers Saddle year after year from the beginning of June, so we took them at their word. We shifted Jock Edgar's hut over, arranged for the County to keep the road clear of snow, bought some skis and boots for people who did not have their own, did a certain amount of promotion, and waited for the snow to fall.

By the end of the winter we were still waiting. There was insufficient snow for skiing, and the skiers had to scramble over the snowgrass half covered in snow for an hour or so to where it lay more heavily on the higher, smoother slopes. The winters of 1945 and 1946 showed us that the winter snowline settled down at nearer 1200 metres; they also taught us that the slopes of the mountain were much more suitable above this altitude and further to the north.

Coronet Peak is not a high mountain, in fact it is only 1646 metres above sea level, but it is ideally suited for skiing. The rock strata lie in such a way that they slope away to the south in a series of gentle dips and hollows which make for fun-skiing. There is an almost complete absence of rocky outcrops, so it is possible to ski over much of the area on a slope of one's own choosing. Its south-facing slopes are reasonably sheltered from the prevailing winds and the direct rays of the sun, with the result that the snow often remains dry and powdery for many days on end. It is also less subject to thaw than less favoured slopes in the area. So Coronet Peak seemed to offer the best possibilities for development, and its proximity to the Skippers Saddle road meant that one of the major problems, that of access, was largely overcome.

Two things were required to attract skiers in numbers to make it worthwhile: the first was a ski-tow of some kind, and the second was access to it. Ski-tows and various devices for transporting skiers up to the top of ski slopes had been developed overseas, but practically nothing had yet been done in New Zealand. Little technical information was available, but the job of running a long endless rope over pulleys mounted on posts and driving it with a petrol engine did not seem insurmountable.

A sheepfarmer from Irishman Creek station in the Mackenzie Country who had turned engineer and later perfected the jetboat, the late Sir William Hamilton, was the first man we approached. We outlined our requirements for uphill transport and discussed the project from all angles — feasible lengths, the speed at which the rope should travel, the type of engine to be used and its power, the types of pulleys to carry the ropes, the types of poles to carry the pulleys — and, last but not least, the cost.

Bill Hamilton turned his inventive mind to the subject and it was not long before he came up with excellent designs and concrete proposals. Instead of using makeshift parts and finishing up with a Heath-Robinson outfit, he proposed to design and fabricate the whole unit, from driving drums, pulley trains, Renolds chain, sprockets, and everything else specifically for the job. At the time, it looked an expensive way of going about it, but the efficient trouble-free performance that the design provided over a number of years proved that the decision to adopt his plans was the right one.

In view of our limited knowledge of skiing conditions high up on Coronet Peak, we were uncertain where to locate the tow and realised we would have to move it from place to place until we found the most suitable area. With this in mind, Bill designed the driving unit and the engine to be installed on a steel sledge which could be pulled from place to place by a tractor; or, if we anchored the top end of the rope to the ground, the tow could use its own power to climb along it.

The next problem to be tackled was that of access. There was no point in putting a rope tow on the best slopes of the mountain if the skiers could not reach it. And some sort of an access track had to be cut to get the tow, its rope, poles and other equipment in, as well as building-materials to provide some shelter for skiers, a small cafeteria and a ski-room.

The cost of the tow and its erection, building, ski equipment and access track was quite a hurdle for a small company to face up to in those days, but the directors realised that if skiing was to be established in a worthwhile way, we had no option but to tell Bill Hamilton to go ahead with the construction of the lift, to be completed in time for installation for the winter of 1947.

It was beyond the Company's resources to build a motor road from Skippers Saddle to the site of the tow, but the line of the future road was surveyed and a contractor with a bulldozer was engaged to cut a track along it that would be wide enough to get the tow into position and provide a walking track for skiers in the winter. Walking on a prepared track was infinitely easier than clambering over snow-covered snow tussock, and we figured that the skiers would be prepared to put up with this in the knowledge that the tow was waiting for them at the top end to transport them up the mountain as many times as they liked to go.

The whole project was a bit of a gamble: it could become a tremendous success or a dismal failure. It could attract a lot of skiers to Queenstown, or it could bring so little additional traffic to our bus services that it would be a financial loss. Many questions remained to be answered, and the decision to go ahead was delayed so long that the autumn was well advanced before we could go ahead with the installation. Traffic on the Company's services had, as usual, fallen to a low level after the end of March, so all surplus staff, drivers, office staff and, in fact, anyone who could be spared, was sent to Queenstown where, with typical enthusiasm, they weighed in and helped with buildings and preparations for the erection of the lift.

Bluegum poles to carry the pulleys for the ropes had to be cut and transported to Coronet Peak. Timber and other supplies had to be loaded up and off trucks and sledges, and considerable manual labour was required to dig holes for poles, foundations for buildings, and lavatories.

As the winter drew on, the days got shorter and snow began to accumulate. The effort to complete the installation was stepped up. On most mornings we were away from Eichardts Hotel at 7 or 7.30, before it was light. Billy Hamilton, who had brought some of his team down to supervise the erection of the lifts, liked starting late and working late, and was a reluctant morning starter, but we finally got under way, drove up to the Skippers Saddle and then walked up to the site of the tow. The day would be spent erecting poles, drilling holes in them to take the bolts for the pulley arms, and manpowering all the bits and pieces, some of them quite awkward and heavy, up the snow-covered slopes to their destination.

It was tough work, and by five o'clock most of us had had enough. But not so Billy! He kept us at it until well after dark when, cold, thirsty and hungry, we put on skis and staggered our way down to the cars at the Skippers Saddle. Bill complained about the quality of the ski-poles we were giving him, and we could never understand why he was breaking so many until we noticed him putting the two together with one hand on the top and one near the bottom and using them as a brake. His unsteady progress down the rough track in the darkness was more than the sticks could cope with.

During the last ten days that we were working on the tow, a bitterly cold easterly wind blew almost continuously, carrying with it fine dry snow. Each day the snow got deeper and more difficult to work in, but by the time the tow was finished and running, about the middle of June, there was sufficient snow for skiing to begin. It was a tremendous thrill for those who had been slaving so hard to see the lift finally go into operation, and transporting skiers way up the mountain. Most of us enjoyed our first experience of being hauled up to the top of the ski-slope, and the fact that we had all been so heavily involved in getting the tow installed, gave us double satisfaction.

This Hamilton ski-tow was the first one to be operated successfully in New Zealand, and skiers came from all over the South Island to take advantage of it. They gave glowing reports of the tow and the wide sunny slopes of Coronet Peak; the papers ran their stories and brought the area much publicity. More and more skiers came into the town as the winter went on, and for the first time since the mining days, the hotels were catering for quite large numbers of winter guests.

The rope on the tow, about 60 mm in diameter, moved quite briskly at 10 to 12 km/h, and although a few people had difficulty in gripping it, the majority soon became accustomed to it and enjoyed the quite exhilarating slide up to the top of the mountain.

The weight on hands and arms and the effort of holding on were considerable, so Bill Hamilton developed a device like a nutcracker to grip the towrope, and this was attached by a short cord to a belt around the skier's waist. He would use his hands to get moving and then attach the device to the towrope and hold it in position. If the skier wished to get off, or fell over, he simply let go.

Inevitably, a few minor accidents occurred in the early stages when we were learning how to operate the tows, but considering the tens of thousands of skiers who used them many times a day over a period of fifteen or more years, the accidents were remarkably few. Most of them occurred through skiers using clips of their own design.

Tickets were not issued but skiers hired a belt with a nutcracker attached for the day and returned it when they were finished with it. Some designed their own nutcrackers and belts to beat the system and get a free ride, while others built ones which, though easier to hold in position, would not release readily if the skiers got into trouble, while others had slip-rings and other devices which kept them shut until released by some positive action by the skier. If he fell over and was dragged, or if a skier fell in front of him and couldn't get out of the way, he would be dragged over him, causing cuts and bruises or even broken arms and legs.

The ropes had a tendency to spin when the clip was released, and rather nasty accidents occurred with clothing and long hair getting caught in it and twisted round and round. The staff were constantly on the alert to stop people using clothing which was a danger but, even so, a few accidents did occur. Early in our experience, before we knew much about these things, a fine-looking teenage girl with long dark tresses flowing over her shoulders was fairly conspicuous amongst the other skiers, and she rode the tow with plenty of confidence. A while after she had ascended, the attendant stopped the lift and reported to the manager that there had been an accident. The manager looked up and down the liftline, but could see nothing. He asked the attendant what reason he had for believing there had been an accident, and the attendant pointed out a large hank of black hair entwined on the downgoing rope. They both knew where it had come from; apart from some loss to the lady's dignity, the damage was not irreparable.

Another incident occurred when a girl went up in the lift wearing a sloppy long-sleeved sweater. She attempted to get off about three-quarters of the way to the top, but the rope grabbed her sleeve, and wound it round and round until it was hopelessly caught. With great presence of mind, she backed off and let the rope have the sweater, and stood there with a rather surprised look on her face, and not much else!

In addition to providing the rope-tow we purchased skis, sticks and boots for hiring out to skiers who did not have their own, and a small room was built to house them. Another small room was built as a cafeteria, where hot soup, pies, tea and coffee and chocolate were dispensed. Somebody gave it the name of the Pie Palace, and this stuck to it for a long time.

As part of the development programme we decided to provide an overseas ski-instructor to help people to get the maximum fun out of the sport, and we were extremely lucky to get the services of an expatriate Norwegian working in Sun

Valley, USA, by the name of Olaf Rodegard. Olaf, energetic, small of stature, and with a permanent, infectious grin, was an extremely smooth and competent skier. He ran a very efficient and friendly ski-school for two seasons and will be remembered by hundreds of skiers who passed through Coronet Peak in those early days, where he worked so hard and cheerfully under what must have seemed to him to be extremely primitive conditions.

The rope tow did a useful job in popularising skiing, for up until this point many people had found the uphill climbing without a lift was just too tough. Although some effort had been made in other parts of New Zealand to copy the American type of rope-tows, using car-wheels for pulleys and makeshift equipment for driving the rope, they were not particularly successful: we claim that the Hamilton tows, professionally designed and built for the express purpose of transporting skiers uphill, were the first successful ski-tows to operate in New Zealand.

Each year the lift queues got longer and longer, and the demand for additional tows grew. The site of a new tow was found to be too low down, and the next year it was moved higher up the mountain. Once again all hands and the cook were called in. Aub Rollinson, the general manager from Timaru, Bill Brown, the manager of the Queenstown branch, and many others, worked with a will to get the lift installed in the new position and the rope run out before winter.

Billy Hamilton had built a small portable tow, powered by a Ford 10 engine, which he believed would be suitable for moving around the mountain to various places and for clubs to use on their own private snowfields, and he asked us to try it out on Coronet Peak. It arrived when the winter was fairly well advanced and the ground was well covered in snow, so we hired a draught-horse to haul it up to the bottom of the steep slope on which it was to be installed, and we intended then to let it winch its way over the rest of the distance under its own power. The snow was frozen hard and the horse had no difficulty in hauling it over its share of the journey. Anchors were driven into the ground, the rope pulled out, and the tow winched its way slowly up the slope, which was getting continually steeper. Everything went well until it reached the very steep top section, when the anchors came out and the tow took off downhill, scattering people right and left and heading at about 90 km/h, straight for the horse.

In spite of the commotion, the horse just stood there looking peacefully into the middle distance and made no effort to get out of its way. Finally the tow moved a few degrees and shot through between the horse and the pile of skis, flew through the air and buried itself deep in the snow at the bottom of a ten-metre-deep gulch. Skiers were scattered all over the slope and it was extremely fortunate that none were hit; as for the old draught horse, it had nearly been a job for the horse repairer.

It took several years of trial and error before we found the ideal position for the tows, which is the one almost parallel with the position of the present double chairlift. Finally two tows, running parallel and using the same poles, ran from a point near the bottom of the chairlift to the halfway station, and a single tow ran from there to within twenty or thirty metres of the top of the mountain. This provided excellent uphill capacity and catered for a large number of skiers each day.

Additional buildings were constructed to house a bigger Pie Palace, ski-rooms and ticket offices and commonrooms for the use of the public. The whole show was very primitive by today's standards, but it worked, and it attracted more and more skiers each year.

Problems with the employment and training of a lot of temporary staff at the beginning of each winter were considerable, for although we had a good nucleus of oldtimers to supervise the new recruits, they could not be everywhere at once. Having sold the Company's board on the merits of investing a lot of money in Coronet Peak, I was keen to make sure it was a success and I was also directly responsible for its management. So I had to fly the Whitney Straight two-seater aeroplane which we kept for communication purposes, to Queenstown once or twice a week to make sure that everything was operating as it should be.

Sometimes when sitting in my office in Timaru I would get a call from Queenstown to go down urgently over some problem or other, and if time was limited I wouldn't bother to change but would arrive on Coronet Peak in a business suit and hat. If the problems were up the mountain, I would don a pair of skis, ride the tow up the mountain, attend to whatever had to be done and then ski down again, much to the amusement of the onlookers.

One day I was standing with one of the staff near the top of the double tows where the two return pulleys were mounted high up on two bluegum poles. The tops of the poles were tied by twisted No. 8 wire back to a rock fifty or sixty metres away, and one of these had been carried away — fortunately without causing any damage — and had been replaced. I considered it was not strong enough. We stood for quite a while watching the stream of skiers arriving at the top of the lift, getting off and skiing down, and noticed with some concern the movement of the bluegum poles. I said, 'I don't think this lift should be operated any longer without those tiebacks being strengthened, or it'll let go and the weight of the rope with twenty or thirty skiers on it will break the poles at base and catapult them downhill among the skiers coming up.'

I was actually saying this when there was a loud report and exactly what I had forecast happened. We rushed to the edge of the steep slope to see how many skiers had been injured but by the Grace of God, there had been a gap in the line and there was no one there.

The tow running to the top of the mountain travelled across a gully where at one point it was four or five metres above the snow. When the lift was lightly loaded, the weight of an average skier would pull it down to allow him to keep his skis on the snow, but when it was heavily loaded, the rope would pull tight and he would become airborne for twenty or thirty metres. There was no particular danger in this, although one or two people did panic and let go when they were over the drop, but landing in the soft snow cushioned the fall and very few suffered even minor injury.

One afternoon I was skiing down the mountain near the drop and overheard a tiny voice from high up in the air call out, 'Hello, Pop!' I looked up, and there, like a bad splice on the rope, was my son Brian, aged about six, his woolly hat at a cocky angle on the side of his head, an elbow hanging nonchalantly over the rope and two skis dangling in space. He and his sisters had been forbidden to use the top part of the lift, as they were so light that at this point the rope traced in a straight line from pulley to pulley across the gully and high enough for them to be seriously hurt if they had panicked and fallen off. But if they were not worried about it, why should we be, so we let them carry on.

Over the years, the popularity of Coronet Peak increased and people came from all over New Zealand and Australia to enjoy its usually powdery snow conditions and the clear cloudless sky of Central Otago. The hotels, motels, camping grounds and businesses of Queenstown became almost as busy in the August holidays as during the summer, and our buses were carrying economic loads for the greater part of the winter. The development of Coronet Peak had achieved its objective! It had turned Queenstown into a major holiday town in the winter and, from this, everyone benefited.

Over the years the Company spent thousands of dollars on widening the road between the Skippers Saddle and the chairlift, and the Company's buses shuttled backwards and forwards with a reasonable degree of regularity, if not comfort. The next stage of development of the road would have been to improve it to the stage where it could be opened to private cars, but this was taken out of the Company's hands.

Although the south face of Coronet Peak had been of value to neither man, God nor beast — too dark, cold and sour for grazing and good for nothing else — it was now a highly productive skifield thanks to the efforts of the Company and its band of energetic and enthusiastic staff. People who had never heard of it before now wanted to get into the act to control it and to charge us a high rent for the leasehold. The Lands Department were only too willing to get rid of it and pass control over to the Tourist Department. For the most part we enjoyed a good working relationship with this Department over a period of years, but one incident did occur which emphasised the gulf between private enterprise and the State departments.

I was in Queenstown one day, having flown down from Timaru on some errand or other, when I met Bob Marshall, the general manager of the Tourist Department, strolling down the street. He greeted me — not very cordially, I thought — and then asked if I was going to the meeting that morning. I told him I knew nothing of any meeting, and asked him what it was all about. He replied that it was about taking over the Coronet Peak road.

Amazed at the fact that neither I nor any of my staff had been asked to attend, I went along and found, sitting round the room, representatives of the Lands Department, the Tourist Department, the Railway Road Services, the ski clubs, and one or two other odds and sods. They were gathered together to discuss the disposal of the road from Skippers Saddle to the Coronet Peak, the road that we had built and spent so much money on! A decision was made that the Railways Department should take the road over from the Company, and that they would put their own buses on it and open it to private cars. The road was, in fact, commandeered, opened to the public and not one penny was paid to the Company in compensation.

Although the road was quite unsuitable for private motorists, they were encouraged to go ahead by the manager of the Railways Road Services, who said, in effect, 'Go for your life! You have as much right to go up the road as the Mount Cook Company — or anyone else.' There was practically nothing that we could do about it. We had put the road in and spent all the money without getting ample legal security.

A complete shambles ensued, with private cars and inexperienced Railways drivers getting stuck all over the place. Traffic virtually came to a halt. At the time we were extremely bitter about the high-handed action of the Government departments responsible, but amends were made later. Our rights to operate our own buses were restored, and private cars were kept off the road until it was improved enough to take them.

By taking over the road the Government had assumed responsibility for its development and maintenance and, following up the example the Company had provided, it spent a large amount of money in reconstructing it and turning it into the fine two-way sealed highway that today gives all types of traffic fast and safe access to the bottom of the lift.

The Hamilton rope-tows had served us faithfully and well, but they were reaching the stage when they could no longer cope with the ever-increasing crowds nor provide the sophistication that people who had skied overseas would expect. The time was approaching when they would have to be replaced by modern lifts of greater capacity, greater comfort and greater safety. As well as this, the Company was planning to start a scheduled airline service from Christchurch to Mt Cook and Queenstown with DC3 aircraft, to encourage people with limited time to travel south. It was highly desirable to do something which would give Coronet Peak an even more vigorous boost along.

To see what the world had to offer, I travelled overseas and skied extensively in Europe, Japan and the States, studying various types and makes of lifts. Many lifts had been evolved in various countries which would meet the requirements of our area: some, like the rope-tows, and T-bars, carry skiers uphill while they stand on the snow; others carry them uphill in chairs, but without shelter; others carry them in comfort in four-seat gondolas, while the most sophisticated of all carry up to fifty or sixty standing passengers in large cabins slung on huge cables which travel over hills and valleys, forests and rocks.

The vertical lift at Coronet Peak was really too long for the skier to be standing on the snow and, as well, as we had found with the rope-tows, it was in places too rough. Furthermore, the comparatively low snowfall meant that too much maintenance would be required on the tracks. A chairlift which would carry skiers above the snow and over obstacles, and at the same time give them reasonably comfortable rides and a rest from the strenuous exertion of skiing, was the answer.

Manufacturers of lifts from several countries were asked to provide information, and some twenty-five lifts were studied. The one we finally selected was of Italian design, built in Grenoble, France, by an expatriate Pole by the name of Pomagalski. We chose it because it was one of the most robust designs submitted and would stand up to the high winds encountered in New Zealand, and occasional icing. It was also one of the smoothest and quietest that I had encountered overseas as the pulleys carried the rope on deep rubber and their multiple-pulley trains — sixteen in one case — reduced noise and vibration to a minimum.

A further big advantage was that it was of a recently introduced design that allowed two people to be carried in each chair, thus doubling a lift's normal capacity and making it more sociable. Before the lift could be ordered finance had to be arranged, as the cost was considerably beyond the normal resources of the Company.

If finance could be arranged for the chairlift, it was also highly desirable that more sophisticated buildings be erected to house the cafeteria, lavatories, ski-storage and other facilities to match the modern chairlift. The directors decided that a public issue of shares be made and that Stock Exchange listing should be sought. In due course the issue was successfully launched, the lift was ordered, and preparations were made to erect it.

Although the erection was a major project of which our staff had had no previous experience, they were determined to do the job themselves and so reduce costs as far as possible. Jack Anderson was the manager of the Queenstown branch at the time. He had had a lot of experience with rope-tows, and was familiar with snow conditions on the Peak; he was a tireless worker, seemed to be able to stand the cold like an Arctic hero, and through years of playing round with motor vehicles in

New Zealand and in the Middle East, he could solve almost any mechanical problem by common sense and improvisation. Ray Robinson had spent a lot of time on sawmills on the West Coast, and driving bulldozers, and was equally resourceful. Jack and Ray were supported in no small way by the three Brough brothers, who were builders and carpenters.

Before the steel towers and top and bottom stations could be erected, massive reinforced-concrete bases had to be built. The top station had to be strong enough to carry the tower holding the 3.96-metre diameter return pulley, and this was built by blasting and excavating the rock and pouring in between fifty and sixty tonnes of reinforced concrete. Tracks had to be cut to the top of the mountain and to the base of each tower but, even with the tracks, the transport of the concrete was a major job; 225-litre drums were cut in half and welded end-to-end to form containers which were fitted to the bulldozers and wheel tractors. During the big pours, even the Land Rovers were used by filling the rear compartment with the wet concrete.

Once the concrete bases had been built with the large steel holding-down bolts in place, the next major job was to get the towers into position and to erect them, and this was no easy task as some of them were 10.6 metres long and weighed about 1.5 tonnes. Ray was an expert on bulldozers and could almost make them sit up and dance a jig, and in typical Kiwi style he used the hydraulically-operated blade to do any heavy lifting, pulling or pushing which was required. He designed and built a derrick attached to the bulldozer blade, and by using the hydraulics and a cable on to the power takeoff, he could lift the pylons off the ground, transport them to the site and erect them.

One by one the towers were erected, and the lift started to take shape. The tower on the top station looked lonely with its massive axle to take the bullwheel, four to five metres above the ground. This large-diameter wheel weighed about half a tonne; it seemed too big for the derrick, and I asked on several occasions how they proposed to get it into position, but received no satisfactory answer. In due course I was taken to the top of the mountain to see the wheel in position, and asked again — 'How ever did you get it there?'

They replied, 'Didn't you ever hear how they built the Pyramids?' They had used a bulldozer to build a ramp high enough to carry the wheel up, drop it on its axle, and had then bulldozed the ramp away again.

With the winter rapidly approaching it was a race against

time, and the boys worked longer hours each day with decreasing daylight and increasing cold, but finally the lift was complete and ready to be put through its tests by the Marine Department inspectors. It has many safety features, including a series of mechanically and electrically-operated brakes to cater for any emergency.

To test the lift, the Department required that sandbags weighing 180 kilos be placed on every chair (120 chairs), first on the uphill side when the brakes were tested, then on the downhill side when they were tested again, and finally with every chair loaded — a total weight of 21.6 tonnes. With the lift travelling at about 17.5 km/h, the emergency brakes were slammed on, the loaded chairs swung backwards and forwards violently, the rope surged up and down four or five metres, and the bottom driving station slid backwards and forwards on its tracks, a most alarming procedure. But the lift stood up to this rugged testing, the Marine Department inspectors gave it their blessing, and when the laborious job of removing the sandbags had been completed, and a few other minor jobs done, the lift was opened to the public in June 1964.

Ray Robinson and his team did a magnificent job in erecting the lift, and it has been going almost without incident, day in day out, winter and summer, ever since. A wonderfully safe and reliable piece of equipment.

As the ski-tows had done, the chairlift gave Coronet Peak a big stimulus and a further rapid growth in business from both Australia and New Zealand. More lifts were installed, a Poma lift in Rocky Gully in 1967 and a lift for beginners and novices in Happy Valley, a couple of years later. These helped to reduce the length of time skiers had to wait, but it was not long before the queues were as long as ever again, and we had to decide to erect a second chairlift running from above the car-park to a slightly lower peak to the south of Coronet.

This new lift was designed by Pomagalski, but most of its components were manufactured in New Zealand and it was a three-seater with high capacity. It is 1128 metres long, has a vertical lift of 381 metres, and a capacity of 1500 skiers an hour. The first chairlift had a vertical lift of 436 metres, was 1342 metres long and had a capacity of 800 skiers an hour. The Rocky Gully Poma has a lift of 214 metres and 1200 skiers per hour, and the Happy Valley one of 122 metres, and 700 skiers an hour.

Coronet Peak is not only endowed with the natural features of good terrain, usually good snow conditions and good weather, but it now has the capacity to transport a large number of skiers up the mountain on some of the most efficient and up-to-date lifts operating in any part of the world.

The growth of skiing has been so rapid that it is predictable that Coronet Peak will reach saturation point some time in the near future, and it is with this in mind, and to provide a longer season, that the Company is at present (1979) investigating the possibility of a skifield in the Rastus Burn Basin to the east of Queenstown.

If this can be developed, the lifts will start from a point higher than the top of Coronet Peak and finish 430 metres higher. This will ensure a longer skiing season, with more reliable snow, as well as a tremendous variety of slopes. It is also capable of being extended in future years into other basins, such as the head of the Doolans Stream and, operated in conjunction with Coronet Peak, could be a tremendous boon for Queenstown by providing two skifields, quite different in character, within fifteen kilometres of the town.

9

Road Services

THE TWO LITTLE DE DIONS that chuffed to a standstill outside
The Hermitage in the early hours of 7 February 1906 had
proved that a motor-car could travel in one day from Timaru
to Mt Cook on tracks formed by horse and bullock-drawn
vehicles. Their arrival demonstrated that the car in its modern
form would be capable of sustaining a scheduled motor service
on the route.

A small company was formed to exploit the idea. It was
called the Cook Motor Car Service, and the subscribers were
RLW, Robert Rhodes and others. They bought larger and
more powerful cars carrying six to eight passengers to operate a
scheduled service between the railhead at Fairlie and The
Hermitage, and were ready to cater for the summer traffic late
in 1906.

After the new cars had been checked over, a trial run was
done from Timaru to The Hermitage and return on 8
November 1906, preparatory to the inauguration of the timetable service. The *Timaru Herald* reported on 10 November
1906:

The Motor-car Service: Later Successful Trials
The party which left Timaru on Wednesday evening in the
motor-car which is to be used on the Fairlie/Mt Cook service
had a successful trip, a final test in view of the opening of the
service to take place about the end of the month. The car, a
24hp Darracq, contained a full load and the whole trip, Mr
Wigley says, was a most satisfactory and successful one.

On the journey yesterday morning, when returning from
The Hermitage, they ran into very bad roads which were
suffering from a plentiful supply of melting snow which fell
on Thursday evening between Mt Cook and Lake Pukaki.
The trip under all considered circumstances was such as to
give the car owners every confidence as to the successful
running within a timetable limit. That is, they had the

experience with their small car of a steep grade on a sloping road and got over without difficulty. . .

Time from Fairlie to The Hermitage 8 hours 50 minutes, the actual riding time for about 100 miles — 6 hours 20 minutes. These times, of course, exceed the timetable fixtures and Messrs Wigley & Thornley intend allowing bigger margins all through.

The party were not in a hurry on the down trip, for there were some final arrangements to be made in connection with the building of bridges and consequently no times were taken, but the whole return trip was done from The Hermitage to Cairns Terrace Garage between 8am yesterday and 9.30pm. Anyone who has been over the roads can readily testify as to the assured possibility of a motor-car service to Mt Cook, and the promoters speak with the greatest confidence of its establishment. Messrs Wigley & Thornley Ltd state that the service is now open fcr tourists from date starting from Fairlie forthwith.

The vehicles chosen were 24 and 40hp four-cylinder six-seater Darracqs, and in the advertising folders of the time they were described as 'fast, comfortable and luxurious'. They were reasonably well sprung, the seats were well padded and quilted, but apart from a rather inadequate windshield, the driver and passengers were completely unprotected from the wind, and rain and the sun, except for a collapsible hood which was strung over folding frames and held down by leather straps and domes; it was usually considered to be more trouble than it was worth and was used only when conditions made the passengers vociferous.

The gear-change lever, which was a long steel rod with a release below the handle to allow the driver to select reverse, was outside the body of the car. It led into a rather complicated-looking gate system, through which the driver had to select the appropriate gear. On the dashboard was a drip-feed oiler system to keep the main engine bearings lubricated; four or six glass tubes allowed the driver to see the oil drip through, drop by drop, and he could regulate the supply by adjusting a valve on the top of each tube.

Ignition was by magneto, and no battery was carried as the spark-coil systems of that era were considered unreliable. Light was provided by acetylene gas generated in a large cylinder on the runningboard and fed to the imposing brass headlamps through rubber tubes. The radiator too was of brass, and it was a daily duty of the driver to polish this and the headlamps, so that the cars looked really flashy in the morning before they started on their long trip to Mt Cook. Later on, when the name of the Company was changed to the Mount Cook Motor Company it was fixed to the bonnets of the cars in big brass letters, painted red on the sides, and these too were polished daily. The cars were painted a dull greeny brown.

Tyres were always a problem, as their life on those stony roads was very limited; they often blew out and were completely ruined on their first trip. Various makes were tried, but it was many years before they had evolved to the stage where they were reasonably reliable. At one stage, to make them last longer, the manufacturers built metal studs into the treads, but I can remember the old drivers saying the studs generated heat and ruined the tyres more quickly than ever.

Supplies of 'motor spirit' (petrol) had to be ordered well in advance, as the demand was still so small that bulk supplies were not available. It was packed in 18-litre non-returnable tins, two tins in one wooden case, ordered by RLW from a Dunedin supplier and railed to Timaru.

When the service first started, passengers travelled from Timaru to Fairlie by train, where they spent the night. Next day, on Tuesdays, Thursdays and Saturdays, they would travel as far as Pukaki in the cars and complete the journey by horsedrawn coach. As the road from Pukaki to The Hermitage was improved and more bridges were put in, the cars travelled farther before transferring their passengers to the coach.

Eventually all the bridges were completed and the cars took the passengers right through. But bridges did not solve the problems of flooded creeks, for rapid erosion in the hills at this period caused by burning and grazing brought down masses of débris which clogged existing channels and forced the water to find new courses which often left the bridges high and dry.

At some places the amount of débris was actually higher than the decking on the bridges. When this happened the drivers had to find fords by wading through the flooded streams, often up to their waists in water, picking out places where the bottom was hard enough to carry the car, yet shallow enough to stop the engine becoming flooded, and slow-flowing enough to stop the car being washed downstream. Usually they were successful in fording the streams, but at times they were not, and got the cars hopelessly bogged down or the engines stopped through water in the ignition, in which case they would have to seek help from the nearest sheep-station.

Fairly early in the history of the Company the vehicles were fitted with winches. When the car became bogged the driver would run out the wire rope for its maximum distance and anchor it to a large rock or dig a hole in the shingle and anchor it to a 'dead man' (a post sunk in the ground), and proceed to winch the vehicle out by turning the handle. This must have been an incredibly laborious process and, although great play was made in advertising the efficiency of the service in carrying these winches, I have never been able to get first-hand information from anyone who had ever used one. I think it probable that the vehicles were too heavy to be winched out by man-power, and in any case it would have been very difficult to find something really secure to which to anchor the rope.

The telephone line was first established from Timaru to Fairlie and then progressively to Burkes Pass, Tekapo, Pukaki and The Hermitage, but for many years there were no telephones along the route, and it was impossible for the driver to phone his base if he should strike trouble. To overcome this, carrier pigeons were kept on the cars and released when the driver wished to get a message back to Fairlie or Tekapo; but here again there is not much evidence of this communications system being very effective. RLW had a suspicion that hawks and the local sportsmen undermined its efficiency.

On thumbing through some of the old 1908 correspondence files I ran across the following letters from RLW to the *Timaru Herald*, explaining that runholders were disappointed that the *Herald* had not been delivered to them with its results of the previous Saturday's general election.

Dear Sir,

We have already pointed out to you that your papers for the Mackenzie should be forwarded here on Monday, Wednesday and Friday night's train, but you seem to disregard the matter entirely, forwarding papers when you seem inclined. There were no papers forwarded to go up by car this morning, people up-country would be anxious to see the results of the election. Kimbell and Silverstream residents are complaining that their papers do not go up with the car. We hope that you will correct the above, and forward letter-headings as soon as possible.

Yours faithfully,

This was followed by a second letter to the *Herald*, on 3 December:

Dear Sir,

You are still sending the papers all to the devil. The people up-country are getting about sick of it. There are no papers here to go up-country tomorrow, there were none for Saturday's trip.

You want to forward by Mondays, Wednesdays and Friday night's train. Have spoken to you on this matter about fifteen times already.

Yours faithfully,

At this time RLW must have been about twenty-eight and had not acquired the polish in letter-writing that he did later on, but as the owner of the *Timaru Herald* was a personal friend, these peremptory missives were probably written tongue-in-cheek.

The *Herald* was sent by rail to Fairlie on the Monday, Wednesday and Friday afternoons to connect with the Mt Cook service on the Tuesdays, Thursdays and Saturdays, and evidently some delivery boy had forgotten to put them on the train. It is hard to realise today that without telephone or radio, the back-country people could learn about national events down-country only by means of private correspondence or the *Herald*. Perhaps they were luckier than we are today?

The service must have been reasonably popular right from its inception. More 40hp Darracqs were ordered and, a few years later, the 60hp Darracq, which carried nine passengers. The service operated only for the six summer months; in winter it was closed down to allow the vehicles to be overhauled and made ready for the next season, while the drivers and others took their annual holidays.

Spare parts were very hard to get, as they had to come by ship from the French manufacturers. It used to take at least three months to receive these parts from the date of ordering. To overcome this problem a lot of equipment was installed in the Fairlie garage to allow parts to be fabricated there. I understand that the first milling machine to be imported into New Zealand was installed at Fairlie. The following newspaper article of about 1912 shows the length to which the Company had to go to keep the cars on the road.

A NOTABLE ENTERPRISE:
MOUNT COOK MOTOR SERVICE

All claims to respect and honour for courage and initiative in pioneering were not exhausted by the early settlers. These qualities have been called for in many directions from time to time to this day, and will be called for frequently in the time to come. A notable instance in recent years surely was the placing of motor-cars on the road between Fairlie and Mt Cook Hermitage, a few years ago. The courage required cannot be fully gauged by the observations of the car tourist on that trip today, so much has the road been improved in the meantime by the bridging of mountain torrents and otherwise. Originally it was a bold enterprise, but the courage of its initiator, Mr R. Wigley, won success and the practical recognition of reliance upon this service he opened, and is maintained under his direction by the Mount Cook Motor Co.

The service has more recently been extended to Queenstown on Lake Wakatipu, through a thoroughly wild back country of such varied nature as to make this one of the most interesting car tours in the Dominion, to make no larger claim.

The Company's motor business has grown remarkably. From an exploratory runabout in two Darracq [De Dion] passenger cars, the plant on the road has been increased to no less than sixteen motor vehicles, including a 4-ton lorry and two or three smaller ones. The mileage covered weekly by the motors runs into thousands, and rain or shine the service is carried on with a remarkably small measure of mishaps, considering the rough nature of some parts of the road and tracks that have to be traversed.

This character of the roads implies great wear and tear, especially on tyres. The Company's tyre bill must be very large. The headquarters are at Fairlie, and Fairlie being so far from established engineering works it was necessary to provide a complete plant for effecting repairs. Mr C. Jones, the engineer in charge, claims that he has the best fitted car-repair shop in the Dominion. There are, therefore, engineers, blacksmiths and carpenter shops at the garage and the repairs undertaken and the alterations made enable Mr Jones to say that he could build a car complete, except making the castings for the engines and the rough castings for the gearwheels. A neat 7hp Tangye kerosene motor supplies power for the machine tools and for a lighting and battery-charging dynamo, and for various other purposes.

Machine tools installed are of the very best of their kind obtainable, and the principal ones are marvels of fine construction, ingenuity and various uses. A Universal milling machine cuts gears, is a planer, and in fact seems to be able to do a vast variety of work through accurate gauges that are fixed on the machine itself. It has no less than sixteen outside drive speeds and an internal arrangement multiply these endlessly almost, giving motions with minute intervals between 6,000ths and one quarter of an inch.

With this tool can be made working tools for the other machines with absolute accuracy in size and shape, one after another. A smaller lathe for finer work is also a beautiful tool. Altogether the equipment is so complete that all repairs, alternations, reconstruction, repainting etc. can be, and are, carried out in this garage of the inland town. The enterprise shown in putting the cars on the road is displayed again in the provision of such fine and complete appliances for keeping them there in good order. The success of this side of the venture is seen in the fact that the cars first employed, now a good many years ago, are still running, in as good or better order than when they started.

It was unfortunate that while one of the vehicles was being painted in a tent in the garage a fire started and destroyed the garage completely and with it a number of vehicles, including the historic little De Dion 'Beetle', and much valuable equipment.

RLW had many interests, and he threw himself into these with a great deal of enthusiasm. One of his lifelong hobbies was photography, and in the back of the garage at Fairlie he had built himself a darkroom where he developed and printed the photographs he took with his then-modern camera, which used the 10 x 12cm glass plates. Many of these plates are still in perfect condition today, and many reproductions in this book have been taken from them.

His darkroom was made of corrugated iron and backed on to the boundary of the Gladstone Hotel next door. RLW often worked late at night on his photographs. With the ten o'clock closing of the pub next door there was a general exodus, and he was irritated by boozers urinating against the wall of his darkroom before weaving their way homewards, so he worked out his own solution to the problem.

He built a spark-coil which would throw a hefty spark of about three centimetres, and he connected this up to some fine wires strung along the corrugated iron. As soon as he heard someone moving outside in the darkness he would pull the switch, and he did this for several evenings, till finally he had no more customers.

About a week after he started he was approached by the local doctor, who said to him: 'Wigs, what the hell are you doing down there at ten o'clock at night? In the last week I've had seven patients call on me, all complaining of kidney trouble, but there's absolutely nothing wrong with any of them. They all complained about getting a violent pain while standing at the same part of your fence. What the hell are you up to?'

RLW explained, with the tears rolling down his cheeks he was laughing so heartily. He must have given the carefree boozers good reason to hurry round to the doctor.

The car service from Fairlie to Mt Cook was a pioneering venture, fraught with frustrations and difficulties that would have daunted any man with less courage and persistence than RLW. The cost of operating these early vehicles over those primitive roads must have been considerable, and although many passengers were carried, there were not enough to make the enterprise profitable. After some years the syndicate was losing so much money that they were not prepared to persevere with it any longer.

RLW sold his share of the farm at Opua and got a loan from his mother, and with these funds he bought what remained of the syndicate's assets. He had disagreed with them on the method of operating the service, and he now proceeded to reorganise it according to his own ideas, forming a new company called the Mount Cook Motor Co. Ltd. The service from Fairlie to Mt Cook was maintained, but he also had visions of extending it from Pukaki, over the Lindis Pass and down the Lindis River — the route used by the notorious sheepstealer, Mackenzie — then up to Wanaka and, later on, to Queenstown.

The Southern Lakes were starting to attract the attention of overseas and home tourists, but the area was difficult to reach: after viewing the prime attraction of Mt Cook, the visitor had to return to Timaru and overnight there, then rail to Invercargill where another night was spent, then take the train to Kingston, and finally catch the lake steamer to Queenstown. RLW's scheme would allow people to travel by road to Mt Cook, then southwards to Wanaka and Queenstown and by lake steamer to Kingston on the southern end of Lake Wakatipu, where they would join the train to Invercargill, thus saving time and taking in much of the most scenic and spectacular country of the South Island.

But if the difficulties of pioneering a route to Mt Cook had been severe, those on the Wanaka and Queenstown route were, if anything, worse. RLW pioneered the first car trip from Mt

Cook to Queenstown on 6 February 1911, travelling over the Crown Range. The road from Pukaki to Omarama, and then up alongside the Ahuriri River to the mouth of the Lindis Pass was flat, like the Mackenzie Plains, and presented no difficulties in good weather. From the Ahuriri the road climbed alongside the Longslip Creek, which it crossed a number of times until it reached the top of the Lindis Pass at over 975 metres above sea level. From the top of the pass the road descended steeply for a while and then went through a series of gorges down the Lindis River, which it crossed five times.

Over many thousands of years this river, flowing through a low rainfall area, has eroded its bed much faster than the surrounding countryside has been eroded, with the result that it now runs through deep gorges in many places, with extremely rugged and steep precipices rising on either side. It drains a large watershed, and after heavy rain is subject to flash floods which can lift its level by four to six metres or more of swift boiling water, making a crossing impossible. In some places floodwaters would cover the shelf cut out of the hillside which passed as a road.

A few bridges were later constructed over the worst parts of the Lindis and one of these, the Black Bridge, just below Morven Hills station, had been designed for horsedrawn traffic. It extended at right angles from where the road was cut out of solid rock on the cliff face on one side, to a level bank on the other. Horsedrawn vehicles had no difficulty in getting round the very sharp bend below the rocks, but the cars were unable to do it without shunting backwards and forwards quite a number of times — and even then, it sometimes proved impossible. The old drivers then overcame this problem by putting a jack under the differential of the car, lifting it as high as it would go, and then, with the help of the passengers, pushing it over sideways. Every time it was pushed over sideways, the back-end would be moved some fifteen or twenty centimetres.

From the Lindis Gorge the going was reasonably flat, through Tarras and then up the Clutha or Molyneux River as it was then known, to Wanaka (then called Pembroke). In the Mackenzie Plains most of the roads, such as they were, were formed easily enough and primarily for the settlers whose sheep grazed the hillsides. The roads through the Lindis and Clutha valleys had been formed to service the many thousands of prospectors and miners who were working the area for gold. Gold-fever caused more opening up of the countryside with roads than would have been possible otherwise, and the tremendous amount of work done to provide access to the diggings, water-races to the claims, and on the claims themselves, could never have been done without the irresistible stimulus of gold.

From Wanaka the road zigzagged up the Cardrona River through the tailings and chaos left behind by the miners, and arrived on top of the Crown Range at 1067 metres. The Cardrona had to be crossed twenty-nine times, and apart from the difficulties presented by each ford, the drivers had to be very careful that they did not become trapped by rising water. From the top of the Crown Range the road descends steeply to the Crown Terrace in a number of zigzags cut into the precipitous hillside, and in some places it is so narrow that the outside wheels of the car were right on the edge of an almost sheer drop hundreds of metres down into the Kawarau River.

Fortunately, the number of vehicles using it was very small, for there was often no room to pass for some distance. The cars had to back two or three times to negotiate nearly all the hairpin bends. Also, the whole length of the road was virtually unmetalled, it scoured badly after heavy rain, was subject to snow for much of the winter and frequently during the summer, and presented difficulties which would make the operation of a scheduled service quite impossible on many days, and extremely difficult even on the best of them.

Despite these formidable hazards the first weekly motor service from Mt Cook to Pembroke (now Wanaka) opened in December 1910 and was extended to Queenstown in November 1912. It was publicised as 'The Grand Motor Tour — the World's Longest Motorcar Service — 300 miles — includes Mount Cook, Lakes Wanaka and Wakatipu, the Crown Range and the Lindis Pass.'

On the first day passengers travelled from Mt Cook to Omarama, where they had morning tea at the old pub which, like most back-country hotels, was a low rambling old place with quite a history. In the winter very few strangers called, and even in the summer few people required meals or accommodation. Only a handful of locals drank there, so respect for the licensing laws was barely superficial. On one trip to Lake Ohau with RLW and some of his friends, we overnighted at the Omarama Hotel and, soon after checking in, were taken to the small dining-room for a meal. After the soup course we were each given a large helping of baked rainbow trout, and most of the party set to with appetites sharpened by the frosty weather.

But one member held back. 'Wig,' he said, 'I don't think I can eat this. I'm an honorary ranger and, apart from the fact that it is out of season for trout, it's illegal to serve them in a hotel.' He probably suspected also that the fish had been speared rather than caught by legal means during the legal season.

Most trading in the country hotels was done at night after station owners, travellers and others had finished their day, which was after the official 6pm closing time. It was a law which was not easy to police, for if a representative of the constabulary started off on his rounds and called at one country hotel, the message that he was on his way would be passed on to the next one by telephone as soon as he was out of the building.

There were occasions, however, when they did reverse their sequence of visits, and they would arrive unannounced and unexpected to find the bar full of illegal drinkers. One of our staff, driving to Queenstown, arrived at Omarama well after dark and decided to spend the night there rather than tackle the Lindis Pass, which was under snow. He parked his car, opened the guests' door of the hotel and walked inside, and was standing there wondering how to check in when the door of the bar burst open and one or two people rushed out, pushed him down the long corridor into one of the bedrooms, where the window was opened and he and several others were bundled outside.

They stood around in the frosty night in silence, and finally he asked someone nearby what was going on.

'A cop has just walked in,' he was told.

'I'm not a cop,' he said, 'I've just walked into the pub to book in.'

After crossing the Lindis Pass passengers lunched at the old Lindis Hotel, another old pub that had a character all of its own, and quite a history. It was built of stone, the local slaty rock which abounds in the district, and plastered on the inside walls. The people who built it must have run out of money or energy before the roof went on, for the doorways were so low that you had to stoop down to get through them. The floors were of earth and the windows so small that very little light came in, which made the building very cool in the hot summer days. Mrs McCormack ran a small unlicensed dining-room there and was very good indeed to our drivers, always providing an appetising meal or cup of tea regardless of when we arrived.

In the early days it had had a liquor licence, and the shepherds, shearers and rabbiters from the surrounding district would congregate there on Saturday nights or when the weather was too bad for shearing. It had a room for the drunks, and those who had spent all their money and could no longer stand on their feet were thrown into this room to cool off.

If conditions on the road created by geology and meteorology were to make life difficult for the drivers, there were also problems for RLW caused by people who objected furiously to the introduction of the motor-car.

On some occasions he and his vehicle were made very welcome. For example, on his first trip from Wanaka to Queenstown he was heading up the Cardrona Valley and, as he passed the Cardrona school, the kids who were out playing at the time got wildly excited at seeing their very first motor-car. RLW, extrovert that he was, stopped and turned round and drove back to the school and asked the head teacher if he could take them for a spin. He took them all for a cruise up and down the road and thereby made some lifelong friendships. For years afterwards when driving through that area he would be stopped by a farmer, a drover or some other inhabitant of the district who would greet him like a long-lost brother and remind him of the joyride he had given them so many years before. He never failed to stop at the Cardrona pub to have a drink and pass the time of day with members of the Patterson family, who were schoolchildren on that epic occasion.

But on his first arrival at Queenstown after having surmounted all the problems of the road, RLW was driving down the main street when he was attacked by the village blacksmith with a sledgehammer. Really aroused by the intrusion of the motor-car, this character was intent on smashing it up and so getting rid of this form of opposition for ever. RLW spoke frequently of the opposition he had had from people who refused to accept the inevitability of the introduction of the motor-car. However, he had a tremendous liking for his fellow man and could make friends almost anywhere, and I am sure he and his opponents finished up at one of the local pubs, discussing each other's problems and agreeing to co-operate.

Although I have had no confirmation of this, I suspect that the Queenstown blacksmith who greeted the arrival of the first Darracq with such hostility, finished up as the branch manager for the Mount Cook Company. His name was Jim Richards, and he was a real character in his own right. When he was not at his anvil, his services were greatly in demand as a juggler and ventriloquist at local entertainments, and he served the Company loyally for a great number of years.

Pressure from the farmers, who were understandably apprehensive that the new noisy, smelly motor-cars would panic their horses and stock and send them crashing through fences and over bluffs, made the Lakes County Council pass bylaws that prohibited the use of all but horsedrawn vehicles over certain sections of the route.

Then in 1911 the Company approached the Council for permission to establish regular motor services between Wanaka and Queenstown, and the Council agreed to relax its restrictions for a trial period. The Company brought its first service car into Queenstown in November 1912 by way of the Crown Range, and in the same year regular services were established. However, the Council required a conductor's whistle to be used instead of a horn, and a person had to walk ahead of the car round bad bends.

The Council closed the road from Frankton to Queenstown to motor vehicles, but the drivers overcame this problem by yoking horses to their cars and hauling them across the four kilometres of forbidden road; later, the horses were used only for the first few chains and were then unhitched round the first bend. The comic-opera side of this situation, with the drivers blatantly breaking the law caused the County to reconsider the matter, and finally in 1915, when other cars were quite frequently seen in the area, the Frankton Road restrictions were removed.

Certain local residents could see no future in progress in the form of the motor-car and forecast that it would spell disaster to the tourist trade. One, writing in 1912, surmised that the livery stables would be put out of business, and that the Skippers drive, 'the finest in our district, would be lost to travellers', as cars could never negotiate such a road. He considered that the increase of tourists from the use of cars on country would be 'very meagre, and the increase to trade from a possible few extra individuals simply means nothing. To introduce motor-car locomotion would not be progress, but simply retrogression. Why then should we endanger the properties and the lives and limbs of our people?'

Finally, in 1915, a poll of ratepayers was held on whether motors should be allowed on the roads or not, and it was won by only 36 votes, with 275 for the cars, and 239 against them. Some sections of the road had 8 km/h speed limits imposed on them but, like the other regulations, they did not last long, for most people in the district could see that motor transport would ultimately be highly beneficial to the district.

RLW was for most of his life a keen trout fisherman, and was adept at the use of the wet fly which produced for him more than the average number of fish, and his trips to the back country gave him an opportunity to angle for the big fish in those rivers. His skill was such that he would not have to revert to the more doubtful types of fishing to get one for the pot, but if the opportunity occurred and he did not have his rod and gear with him, I'm sure that his sense of fun rather than fear of the law would have guided his actions.

He used to tell a story about a poaching episode which took place in one of the clear streams at the head of Lake Pukaki, and the way it was embellished suggested strongly that he was present, if not an active participator. A local resident, either a member of the Public Works roading gang or a hand on one of the local stations, was in the habit of getting himself an occasional trout for a meal by dynamiting the pools. He prepared the charge, lit the fuse and tossed it into the water — but his dog, which he had forgotten to tie up, thought he was having a game, and dived in and retrieved it. Seeing what was happening, he decided to separate himself from his dog as far and fast as possible before it swam ashore and delivered the explosive at his feet! He headed across country just as fast as his legs and the rough ground would let him, but the dog closed on him with every step. He kept yelling curses at it, but the dog, who thought the boss was turning on a jolly game for his entertainment, kept closing on him. Finally the charge went off but without material detriment to the would-be poacher. His dog, alas, did not survive.

Passengers chugging along the Mackenzie Plains from Burkes Pass towards Lake Tekapo were struck by the dramatic change from the arid plains to the sight of the chalky-blue Lake Tekapo, with its backdrop of snowy mountains. This view, one of the best of the whole area, never fails to impress me with almost dramatic force, although I have seen it literally hundreds of times. It is said that the South Island is a land of contrasts, and nowhere is this better illustrated than on the approach to Tekapo.

Towards the turn of the century, a single-span bridge was built over the Tekapo River, which ran wide, deep and turbulent for some kilometres below the lake. On the other side an hotel was built of local stone and, as with the Lindis Hotel, the masons must have become tired or run out of pay before the walls reached a reasonable height, for one had to stoop down to get under the doorways and into the bar, and the main entrance was not much better. The floors of the bar were plain earth, a barrel of beer sat on one end of the counter, a few bottles of spirits were in the centre, and at most times it did a very desultory business.

But at certain times of the year the shearers and shepherds from the surrounding sheep stations would foregather there, and some riotous parties ensued. On occasions, the shearers would declare the sheep black — that is, too wet to shear until a day or two had elapsed and they had dried out. The men would then adjourn to the Tekapo pub and rapidly rid themselves of their hard-earned wages.

Tommy Burnett, who owned Mount Cook station, refused to stand by and see the shearers fleeced. He bought the hotel and closed it down for a period long enough for its liquor licence to lapse. It did continue to provide meals and accommodation, and provided useful service until it was replaced by a more modern building about 1913.

At one stage the Company owned the hotel, as it was so important as a staging post, to cater for the passengers on the cars for meals and beds. RLW always called in to pay his respects to the landlord and his wife, and on one occasion he had ordered drinks for some friends when he noticed the landlord's wife behind the bar using her pocket handkerchief to polish the glasses she proposed to serve them with.

He said, 'Hey, Mrs Robinson, you're polishing those glasses with your handkerchief.'

She replied, 'Don't worry, Mr Wigley, it's a dirty one.'

Bill Vance, an historian of South Canterbury, in an article dated about 1960, recalled that with the demolition of the Tekapo hotel, South Canterbury would lose an important link with some interesting early history of the district. As well as the hotel, the bridge which crosses the Tekapo at this point would also be demolished after serving the district for more than seventy years, to be replaced by a motorway on the dam, a short distance below. He writes:

'Since the coaching days of the 1870s many overseas notables have stayed at Tekapo, including the Duke of Gloucester who laid the foundation stone for the famed Tekapo Church nearby.

A renowned early squatter, John Rutherford of Opawa station, once drove Lord and Lady Onslow to Tekapo with a six-in-hand. One of the greatest horsemen of early New Zealand, John Rutherford is remembered for his ability to catch and hold a yearling horse by the hind leg with one hand.

The first Tekapo House was built in the early 1870s by the Mount Cook Road Board to provide accommodation for travellers to The Hermitage and up-country stations. It was the centre of social life of the district until it was pulled down and the present building erected on the site in 1919.

Coaches and wagons were the only means of transport in the days of the first Tekapo House. A local disaster, often recalled by early residents, was the time when a wagonload of nine-litre whiskey jars overturned before reaching Tekapo. The locality is still called Whiskey Cutting, and it is said that the remains of broken stone jars can still be found in the gully nearby.

In the coaching days of the old Tekapo House, one of the best-known coachmen of the time was George Shaw. He drove for many years for the coaching proprietor of that time, Keir Frane. During Shaw's time the mail never failed to get through, in spite of the floods, frosts or snows of the Mackenzie winter. The late Charlie Elms, for many years manager at The Hermitage, made a wager with a local resident about the veracity of this claim. When earlier records were consulted at The Hermitage, the claim was found to be true.

The memory was treasured in the Mackenzie of Mrs Louisa Smith, much respected and loved by those who kept the first Tekapo House, and her cooking is still spoken of as one of the marvels of the district. In her time, Tekapo House was regarded as another home by runholders and their families, who used to stay there on their journeys up and down the country.

Another notable character of the district was described by one wellknown runholder as 'A very nice pretty little thing between 25 and 30 stone' (130-150 kilos). She took up much more than half the seat of the gig in which she and her husband used to attend the local sales, and he was often obliged to sit nearly on the mudguard. She was known more than once to break into the local council meeting and throw the members out if they did not resolve in accordance with her wishes. Those who bid against her at cattle auctions had

well beware: she would search the stockyards with a whip,
saying darkly at intervals, 'Where *is* that so-and-so man?'
Once, when bound over to keep the peace, she rebuked the
local Justice of the Peace with the words 'You drunken
so-and-so! How many times have I had to drag your carcase
off the roads?'

An insurance agent once visited her farm. The lady did
not like insurance salesmen and, turning to her daughter,
said, 'Alice, fetch the so-and-so gun!' She met her death by
accident. A neighbour held a gate open for her to drive
through in her gig. She lashed the horse forward and the
harness broke, the cart tipped back and she was flung on her
head.

Another character, James Smith, was known as Night-
and-day Jimmy and was for many years a wagoner on the
Mackenzie roads. In his dray he had all sizes and kinds of
horses, and earlier residents recount that they were shod
with any old shoes he could find, regardless of size. A settler
once visited Jimmy, who also ran a bit of a farm. After some
talk Jimmy asked his visitor in for a feed, and filled a billy
with eggs and water. When the eggs were cooked, Jimmy
poured the water off into the teapot to make the tea, tipped
the eggs on the table, pushed half across to his guest and ate
the other half himself — about three dozen altogether.

A coat he left behind on a visit to a runholder in the
district was so dilapidated that it was thrown on the rubbish
heap. Some weeks later Jimmy collected the coat from the
rubbish tip, still with £75 in the pockets. He used to camp at
night under his dray, with a tarpaulin hanging down and a
good fire underneath, even when carting petrol.

Fred Ambrose was one of the most remarkable of the early
swaggers, those restless souls who called in at stations to
work for a meal or two before moving on. Fred, though a
very small man, walked so quickly that no one could keep up
with him. He was noted, furthermore, as a mountaineer, for
with the renowned Mt Cook guide Alf Brusted he made a
number of traverses to the Copeland and other mountain
ranges.

He thought nothing of swimming treacherous Mackenzie
rivers in flood, and this with a huge swag that contained,
among other personal things, a gramophone, an accordion
and a camera. As with most of his kind, responsibility was
not to his liking. He was once nearly reduced to nervous

prostration because he had to feed a few horses for an absent runholder.

Fred Ambrose must have been round the Mackenzie for a very long time, for he was still on the roads when I started driving through the Mackenzie Country in the early 1930s. He was quite independent and would never accept the lifts I would offer him if I happened to be travelling with an empty bus. He would chat for a moment or two and then stride briskly on again.

Further down the line was the Pukaki Hotel, built near where a punt had carried traffic across the river until it was replaced by a bridge. This hotel, too, was a most hospitable place. It served meals to passing travellers, and cars which had been turned back from The Hermitage through flooded creeks or snow would spend the night there. The hosts for many years were Mr and Mrs Graham, and it didn't matter at what time of the day or night we turned up, they always had a meal and a bed for us.

Mrs Graham, a tall, handsome, blonde woman, came from Alsace and had married her husband at the end of the First World War, when he was with the occupation forces on the Rhine. She had a strong and sometimes unpredictable personality. She could turn on all the charm in the world but on other occasions she could show a very brusque front — that hid a heart of gold and a warmth of hospitality. On one occasion when several cars had attempted to get through to Mt Cook and were turned back at Pukaki, she did her magnificent best and fed everyone, but she could provide beds only for the most needy. We drivers slept in the backs of our buses, but one young couple had nowhere to sleep. They had divested themselves of their wet clothes and were walking round in dressing gowns, and they asked Mrs Graham 'Where will we sleep?'

She pointed to a settee, and a couple of blankets, and said 'What's wrong with that?'

The girl said, 'But unfortunately we're not married.'

Mrs Graham said, 'That doesn't matter — you have your dressing gown on.'

On another occasion, a rather fastidious English tourist stayed at the hotel overnight on his way to Mt Cook. The lavatories were single-hole things out in the yard, and were usually oriented so one could leave the door open and enjoy the view. This English tourist complained bitterly to Mrs Graham about the flies there, and her retort was, 'Why don't you go at mealtimes? They're all on the dining-room table then!'

Over the years the restaurants and wayside inns patronised by the Company for its passengers have not always provided the standard of service and cuisine which we required and this has caused some inconvenience because timetables have had to be changed to fit in with changed meal stops. One luncheon stop was terminated abruptly by Aub Rollinson very soon after partaking of part of his last meal there. He had been sitting at a table with two or three others, and was enjoying a juicy, well-grilled steak. At the next table there was a large woman with two or three small children, the youngest of whom was bawling his head off. She tried to quieten him down but to no avail and finally, in desperation, she opened her blouse and extracted the apparatus for breast-feeding, but the baby would have nothing to do with it.

Aub was somewhat shocked by this performance, but even more so when the lady picked up the sugar-basin, took the top off it and dunked her breast in the sugar. This particular inn was removed from the list of meal-stops immediately afterwards.

It was not long before the Grand Motor Tour, the trip from Fairlie to Mt Cook, Mt Cook to Wanaka and Queenstown was reasonably well established and getting the support of the Government Tourist Department, Thomas Cook, and other international agencies. Quite a number of overseas visitors used this service and many wrote articles for their newspapers on the beauties of the scenic areas they had passed through.

Although the private car was becoming more and more popular each year, there were few owners who would venture into the wild back-country for personal pleasure or under charter to tourists, and so the Mount Cook Motor Service provided virtually the only access to these areas. As well, back-country stations and villages relied on the Company to bring in the mail, newspapers and stores of all kinds, and for them it provided an essential service.

Many of the stores and day-to-day necessities on the back-country runs were ordered by mail, but many of the wives preferred the more personal service of the drivers. At a point where the main road passed closest to the stations a post would be erected on which the green canvas mailbag would be hung on a hook. Alongside would be a box to hold the bread, groceries, and other stores delivered by the car. On his return journey the driver would pick the outgoing mailbags off the hooks without having to get out of his car, and many of these hooks were so designed that the mailbag could be retrieved on the gallop, so to speak, with the driver grabbing them on the way past without stopping the vehicle.

Often the womenfolk would leave notes for the driver, or would wait for his arrival to have a yarn or give him their instructions in person, as to the shopping they wanted him to do — a reel of blue cotton, a bottle of ink, a bottle of iodine and some bandages from the chemist, a tin of baking powder, and so on through the list. The driver would finish his journey, wash his car down for the next day's journey, and then go round the shops buying the various items, labelling them to the rightful purchasers, and accounting for the cash. Only then would his day's work be over.

Even today, the driver of the coach through the back-country is called on to do a variety of shopping jobs; although it can be rather irksome at the end of a long day, a request is very seldom refused.

In the days of the bullock or horsedrawn wagons, a whole year's supply of stores would be taken in to the stations by the wagons taking out the wool or grain. Every possible thing which might be required in the next twelve months had to be remembered, for there were no regular mail services, and people living on the stations left them only infrequently. Anything left off the list could add to the problems of the station owner or the housewife, for it could mean a special excursion on horseback or buggy to the nearest town to make the purchase. As a result of this, each large station ran its own store, whose stock might rival that of any small village store in the amount and range of merchandise on its shelves. As a kid I used to be fascinated by all the sights and smells coming from the ceiling-high shelves when I was allowed in to watch the daily issuing of supplies.

Scheduled services through these areas have, to a large extent, rendered these stores unnecessary, and many stations now receive their supplies daily. At one time every station had its own old-fashioned baker's ovens, and the baking of bread with its mouth-watering smells and the crunching of delicious chunks of hot crust have almost completely disappeared. Many stations do not even kill their own mutton and beef, while the placid old milch cow peacefully chewing her cud near the homestead has also largely disappeared.

Recently, while talking to one back-country station owner, I said I was surprised that with all the lush pasture round his homestead he had dispensed with the old milch cow which used to provide him with so much beautiful, sweet-smelling fresh milk, rich cream and butter. He replied that it was far cheaper to buy the exact quantity of milk from town by the bottle and to pay the freight on it, as it would cost him more than $4000 a year to run a cow. ($2000 for wages and board for cowboy, $1000 for hay and $1000 for condensed milk.)

The result of all this is that service vehicles today carry a tremendous assortment of goods of all kinds. A load out of Christchurch or Timaru will often be carrying a greater weight of freight than of passengers.

Daily deliveries of goods to these back-country stations have actually given them in most cases a better service than is enjoyed by city people, and has done a lot to remove their sense of isolation. Thus what was provided originally for tourists has also been instrumental in getting roads and bridges improved throughout the back-country and has provided a facility that has made life much more livable for those that dwell there.

With the introduction of the Grand Motor Tour, traffic built up and continued to build up until the outbreak of the First World War, and even in those far-back days the cry was much the same as that heard today — 'There's not enough accommodation for tourists!'

Transport is flexible, as extra vehicles can be put on to cater for extra traffic, but (in the more reputable establishments) hotel beds can cater for only one occupant in the twenty-four hours.

10

Freights and Floods

THE ACTS OF GOD AND MAN which destroyed the old Hermitage
not only eventually solved the accommodation problem but
also started the Company on its first purely freight transport
operation.

For thousands of years the Mueller Glacier had collected the
water from its thawing ice, from rainfall and from tributary
streams fed by thawing snow on the mountainsides, and
through a system of creeks and rivers on its surface, dropped
the water down frequent crevasses to its rock bottom. Here
tremendous rivers flowed during the summer, their courses
relatively unimpeded until they hit the shingle of the terminal
moraine which caused pressure to build up and the water to
emerge as a tremendous geyser rising six or seven metres or
more above the surrounding ground. The sight of this erupting
water gave a vivid impression of the tremendous forces
involved.

Movement of the ice, erosion of the bed of the glacier or the
choking of existing channels by débris, forced the river to
change its course and make a new channel for itself between
White Horse Hill and the Sealey Range. After breaking
through the old terminal moraine wall, the river followed a
thousands-of-years-old course down the valley between White
Horse and Foliage Hills and flooded one wing of the old Hermitage. The building was not severely damaged and when the
river had reverted to its previous course, it was repaired and the
operation catered for tourists again.

However, a year later it was largely destroyed by fire and so,
with the risk of further flooding always possible, the decision
was made to build a new Hermitage on a risk-free site. The site
chosen was the one in use today, alongside Glen Coe Creek at
the foot of the Sealey Range. It gives unrivalled views of Mt
Cook and Mt Sefton, which were not visible from the old site.

The new building was started about 1912 and finished about

1913, and although the Company was vitally interested in the increased accommodation it provided for the car passengers, it was also interested in another aspect: up until this time, all heavy carting to the Mackenzie Country had been done by wagons which were later superseded by RLW's traction-engine trains. He was interested in all forms of transport through the area, and he tendered for the cartage of the large quantity of building materials which would be required for the new Hermitage. On winning the contract he made arrangements to import a Leyland motor lorry to do the job, for he reasoned that this vehicle would travel from the railhead at Fairlie to Mt Cook in the day far faster than the horsedrawn wagons could do it and would carry a far heavier load.

According to his calculations it would not only give better service to the contractor building The Hermitage but would be much more economic, at the same time giving the Company a big enough job to establish a lorry service which would take over the carting of wool and other general cartage in the Mackenzie Country from the traction engines and remaining wagons.

RLW claimed that this lorry was the first to be imported as such into either Australia or New Zealand, and it certainly must have been a very early model, for when the Leyland Company located the old vehicle in a dump near The Hermitage a few years after World War II they salvaged the engine for their musuem of early vehicles in England.

The Leyland, or the Red Lorry as it was known for twenty years or more, had a four-cylinder engine which turned over at a leisurely speed more suitable for a steam engine than a petrol combustion one, and it pushed the vehicle along at about 30 km/h. It had solid rubber tyres, which gave the driver sitting in the small boxlike cab a singularly uncomfortable ride. The 155-kilometre trip from Fairlie to The Hermitage must have made a very long day.

The first driver of the Red Lorry was Charlie Elms who, tired of being head teamster at Holme station in South Canterbury, wanted to try something a bit more modern and exciting. He stayed with the Company and served it in various capacities until he retired about 1944. He was branch manager at Fairlie for quite a long period before taking on the managership of The Hermitage, where he did a rugged job under the very difficult conditions of the Depression.
on the managership of The Hermitage, where he did a rugged job under the very difficult conditions of the Depression.

Three historic staging-posts. *Top*, the Burkes Pass Hotel. *Middle*, the original Tekapo Hotel. *Bottom*, the Pukaki Hotel. The Tekapo and Pukaki Hotels are now submerged by the high dam. The Darracqs feature in each photo, and 'The Beetle' is in attendance at Pukaki.

Top, the Company's headquarters at Fairlie, RLW at the wheel of a Darracq. *Middle*, RLW was a passionate upholder of the doctrine that 'the mails must go through'. On this occasion he is preparing to deliver them by packhorse. *Bottom*, The Ministry of Works construction camp halfway between Pukaki and The Hermitage. As a coaching meal-stop it became known as The Rest, but the camp's inmates christened it Hell's End.

One of the Company's first Cadillacs at Queenstown. The runningboard carries the acetylene-gas generator for lighting, a reserve tin of engine-oil, and a brand-new tyre still in its warehouse wrapping.

The 60hp Darracq, last of these French-built cars in Company service. Note the steel-studded tyre on rear wheel.

Top, Darracq and Cadillac at Cardrona. The lady's bonnet carries a thick veil as a protection against the all-pervading dust when the roads were dry. *Middle*, Company convoy to The Hermitage, 1911. *Bottom*, the service direct from Timaru to Mt Cook was inaugurated in 1919. The 60hp Darracq outside Timaru's Hydro Grand Hotel is now on an extended chassis.

RLW overcame communication difficulties by using a hook-in telephone to contact The Hermitage when vehicles were held up by flooded creeks.

The first heavy motor truck in use on New Zealand roads. The Leyland 'red lorry' loaded up at Fairlie with luggage and stores for The Hermitage. Charlie Elms (*left*) is the pilot.

'Big Bertha', a 90hp fire engine, was adapted to carry 40 passengers. Driver J. Bennington, on the right, must have found that starting the huge engine by hand was mighty hard work.

One of the Hudson convertibles that replaced the horsedrawn coaches on the awe-inspiring Queenstown-Skippers run.

'Three-score years and ten' – plus one. The 1979 48-seat 6-wheel luxury coach built in the Company's Christchurch workshops on an MC-Denning chassis towers above the 9-seat Darracq rebuilt in the workshops on an original 1908 chassis and engine.

Three pioneers of road transport. *From left*, J.T. Harvey, founder of Hawke's Bay Motor Co., which is now part of the Mount Cook Group; RLW; and Tom Newman who, with his brother, founded Newman Brothers of Nelson.

The next generation, in 1950. *From left*, Fred Tebay, managing director of the Hawke's Bay Motor Company; Jack Newman, managing director of Newman Brothers; and Harry Wigley.

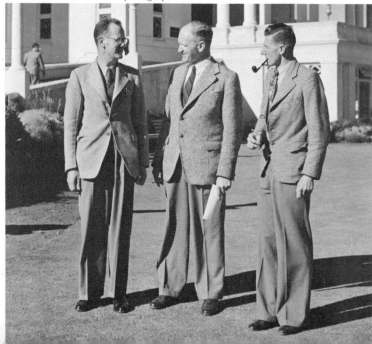

Charlie was well known and respected by hundreds of people who passed through The Hermitage, and by the people of the Mackenzie Country, who recognised him as one of the outstanding characters of his time.

It was not long before the Red Lorry had completely taken over the general freight carting on the Mount Cook Road. There will be few people alive today who can remember having seen a bullock team in action, and only a very few of us can remember seeing the wagonloads of wool being pulled by fourteen to sixteen huge Clydesdale horses, straining gallantly into their collars with tremendous muscles rippling their rumps. The creaking of the harness, the thud of hooves on the soft ground, the crack of the driver's whip, the clanging of the large wooden wheels as they slid backwards and forwards on their axles, and the smell of leather and sweating horses — these are things never to be forgotten.

In a very few years the lorries had replaced horses on the roads and the tractors had replaced them on the farms, and the great Clydesdales virtually disappeared from the landscape. For many years we were proud to show visitors the magnificent thoroughbred Clydesdales at Andrew Grant's stud at Fairlie, where visitors were always welcome. Then, after a period when it seemed as though we would never see the Clydesdale breed again, in recent years another stud was started there to produce horses purely for show purposes, and many people now get great enjoyment out of seeing these 'vintage' beasts.

Slowly but surely the passenger and freight services to the Mackenzie Country became established. The 1914-18 war brought most of the passenger traffic to a standstill, but the trucking of wool and other freight continued, and enabled the Company to survive this very difficult period and to emerge afterwards ready for further development and further growth.

Over the years the roads had been slowly improved by spreading shingle on the worst places, making new cuttings on hillsides for easier grades, and building bridges, but in the main the back-country roads still consisted of three deep tracks — two for the wheels and a centre track made by the horses' hooves. In between the tracks were two high grass-covered ridges over which one had to climb when passing another vehicle. Nevertheless, the roads had been improved to the extent that RLW decided that the cars could do the trip from Timaru to Mt Cook in one day instead of spending the first day travelling by train from Timaru to Fairlie, where a night was spent, and completing the journey to The Hermitage on the second day. The new service began on 2 November 1918. The extension of the Company's terminus to Timaru made it desirable to shift the head office there also, and this too was done before the end of 1918.

An effort to bring Queenstown closer to civilisation was made in 1934 when the Company started a service that connected with the trains at Studholme Junction (on the main line south of Timaru), over the Lindis Pass to Cromwell, where it connected with the Company's existing Cromwell-Queenstown service. This new service brought Queenstown within one day's travel of Christchurch.

As the roads and the vehicles improved still further, the Timaru-Mt Cook timetable was amended to allow the cars to pick up passengers off the Christchurch express train at 11.30am and then proceed to The Hermitage, where they arrived at 6pm, thus allowing the journey from Christchurch to Mt Cook to be made in about nine hours. North Island visitors using the Wellington-Lyttelton ferry could travel from Wellington to Mt Cook in almost exactly twenty-four hours.

The services continued along these lines until 1946, when a licence was granted to the Company to operate direct from Christchurch to Mt Cook via Geraldine, which again decreased the travelling time considerably. This service was linked with the Mt Cook-Queenstown service, allowing passengers to do the 514-kilometre journey from Christchurch to Queenstown in one day by coach.

This pattern, with modification from time to time to suit the needs of places en route, is the basis of the service today, though the modern coaches used are a far cry from the little tourers used in 1906. Great six-wheeled vehicles weighing 12,000 kilos carry forty-five passengers and 2,000 kilos of freight, and travel over the modern sealed roads between Christchurch and Queenstown at a speed which allows them to complete the journey almost as fast as it can be done by the private motorist.

Very occasionally services are disrupted by floods or heavy falls of snow, but the modern equipment used by the Highways Board and the county councils soon gets traffic flowing again, and any delays are of short duration.

It's a far cry from the days when RLW took the attitude that 'the mails must go through'. It was a tradition which he maintained for very many years, but I could never see that it justified the considerable damage to the wear and tear of the vehicles. However, to get a car across a creek in high flood was a challenge which RLW could never resist, and he insisted that the drivers make every effort to get their passengers and freight to The Hermitage, for not only did The Hermitage need every night's board it could get, but fresh milk, vegetables and other supplies were needed to keep the dining-room supplied.

At certain times of the year, particularly in the spring, when the warm nor'-west wind and rains cause rapid thawing of the winter's snowfall in the ranges, creeks which are often quite dry or normally carry trivial amounts of water easily negotiated by the buses, can become raging torrents in a matter of a very few hours.

Many of these creeks pour out of gorges in the mountains and cascade down their rocky beds at great speeds, throwing up metres-high pressure-waves, scouring their banks and carrying down a tremendous lot of débris. The water quickly becomes discoloured, and then very muddy as its load of débris builds up. The roar of the water becomes so loud that it can be heard for some distance away, and almost drowns out speech in the vicinity, but above this continual roar can be heard the crashing of huge boulders being rolled and tumbled along the bottom of the creek. In many places it is quite impossible for man or horse to cross, and quite out of the question, of course, for a motor vehicle. Apart from the speed and force of the water, the big boulders being rolled along by the current claimed many lives in the old days.

When a driver encountered a flooded stream it was his responsibility to assess the chances of getting his vehicle safely over. His first step was to pick the most promising ford in the vicinity and then wade over it to test its suitability, walking downstream for a kilometre or more to where it had fanned out into a number of streams and had lost some of its velocity and volume.

The ground on the approaches to the selected ford had to be firm enough to carry the vehicle, as did the bottom of the ford itself. Often newly-eroded shingle from higher up the stream would lie loosely on the bed of an otherwise promising ford, and it was all too easy to drive into a patch of this and get the vehicle completely bogged. On the other hand, if the crossing consisted of too many big boulders, the vehicle could get perched on one of these on its belly, leaving the wheels spinning harmlessly in the water. The driver had to assess all these problems, wading through a number of freezingly cold streams and testing each ford. Sometimes he would decide that he had a better chance of getting his vehicle across without its passengers adding to its weight, and so he would drive it over and then go back for his passengers and carry them over, one at a time, on his back.

It was never easy to judge the fords accurately, for the dirty water obscured the bottom, and all the driver could do, stumbling round and trying to stay on his feet, was to make an intelligent guess. If he thought the ford was negotiable he would put a canvas sheet over the radiator and disconnect the fanbelt to stop water being thrown all over the ignition and into the carburettor. If there was a possibility of the ford being soft he would charge at it, and water would fly over the top of the car, completely obscuring the windscreen. On such occasions the cars would be jolted and bounced around so violently that one wondered how they ever held together. Hold together they did on most occasions, but the wear and tear had to be reckoned with at a later date.

This 'mail-must-go-through' attitude sometimes made the drivers take on streams which, in their more prudent moments, they would have left severely alone. The excitement — and there certainly was a lot of excitement involved — the challenge, the fear of what the other drivers might say, made them do things in a fit of recklessness which they should never had attempted. I believe RLW enjoyed the excitement of the challenge more than any of us, for he was very frequently on the spot, wading through the water himself and urging the drivers on.

On one occasion, when he was approaching sixty, he was lucky not to lose his life. Four or five busloads of passengers, among them a number of schoolchildren, were travelling to Mt Cook for the skiing; torrential rain had caused the creeks to rise rapidly and one, known as The Twins, was impassable. It had gouged out a narrow gut through which it was quite impossible to get a vehicle, and as there was no way to get up or down to attempt other fords, it was decided to get a rope across to give the drivers something to hang on to while they carried their passengers over. The stream was in an extremely dangerous condition, very deep, very muddy, very swift, and with big boulders trundling along its bottom, obviously a highly unsafe place to try and cross.

Against the advice of the drivers round about, RLW insisted on putting a rope round his waist, getting several of them to hold the other end, and then attempting to wade across. He hadn't gone far before a large boulder hit him below the knee and bowled him off his feet: he disappeared from sight and, as the drivers were unable to hold him, he was swept swiftly down the stream. After being bowled along for fifty or sixty metres, completely submerged, he rolled over and over in an attempt to reach the bank and was finally thrown up on to a shinglebar more dead than alive, badly bruised and shaken, full of water, and only semiconscious. He was pretty sick for a number of days afterwards. After this, he lost some of his enthusiasm for tackling mountain streams in spate.

For many years all the maintenance work on the Pukaki-Hermitage road was done by a character by the name of Jimmie Smith. Jimmie was a guide at The Hermitage in the early days and left there to join the Ministry of Works in charge of the road. Jimmie was a squat, powerful man, and in the days when I knew him he had a snowy white beard and hair, unfailing good humour, and was living with his wife at The Rest, halfway between Pukaki and The Hermitage. He never failed to help drivers in trouble, or to take them into the cottage for a cup of tea, scones and cakes cooked by the equally hospitable and cheerful Mrs Smith.

Jimmie patrolled the whole fifty-nine kilometres from Pukaki to Mt Cook, riding a pushbike with a shovel tied to its bar, and we were likely to encounter his ruddy cheerful face anywhere along the road. His main job was to keep small creeks diverted from the roads, smooth out parts which had been scoured by heavy rains, and do any preventive maintenance work which would keep the road passable. Any heavier work which required the transport of boulders or shingle would be done with his horse and dray, and it was really amazing how much he accomplished with this small amount of primitive gear.

No matter what time of the day or night, or what the weather conditions were, Jimmie was always willing to come out and help a driver across the streams nearby. The cold never seemed to affect him, and with his encyclopedic knowledge of every stream and ford he was a tremendous help. One day, when I had not been driving for very long, I was asked to take a straight-eight six-seater Studebaker car, which was RLW's pride and joy, to The Hermitage with Chief Justice Sir Michael Myers and his wife and son as passengers.

There had been some rain and I wasn't expecting any great trouble with the creeks, but with my very important passenger on board I decided to make sure by taking Jimmie along with us to The Twins creek. When we got there the stream was high and discoloured, but the usual ford seemed to be OK, although the water was flowing over the lower end very swiftly. Jimmie waded across the bottom end of the ford; the water wasn't much above his knees, so he signalled for me to come over.

Instead of following the route that he had taken, I started from a point a few metres higher upstream to get the advantage of the current and to avoid being swept over the ford on to a very rocky rapid below it, for the force of the current in these streams can be quite strong enough to sweep a heavy vehicle downstream. As the water seemed so shallow, I didn't even take the precaution of covering up the radiator and disconnecting the fanbelt.

As soon as the front wheels touched the water I put my foot down on the throttle and charged in and, to my horror, the radiator plunged under water and a solid brown mass hit the windshield. The engine kept going for just long enough for the front of the car to reach shallow water, but the back wheels were well down and the water was halfway up the back squab of the back seat. Sir Michael Myers and his lady were sitting there with slightly surprised looks on their faces while their handbags and briefcases and bits and pieces were floating around them in the water. It was a most embarrassing moment that took me years to live down.

What had happened was that something had caused the stream to scour a deep hole on the side of the usual ford. Jimmie had not known it was there and so was unable to warn me, but I learned from that experience never to attempt a flooded stream without walking through myself exactly where I proposed to drive the vehicle.

One of the most embarrassing aspects of the whole business was that the stream subsided as quickly as it had risen, and an hour later it was not much more than an ankle-deep trickle over the ford. Sir Michael and his family walked with me over to the Glentanner station, where we were made welcome by the Robertson family, who plied us with the usual back-country hospitality. They lit a roaring fire and the Chief Justice made himself at home by standing in front of it, attired only in his singlet and long-johns, trying to dry the seat of his pants.

He did not seem to bear me any malice, but I have no doubt he had plenty to say to RLW, who also had plenty to say to me in due course!

Frequently, when conditions were known to be bad, a bus would be dispatched from The Hermitage with a number of drivers and guides on board and equipped with picks, shovels, ropes and other equipment for helping cars through the creeks. It would be driven from creek to creek, where banks would be broken down and fords located, and would finally meet up with the oncoming vehicle. This arrangement made things very much easier; it saved the driver the trouble of having to find a ford the hard way, as there was plenty of manpower about to push and shove if he got stuck, and there was always the second vehicle there if the worst happened.

Almost invariably it would be raining in torrents and blowing a gale when these flooded creeks were encountered, and with the service timed to arrive at Mt Cook between 6 and 7pm, it didn't take much of a delay to ensure that we were still on the road after dark. Conditions were, therefore, just about as unpleasant as they could be. When we finally arrived at The Hermitage we were almost invariably soaked through and had been this way for several hours, and it was a great relief to get a drink or two and a hot bath and a meal. However, we were all young and hardy, and did not suffer unduly from it.

On the occasions when passengers had to be unloaded and left to get across the streams as best they could, some interesting sides of human nature could be seen. Most men rolled up their trousers and gave us a hand in carrying the female passengers and bags, but a few were completely out of their element and quite upset that the cars had failed to deliver them safe and dry at The Hermitage. One English tourist, who was quite young enough to have forded the stream on his own, insisted on being carried, and as well as being a good deal heavier than most of the drivers, he complained continuously and bitterly, and threatened to report us to the manager of the Company, the Government Tourist Department, and various other people, when he ultimately reached his destination. It was just his bad luck that when, on crossing one of the deepest and roughest streams, the driver carrying him quite accidentally stumbled and dropped him into the freezing cold water. When he emerged, he was shivering too much even to complain.

We had no real objections to carrying some of the attractive young female tourists, and somehow or other, these always seemed to be the first ones to get across.

The chill stream often left its bridge and crossed the roads in quite a number of channels spread over a kilometre or more and, owing to the soft soggy ground round about, it was often necessary to transport the passengers from the original vehicle on one side to a relief vehicle on the other. On one such occasion all the passengers had been carried or had found their own way over, except for one youngish woman who must have weighed at least 100 kilos. She was too heavy to carry so had no option but to walk, and with one fat arm draped round a driver on either side, she started off. Before long she started screaming and shouting, and became quite hysterical. The two drivers half-dragged and half-carried her across. She lost a shoe, and got accidentally dunked in the water a couple of times, and was a very sorry sight when she reached the other side, but fortunately it was not very far from The Hermitage, where she was soon able to get a hot bath and dry clothes.

As I have explained, the amount of débris brought down by the streams could fill up the old watercourses and channels and cause them to change their courses, with the result that many of the bridges were left high and dry, and often hundreds of metres away from the nearest water. Even when the water was flowing under them, they could be quite dangerous, as the force of the current tended to erode the approaches and the piles.

Hughie Fergusson, who was with the Company for the greater part of his working life and was one of the best and most skilful ever to drive for us, had an alarming experience on the Wales Creek bridge. He was driving a twelve-seater Hudson bus from The Hermitage to Queenstown and had covered sixteen kilometres or so of his journey, crossing a number of flooded streams without much difficulty. On approaching the Wales Creek bridge he slowed right down to make sure that the approach had not been damaged and, as it looked safe enough, he drove slowly towards it.

Just as his front wheels hit the decking of the bridge the approach subsided, leaving the front bumper hanging on to the decking of the bridge, and the back wheels on the approach, with a gaping hole, three metres deep, in between. Water had eroded the approach and, unknown to him, it had been undermined and gave way under the weight of his vehicle. The river continued to erode and before the stream went down, it had washed away nearly all the approach to within a short distance of the back wheels. Fortunately the vehicle was not damaged and no one was hurt, but it was some time before the approach had been filled up again and the vehicle salvaged.

The damage to the bridges en route was not always attributable to flooding, and from time to time the Company was in trouble with the Mackenzie County Council for damaging them.

Jack Liddy was a dour, stalwart character who took over the truck-driving from Charlie Elms and worked for the Company for many years, right up until he retired. He drove a Leyland lorry of a later vintage than the original one, but it too was shod with solid rubber tyres, was very heavy to drive, and gave an uncomfortable ride. It would take Jack the whole day to drive from the railhead at Fairlie to Mt Cook, and by the time he got there his arms were so tired that he barely had the strength to pick up his knife and fork to eat his evening meal.

This truck was later superseded by one with pneumatic tyres and considerably heavier, but Jack still found that the trip in one day was as much as he could manage. We later tried to talk him into taking a more modern vehicle with a much higher performance, but Jack would have no part of it at all, and stuck to his old Leyland, even though it was almost killing him.

Finally we persuaded him to do a few trips to Mt Cook with a modern Bedford truck and this, most reluctantly, he agreed to do. I happened to be at The Hermitage when he arrived there after his first trip, and he was absolutely astounded. He said, 'I've done the trip in only half the time and my arms aren't even tired!' It wasn't long before he had as much affection for this new truck as for the old one, and was doing the return trip in the one day.

Jack was a very conscientious chap, and in spite of his rather gruff manner he had a heart of gold. He would never go into one of the back-country stations without ringing first to see if there was any shopping he could do for the housewife. He was gentleness itself with stock, and drove his vehicle as carefully as he could to avoid any undue wear and tear. He certainly would never wilfully overload it.

So he was most embarrassed by one incident which caused some friction between the Company and the Council. He was heading into the back-country with a load of coal in sacks. It was easy to estimate the exact weight of the load, and under Jack's care it certainly would not have been an overload. However, when crossing the Opihi Bridge about fifteen kilometres from Fairlie, the decking gave way under the rear wheels, which crashed through and landed on the riverbed, some three metres below. The lorry made quite a sight sitting

at a 45-degree angle, with its rear wheels on the riverbed and
the front wheels on the decking of the bridge.

Snow caused a lot of problems during the winter, for it fell
frequently through the Mackenzie Country and there were
very few graders or snowploughs obtainable to clear it. It was
not unusual for falls of sixty to ninety centimetres to occur,
when the services would come to a complete halt for several
days until the snow thawed or was cleared.

Up until the mid-1930s there was so little traffic on the road
that it was difficult to get accurate reports on the snow conditions along the route and the driver would have to push on,
often through unbroken snow, until he completed his journey,
or had to turn round and retrace his steps if he found the going
too tough. If a vehicle had travelled in the opposite direction
within a recent time it was possible to follow its tracks and
make reasonably good progress, but if no vehicle had been
through, all would be unbroken white. With none of the present-day fluorescent markers to show the verges of the road, it
was very easy to lose it and drive into ditches or banks.

I can remember Hughie Fergusson once complaining about
the depth of snow and the roughness of the road between
Burkes Pass and Tekapo. This rather surprised us, as we had
travelled over the same section of road an hour or two later
without any difficulty. The answer was provided by his wheel
tracks which, in the bright sunshine the following morning,
showed that, in the bad visibility of the snowstorm, he had
travelled on the rough ground about fifty metres off the road
and parallel to it. The snow remained on the ground for quite a
number of days after this episode with the tracks there for all to
see, and poor Hughie stopped a lot of ragging over it.

RLW's policy of 'the mails must go through' applied to snow
as well as to flooded creeks, and on many occasions he would
send us away from Timaru with a carload of stores for The
Hermitage and enough provisions for ourselves to stay on the
road for two or three days if snowbound. Chains would be
fitted to the vehicle when it could no longer proceed without
them, and by a process of charging the snow ahead, backing off
and charging again, slow progress was made, and a track
established in which other vehicles could follow.

On occasions I, and other drivers, have spent up to three
days on the road, either sleeping in the vehicle or at wayside
stations until we finally got through. But as with the flooded
creeks, while the drivers enjoyed the excitement of it all, the

wear and tear on the vehicles was enormous and, in retrospect, I do not believe it was ever justified. Today we would certainly not subject our vehicles to this type of usage unnecessarily and, of course, present-day passengers would never put up with it.

So developed the story of motor transport through the Mackenzie Country and Central Otago. Rough roads, lack of bridges, lack of facilities and foods, frost and snow, all were surmounted.

For RLW and his gang of pioneering drivers it was high adventure, and it was, still like that, to a large extent anyway, when I started driving in the early 1930s. But this phase is now in the remote past, and today anyone who tries to make the job look like a death-or-glory operation will soon find himself in trouble.

Rugged transport pioneering has given way to a system of smooth routine that gives uneventful and efficient service to the public and the farming community.

11

Landlines and Other Ventures

THINGS did not go very well for the Company nor for RLW during the years of World War II. Traffic slowed down to a trickle, and it was only military personnel on leave and people working for the Ministry of Works hydro-electric schemes at Tekapo and Pukaki and other points who provided enough traffic to keep the service going at all. The depression of the 1930s had seriously affected the flow of tourist traffic, and it had not recovered sufficiently to get the vehicle fleet back into first-class order when the war struck in 1939.

From then on, spare parts became more and more difficult to get, all heavy motor vehicles were conscripted to military use and it was impossible to get new ones, so the fleet continued to deteriorate. A further factor was overloading. Petrol rationing prevented extra services and extra buses being put on, so when passengers and freight turned up they were simply piled on board, and if there was no seat available for a passenger he had the option of walking, or sitting on his suitcases in an over-crowded coach. Many services were curtailed and the only routes operated were Timaru to Mt Cook, and Studholme Junction to Queenstown, both on a tri-weekly basis.

From about 1943 until 1946 or 1947 the hydro-electric dam was being built at Lake Tekapo and a sizeable camp was established there to house the several hundred workers employed on the scheme. The Company operated a tri-weekly service to Timaru, leaving Tekapo early in the morning and returning in the evening, to allow people to do their shopping, visit doctors and dentists and so on, and this created a separate set of problems for us with both the unions and the passengers.

Passengers were allowed to carry so many kilos of luggage without charge, but anything over this was charged at excess baggage rates. Some women would front up to the bus with large suitcases so heavily stocked with about six months' provisions that the driver would have difficulty lifting it off the ground, let alone on to the bus. A suitcase would be put on the scales and a charge made for the excess baggage, and then the argument would start, with the passenger claiming that the suitcase contained nothing but personal luggage, and the staff insisting that it obviously contained winter stores. More pass-engers would join in the argument and take the side of their mate and finally, to let the bus get on its way, an arbitrary decision would be made.

Often families would travel together, and while the wives were busily shopping, some of the husbands would dive into the pubs and roll back to the depot at three o'clock consider-ably the worse for wear. Drivers then had the unenviable job of getting them on board and separated from their bottles of beer, for not only did they have trouble in drinking while the bus was travelling and spilling beer all over themselves and the bus, but they would get fuller as the journey progressed and become belligerent, or demand frequent comfort stops or, worse still, let go in the bus.

On one occasion the bus pulled up at Tekapo House where a number of people were standing around awaiting the arrival of other passengers and stores, and one character climbed out and in full view of the public relieved himself against the front wheel of the bus. The law, apparently, permits a driver, but not a passenger, to do this against the off front wheel of a vehicle; this curious indulgence is a relic of the horsedrawn-days, when it might be unsafe for a driver to leave a restive horse unattended.

On the journey home the driver had to stop outside the hotel at Fairlie and again at Burkes Pass to unload freight, and it was not long before several of the passengers on one pretext or another left the bus and went into the pub, often with their wives protesting volubly. The wives did help to get the hus-bands back on the bus in due course, but the driver would be abused by the drinkers for not letting them out, and by the other passengers for letting the drunks out, so he was in trouble either way.

Squib McWhirter was taking a load of passengers back to Tekapo one afternoon, and he had been told that in no cir-cumstances was he to stop at Burkes Pass. He duly carried on past the hotel, then found an irate male passenger standing over him brandishing a full bottle of beer and threatening to crown him if he did not stop. The gods are on the side of the big battalions, so Squib quickly stopped and let the gentleman off the bus, much to the disgust of the wives on board. They insisted that Squib should drive on, so he closed the door and drove on to Tekapo, leaving this passenger in the hotel. Needless to say, Squib was not too keen on driving more of these passengers to Tekapo and he used to go through Tekapo as smartly as possible and make himself very scarce.

Over the war years RLW himself had not fared much better than the buses. As well as having the worry of trying to keep the firm going, he was very short of staff and insisted on doing more than his share each day in loading the buses with luggage and freight, a job far too strenuous for someone of his age. His health had been deteriorating a lot, and he had aged considerably. Another factor which worried him was that, after all the years he had spent pioneering road and air transport, none of his three sons were intending to carry on the business.

The youngest was by now a doctor, and Sandy, who had been branch manager at Queenstown before the war, had decided to go sheepfarming, and my own interests were strongly slanted towards aviation. Knowing of his disappointment, I agreed somewhat reluctantly to toss in any idea of a career with the Air Force, or the airlines which were then developing, or in commercial aviation, and go back to the firm. From then onward his spirits picked up considerably, and he started writing and giving me all the day-to-day details of the Company's operations, its problems and his plans for the future.

He said: 'I'll walk out one day, and you can walk in the next.'

'But I've been away for over six years, and I don't know anything about it.'

'You won't learn anything so long as I'm hanging round.'

Finally the day came when I was discharged from the Air Force, my family and I returned to Timaru, and I started in at the office and into the strange world of commerce whose existence I had forgotten all about.

A short time afterwards, RLW went into hospital in Dunedin for an operation and never returned.

From then on I was on my own, in charge of a run-down firm with run-down equipment. The only thing bright and shining about it was the loyalty of some of the old employees such as Aub Rollinson, Jack Liddey, Squib McWhirter, Jack Anderson, Spike Woods and Keith McGowan. The fleet was down to about half a dozen worn-out buses and a few trucks, the rental cars had gone, the travel offices had gone. Prospects for an

early recovery of the tourist industry were far from encouraging, and the whole scene was grimly depressing. What a
contrast from my last job, where I was C.O. of an Island base
serving several squadrons of aircraft, serviced by a station
strength of nearly 2,000, burning 135,000 litres of aviation fuel
a day, and where one of the smallest units was the transport
section, which had 140 fully-serviced vehicles.

It was also bitter to reflect that the Company, which in 1930
had been the biggest tourist organisation in New Zealand, had
slipped to such a low level. In that year it had been operating
motor services from Timaru to Mt Cook and Queenstown, had
the Cargon Hotel in Auckland, and Brents Hotel in Rotorua; a
subsidiary company had built the Chateau Tongariro, had
leases of The Hermitage at Mt Cook, and owned the White
Star and Eichardts hotels in Queenstown. It had travel offices
in Auckland, Wellington, Christchurch and Dunedin, as well
as in Sydney and, when the war began, it had owned some
eighty rental cars.

The Depression had forced it out of most of its hotels, and
during the war years the rental cars and the travel offices had
been sold off, leaving nothing but a few bits of real estate in
Timaru, Fairlie and Queenstown, and a few broken-down
vehicles.

The troops returning from overseas were given warrants to
travel on various services anywhere throughout New Zealand
on furlough, on their own or with their wives or in small
groups, and many took advantage of this. They travelled to Mt
Cook and Queenstown on the Company's services, and
provided enough traffic over the next eighteen months or two
years to allow us to extend our routes and buy new buses.

The service which ran tri-weekly from the railway at Studholme Junction, fifty kilometres south of Timaru, to Cromwell
and Queenstown, was extended to Timaru, and this carried
not only tourists and people on holiday, but people working on
the sheep-stations and farms along the route, and employees at
the big State hydro-electric schemes which were starting up
through these areas.

The service from Mt Cook to Wanaka and Queenstown,
suspended during the war, was recommenced in 1945. The
journey from Christchurch to Timaru by rail and then from
Timaru to Mt Cook by bus was still a lengthy one. Passengers
left Christchurch, often after a night on the Wellington-Lyttelton ferry, at 8.30am, and arrived at Timaru at 11.30pm.

After lunch the bus departed for The Hermitage and arrived there at 6 or 6.30pm, which meant at least ten hours of travelling. To overcome this the Company obtained a licence to run buses directly from Christchurch to Mt Cook via Geraldine; this cut down the route by nearly fifty kilometres, and the elapsed time considerably. The service began in November 1946 and was later co-ordinated with the Hermitage-Queenstown service to give a through service by bus from Christchurch to Queenstown in the one day.

Traffic continued to expand, and the frequency of the service was increased from three days a week to six, then seven, and this has been the pattern ever since. The first new vehicles to be put on the road after the war were Bedford twenty-one-seaters and, as demand grew, these were increased to twenty-eight-seaters, thirty-five-seaters, and today forty-eight-seaters.

Though traffic on the services did grow steadily over the years, it suffered one or two serious setbacks. In 1944 our lease of The Hermitage expired. The Tourist Department now controlled it and, by putting some of the staff in the former guest-rooms and closing down a number of rooms which they considered substandard, they had reduced the number of beds the Company had made available to tourists from 200 or 220 to about 45, with very drastic effects on our coach services into The Hermitage.

For many years before the war the Company had been operating 'Landcruise' party tours with seven-seater cars and, from under the same roof, Group Travel had been operating group tours on our twenty-seater coaches, the only ones in New Zealand at that time. The Tourist Department had been the main selling agency overseas and within New Zealand for our tours, but now decided to set up its own tours in competition.

They then block-booked most of The Hermitage accommodation for their own coach tours, which left practically no accommodation for our Landcruises or for people using our scheduled services, with the result that for two successive seasons our scheduled services carried less than a passenger and a half per day between Pukaki and The Hermitage. After all the years of pioneering and publicising the route, it was disappointing that the Government Department which should have been supporting the Company and selling its wares had now become its major competitor.

It was disappointing too that just when the tourist flow was starting again and the Company should have been enjoying the benefit of the near-monopoly it had developed through blood, sweat and tears over forty years, its very survival was now being threatened by an organisation whose loyalty it should have been able to count on. The Tourist Department's control of accommodation at Mt Cook, with its ever-increasing promotion of its own tours, and its overseas policy of selling its own tours in preference to those of the Company, finally forced us to abandon our own coach tours and lease our coaches to the Department.

When our lease of The Hermitage ran out in 1944 the Tourist Department had its own problems in getting suitable staff, even though they had so drastically reduced the guest accommodation. Many of the Company's drivers and other staff who had been happy to be called in to act as temporary barmen, guides and spud-peelers, now watched with disgust the way in which The Hermitage was being run down, and it wasn't long before they and the manager were in strife. He seemed to have a drinking problem, and let the food and living conditions particularly for the staff, deteriorate seriously.

Complaints by the drivers met with no sympathy, so one night they decided to let him understand quite clearly that they thought the show had become fit only for pigs. The manager was running a pig farm, and it was said that these animals got more and better food than the guests, and it was also alleged that he was killing and selling the pigs in the interest of his own pocket. Dozens of these young weaner-pigs roamed around in the scrub surrounding The Hermitage, and Aub Rollinson and some of his mates decided to muster some of these up and liberate them in the corridors outside the manager's quarters.

The Hermitage was a long building and the corridors, covered in highly polished linoleum, extended from one end to the other. They let the pigs go upstairs and downstairs, where they slipped and slithered over the polished lino and set up a squealing that would have woken the dead. It wasn't long before the manager, in a fuddled state, poked his head around the corner, still wearing his long nightshirt and long tasselled nightcap. The boys obligingly said 'We'll catch them for you', and took off down the corridor after the squealing pigs, scattering them right and left. They opened one bedroom door and the pigs dashed in, and what with the shrieks of the occupant of the room and the squeals of the pigs, quite a din was generated.

As the pigs and drivers were careering up and down the corridors, the barman of the day, who kept a tame kea in his bedroom, concluded it had got out and came rushing out of his room to recapture it. In his excitement he took off in only his shirt tails and nothing else, to be met by the screaming pigs careering down the corridors and bedroom doors being opened in all directions by guests agog to see what the hell was going on.

Ten years after the war the Company was still struggling. One was beginning to wonder whether it was worth while keeping on. Apart from all the setbacks already mentioned, it had had to close down its coach tour operations and it had been forced to abandon its development of skiing at the Ball Glacier which had provided its winter traffic. No wonder we found the prospect depressing. . .

Aub Rollinson, who had operated the Landcruises before the war and afterwards, was an incurable optimist. In 1946 he became our general manager, and if we couldn't beat them, he reasoned, we should join them. So we built coaches to cater for the coach-tour operators, we developed the skiplanes to take a dollar off every person who passed through the Hermitage area, we developed Ohau Lodge to provide our own accommodation, and Coronet Peak to take the place of the Ball Hut to give us winter traffic.

In 1956 The Hermitage was destroyed by fire, and out of the ashes rose a bigger building, which has been increased in size ever since, until today there are over 600 beds in the Mt Cook area allowing a reasonable balance to be maintained between people travelling on the scheduled air and road services, and on coach tours. The popularity of the skiplanes increased by leaps and bounds, and not only provided a profitable sideline for the Company, but proved to be a major drawcard to the Mt Cook area.

As traffic built up we put bigger and bigger coaches on the road, with more and more power to climb over the mountain passes and give higher cruising speeds, and today those magnificent six-wheeled Mt Cook-Denning coaches glide quickly, effortlessly and silently from Christchurch to Queenstown in almost airline comfort.

These great machines, evolved by Alan Denning of Brisbane, are built under licence in our own body-shop in Christchurch and are powered by the famous General Motors Detroit diesel engines. The steel frame carries the body, the cargo compartment and the rear-mounted engine, and is mounted on airbags which gives such smooth and vibrationless riding that they eat up the distances as effortlessly as any high-powered private car. At 120km/h they are just as smooth and silent as they are at lower speeds (or so I have been informed, but of course our 80km/h legal speed-limit would prevent most of our drivers experiencing any higher speeds). These big Mt Cook-Dennings are being used on our trunk routes from Christchurch to Queenstown, and from Wellington to Auckland, and will go on to other major trunk routes as they come out of our body-shop.

A slightly smaller version, with the same handling and riding characteristics, is being developed for our coach tours, and we expect them to serve us faithfully and well for many years to come.

Many changes have been seen on the coachlines over the years, and as roads have been improved, their importance in the transport field has not diminished. The aeroplane has complemented the bus on the roads but has not supplanted it, and coach-development will continue. What shape it will take by the year 2000 is anyone's guess, but one thing that is certain is that it will still be there catering for public transport, possibly even taking the place of the private motor-car if our energy crisis gets any more severe.

In the mid 1930s road-transport licensing authorities were set up to ensure the orderly development of the motor transport industry and to cut out wasteful competition, and some rare old battles took place between the various operators to secure rights on routes already established, and on new routes. The new roads, from Queenstown to Kingston and from Lumsden to the Eglinton Valley and ultimately to Milford Sound, were cases in point.

The railway ran from Invercargill to Kingston, whence passengers and freight were transported to Queenstown by the lake steamers operated by the Railways Department. In the early 1930s, at the height of the Depression, the Government decided to build a road from Kingston to Queenstown to create employment and to help the general development of the area.

The Company hoped to get the licence over this route to link it with a service it was operating from Lumsden to the road which was being built through the Eglinton Valley and ultimately to Milford Sound. This service had been developed originally by a man by the name of James Campbell, who was getting on in years and was desirous of selling out. The Railways Department had been negotiating with Campbell for some time but had been unable to reach agreement with him and had gone cold on the idea. RLW grasped the opportunity and quickly completed a deal to purchase the enterprise. The Railways, understandably, were not too pleased.

A year or so went by and the Kingston-Queenstown road was nearing completion, and then the whole situation was changed overnight by the landslide election of a Socialist Government. Its policy included, among other things, the nationalisation of road transport. They directed that all licences to operate over new roads were to be given to the Government Railways Road Services, on the grounds that the Government had built the roads and that a Government Department should therefore reap the benefit of them. Regardless of this, we applied for a licence, as did the Railways, but the Authority said that it must conform with Government policy, and therefore awarded the licence to the Railways.

The Railways then approached the Company to buy the Lumsden-Eglinton Valley service, but RLW refused to sell. The Railways took a strong line and said: 'Sell out to us at our price or we'll run you off the road', and so disappeared our bid to extend our tourist routes from Mt Cook to Queenstown, Te Anau and Milford Sound. This was the first road service to be taken over compulsorily by the Government and it was the first of many which have remained under Government control ever since, even though a succession of ostensibly private-enterprise Governments could easily have reversed the trend.

To complete the accommodation chain and to link in with the Eglinton Valley service, the Company bought a motel-type operation at the top end of the Eglinton Valley, known as Cascade Camp. Negotiations had been going on for some time, and when the day for taking it over arrived, I flew the company secretary — at that time Dooley Coxhead — down to Lumsden where, typically of flying operations in those days, we had nothing arranged but had to select a suitable field from overhead on arrival. We travelled by car to Cascade Camp and returned later in the day to pick up the aeroplane and fly over to Queenstown, where we landed on a farmer's paddock close to where the present Frankton airfield is today. The aeroplane we were flying was a little BA Swallow, a low-wing monoplane which could land as slowly as 40km/h and could become airborne under normal conditions in a very short distance.

We spent a night in Queenstown, where Dooley had a few jobs to do, and we left first thing in the morning with the idea of getting back to Timaru by lunchtime. It was mid-winter and the sky was an unbroken blue, with a hard white frost on the ground, and when we reached the Swallow we found that it too was covered in frost. Dooley has a big frame and carries a fair bit of beef, but the paddock was reasonably long, so I had no hesitation about flying out of it. The engine was warmed up, we climbed in, I taxied down to the end of the paddock which would give us the longest takeoff run, and opened the throttle.

The little aeroplane travelled faster and faster, but she showed no sign at all of lifting off. I wasn't unduly worried and was certain that at any second she would float off as she had always done before. I eased the stick back, but still nothing happened. By this time the fence was coming towards us very fast indeed, so I pulled the stick right back, the tail hit the ground with a smack, the wheels did not leave the ground by as much as a centimetre, and a second later we were crashing through the fence, shearing the end off one wing and doing considerable damage to the remainder of the aircraft. A fairly shattering experience for the aircraft and for my dignity!

The reason why we failed to be airborne was that the thick frost covering the wings had distorted their natural camber and destroyed the lift. In Canada and other colder climates overseas this was a well-known hazard, but it was the first time it had happened in New Zealand, and I had had no idea that the consequences could be so serious.

During the 1930s the Railways Department were moving through the country systematically taking over road services large and small, but by the time war was declared in 1939 the buying spree had lost a lot of its impetus as the Government was becoming involved with more important matters. The main companies which survived were: Newman Bros. of Nelson, Gibsons Motors of New Plymouth, the Hawke's Bay Motor Co. of Napier, and the Mount Cook Company, and they all had their own special reasons for not being gobbled up. In the case of the Mount Cook Company it was no doubt to some extent because it was carrying out the Labour Government's policy in organising cheap group travel for various sections of the community, and therefore had the blessing of the Hon. W. E. Parry, who was then Minister of Tourism.

The concept behind the formation of the Group Travel Association was that a number of hotels and coach and sight-seeing operators should pool their resources and make them available to certain groups in the community at the lowest possible cost, to generate profitable traffic in the off-season and, with the resultant lower fares and tariffs, to make holidays available to those who could never otherwise have afforded them. It was this latter aspect which appealed to the Hon. W. E. Parry and his Labour Party colleagues, and he not only gave the scheme his wholehearted moral support but made funds available to the Association to promote it.

Dooley Coxhead was responsible for the early development of the Group Travel Association and it was he who persuaded Bill Parry of its value. He got round and actively canvassed the Workers' Educational Associations, Women's Institutes, and similar organisations to avail themselves of the very cheap travel which would allow them a holiday seeing their own country in the company of kindred spirits. Dooley worked very hard in getting the organisations established and running, and over a period of years, until stopped by the war, it carried many hundreds of people on holidays throughout New Zealand. Group Travel Ltd. was based in the Company's office at Timaru, and the organisation and operation of the tours, as well as supplying transport, occupied a considerable part of the time of the staff.

After the war more and more operators started in the coach tour field in direct opposition to Group Travel, which reverted to a straight trading operation. It was taken over by Dooley's brother Norrie, who ran it very successfully until about 1970 when, after Norrie's death, it was taken over again by Dooley.

Group Travel was the pioneer of party tours in New Zealand, and it played a crucial part in keeping the Company afloat in the most critical years before and during the War.

Round about 1937 or 1938, when it seemed inevitable that the Railways would soon be taking over the Company, RLW suggested that a few of us might like to start some sort of a commercial operation within the fabric of the Company which could remain independent if the Railways took over the coach services. A line of business closely associated with the one in which we all had a considerable amount of knowledge, the tourist industry, and which now suggested itself, was rental cars.

For many years a number of secondhand car dealers had used secondhand cars in various stages of disrepair to hire out to people in temporary need of a vehicle, but such business was not organised to cater for the overseas tourist or the New Zealander wanting the short-term use of a car.

Our plan was to follow the development of car rental in North America, to buy a fleet of new cars expressly for the purpose and to organise their distribution and operation to make it a self-supporting and profitable business enterprise. The only conditions that RLW laid down were that he would put up the bulk of the capital and several senior members of the Company's staff should put up a smaller amount each; none of us should draw salaries or travel expenses, but we could work in the firm's time and use some of the firm's resources to get the operation built up to stand on its own feet as quickly as possible.

Dooley Coxhead was the manager, and other members were Tui Elms, Norrie Coxhead, Mick Bowie, Eric Hunter, my brother Sandy and myself. The Company was called Mutual Rental Cars and Dooley managed this from his office in the Mount Cook Company in Timaru, while I travelled up and down the country appearing before the licensing authorities to get the necessary licences.

Dooley organised a deal with Dominion Motors whereby we bought new Morris 8s, used them for a year, then traded them in for new ones at a set price. For the first time brand-new cars were available for rental; they appealed to the general travelling public as well as to tourists, and so the business grew quite rapidly. When the war broke out, the Company had in its fleet eighty-odd rental cars of which about half were fully paid for, and the balance at various stages of hire purchase.

During the war Dooley got a job with the Mountain Warfare Section of the army under Major Yerex, with the rank of captain, and was able to travel freely round the country on army business. While on this duty he managed to find some time to keep an eye on our rental car and travel interests.

He also bought-in the shares of those shareholders killed in action and of those who, on returning from overseas service, were in need of ready cash, and eventually he became a majority shareholder. About 1944 he managed to strike a deal with RLW to take over the rental cars and also the Mount Cook travel offices in Christchurch and Dunedin where the rental cars were based, the travel offices in Wellington and Auckland, and also Group Travel Ltd., in exchange for the shares he held in the Mount Cook Company and so finished up owning these subsidiary businesses.

During the Depression and the war, the Mount Cook Company had run down to a pretty low ebb, and with the severance of the rental cars, travel offices and Group Travel, the Company lost some of its few remaining assets that had any potential for postwar development.

During its seventy years of operation the Company has used a great variety of vehicles of all shapes and sizes and makes. After the first rather primitive Darracqs came Studebakers, Cadillacs and Hudson cars, and Leyland lorries. The cars were mostly large standard six-and eight-seaters which were being manufactured in large numbers in the States from about 1916 onwards.

Early in the 1920s the standard six-and eight-seater motorcars had become too small for the growing needs of the scheduled services, and operators started to cast around in a search for something bigger and more suitable. Motor lorries were too big, too slow and had not yet been fitted with pneumatic tyres, and there was nothing in between which was at all suitable. The operators attempted to solve the problem by chopping the standard motor-car in half and extending chassis and body sufficiently to allow the installation of one or two extra rows of seats, thus giving an 11- or 12-seater with some of the performance and comfort of the private motor-car. They were now completely enclosed, with wind-down windows, and were a tremendous improvement over the old open Darracqs and other models of early vintage.

Although they were fitted with heavier wheels and tyres to carry the extra weight, the original engines, transmissions and brakes had to be used, and if the brakes were inefficient enough on the private motor-car, they were a great deal worse on a vehicle which was half as heavy again as the original. This led to driving techniques evolved to cope with this brakeless situation.

Brakes, in those days fitted on the rear wheels only, were not very effective at the best of times and became almost useless if they were not constantly adjusted or if they became wet. Four-wheel brakes were not introduced until the early 1920s; efficient hydraulic boosting systems weren't introduced until the early 1930s, and up to that time the drivers frequently had to make long trips with virtually no brakes at all.

On the assumption that he could not rely on these brakes anywhere or at any time, the driver had to memorise almost every metre of the road, so that he could anticipate when he could build up to a reasonable cruising speed and when he had to allow the vehicle's speed to die off to take corners, to stop for gates or mailbags or to ford creeks, without relying on his dubious brakes. Lower gears had to be used continuously to slow the vehicle down and steady it, and the drivers became expert at double declutching and changing gears in the old-type crash gearbox at any old speeds.

Practically all vehicles are fitted with syncromesh or automatic gearboxes these days, and a modern driver hardly needs to learn about gear-changing, but with the old-style crash gearbox, one had to use clutch and throttle to speed the engine up to match the speed of the next gear being selected in order to engage the gears. If the speed was not matched almost exactly, the noisy crash of the gears could be heard all over the bus, the gears would not engage, and the driver would have to have another shot at it. The drivers became adept at smooth changes — indeed, they couldn't afford to miss their change as the gearbox was virtually the only reliable brake they had.

It is astonishing that more accidents did not occur; but there was very little traffic on the roads, and for most of the journey the approach of other vehicles could be seen by the clouds of dust, if in no other way, from a tremendous distance away. Also, the road speeds were very low, and even in the mid 1930s RLW considered 55km/h the maximum safe speed for any vehicle. Considering that the roads were all surfaced with loose shingle, which tended to get swept into quite high ridges between the wheeltracks, and that they were full of deep potholes, it was almost impossible to exceed 55km/h without shaking the stoppings out of one's teeth. At such leisurely speeds an experienced driver could control the vehicle on the gearbox alone.

When an emergency did occur it was the most helpless feeling in the world to have the vehicle charging on, regardless of panic measures with transmission and brakes. Returning to Timaru on one occasion with a service bus which had been held up for three or four hours at flooded streams, I knew I had no brakes whatsoever and was driving accordingly. On rounding a bend near Albury, starting a gentle downhill slope, I saw a man with a mob of sheep about a kilometre away. I threw out all the anchors, changed gears and did everything possible to get the bus to stop, but it trickled on at 20km/h, then 15, then 10, and nothing I could do would make it go any slower than that. At this speed it ploughed through the tightly-bunched sheep, and unfortunately several were damaged beyond repair.

Stopping at the Company's office at Timaru was always likely to be a source of embarrassment, for it was always the

first port of call on arriving in from Mt Cook, to drop the
passengers off and hand them over to a member of the staff
whose job it was to put them on the train.

The office was about a hundred metres downhill from the
northern end of Stafford Street, and the technique we used was
to slow right down and change gears before starting on the
descent, so the bus could be stopped right outside the office.
Occasionally, through wet brakes and a bigger than usual load,
or even a following wind, the vehicle would refuse to get below
about 5km/h and would carry independently on its way for
another twenty or thirty metres — to the surprise of the passengers and the guffaws of the waiting office staff. Nevertheless,
the drivers learned to live with this situation and became very
skilful, with the result that very few serious accidents occurred.

About 1924 the Company went over to heavier, commer-
cial-type passenger vehicles, British Leylands and, a year or so
later, Studebakers. These had bodies built with square rec-
tangular tops like glasshouses, and the passengers rattled their
way up to The Hermitage if not in modern luxurious comfort,
at least protected from the weather. One Leyland, which
joined the fleet about 1926 or 1927 was a thirty-seater, the
biggest passenger vehicle on the road in New Zealand at that
time. The chassis had been brought into New Zealand for
conversion to a fire engine, and it had a tremendous great
engine capable of pushing it along at speeds unheard of in
those days. RLW was much impressed by this vehicle and
decided it was just the answer for quick travel between Timaru
and Mt Cook; he had built on it a thirty-seat body in the style
of the times, with rows of bench seats extending for the full
width of the vehicle and with a door to each. The chassis was so
long that even with the thirty-seat body on, there was still a
metre sticking out the rear end.

Big Bertha, as she was called, was driven by one of our oldest
and most experienced drivers, Jimmie Bennington, and no one
else was allowed to touch her. Typical of the buses of those
days, it had no speedometer, so Jimmie could only guess at the
speed he was travelling, but he maintained that he could
scarcely get into top gear much under 65km/h and that at
under this speed she was excessively heavy to steer. Whatever
his cruising speed was, it must have been high for those days,
for I remember another driver, following Jimmie in a car,
telling us with awe that he was doing at least 75km/h.

Unfortunately Big Bertha was not destined to last long on
this service, for her relatively high speeds and the bad state of

the roads caused her large tyres to blow out far too frequently. Blowouts became so frequent that her two or more spare tyres were often used and then another vehicle had to be sent out from Timaru with more. Finally a right-hand front tyre blew out on a left-hand bend on the road between Pukaki and The Hermitage, and Big Bertha plunged down a two-metre bank and finished with her nose submerged in a swamp. No one was injured, but after the vehicle was salvaged with some difficulty it was taken to Timaru where, as the Depression had started and there was no work for it, it was stored until finally sold to a coalminer at Mt Somers, who put railway wheels on it and used it to shunt wagons up and down his private railway line.

The long bench seats with a door at each end allowed the maximum number of passengers to be crammed in, but the doors rattled badly and passengers would bang them too hard and break the glass, or they would rattle open and hit the side of a gate or a bridge, doing considerable damage, so that the original seating-arrangement was finally discarded in favour of the modern type with an aisle down the centre. The long seats did have certain advantages however, for they made good bunks when it was necessary to sleep out on the road.

When the Company took over The Hermitage it ran excursions for passengers from Christchurch, Dunedin, and other places and at times like Easter all the buses in the fleet were used and all the accommodation at The Hermitage was fully taxed. The drivers, particularly the itinerant ones, were not asked if they would give up their rooms to guests, they were simply told, 'You'll sleep in your bus.' We drivers used to take it for granted and to take it in good part if such trivial hardships ensured the Company received the maximum revenue over these holiday periods. I certainly can't remember anyone ever grizzling about them. After all, a certain holiday spirit pervaded, and if a driver was asked to peel spuds or act as a barman or run drinks in the dining-room, he accepted it as part of the job and part of the fun.

Even the more elderly drivers, such as Jimmie Bennington, cheerfully accepted all this, and it wasn't discomfort that finally persuaded Jimmie that he'd had enough of sleeping in buses. He and some of the others who had to make an early start the next morning liked to get to bed reasonably early, and they would be sound asleep when they would be disturbed by someone getting into the bus. Of the 150 or 200 holidaymakers in the area, there were always a few couples looking for somewhere to park up — and what better place than the long seat of a bus? It was very difficult to sleep soundly when, two or three seats away, a couple are noisily making love. Jimmie decided to solve this problem by buying a length of rope and tying all the doorhandles together, but this was foiled by someone with a sharp knife who cut his rope to pieces and used his bus.

On the other hand, some of the couples provided some very amusing moments for the driver stretched out along the back seat, if he still happened to be awake and was receptive to that type of late-night entertainment.

One of the best-loved and most respected drivers of the early 1930s was Aubrey Rollinson, who has spent most of his working career with the Company. His main loves in life were his wife Bet, the Company, and rugby football. Aub was a star rugby player in his day, first for the Timaru Boys' High School and later in representative football; but for some accidental damage to a knee he would undoubtedly have gone on to become an All Black.

He joined the Company at the height of the Depression, in 1932, as a driver and courier on the Landcruises, and became its general manager soon after the war, continuing in this capacity until he retired at the age of sixty. In over forty years for the Company, he had had enough experience to fill a book of his own.

During the war there were no replacement vehicles, and the ones on the road were becoming badly run down through lack of spare parts and continual overloading. One of these driven by Aub had an engine failure on the way to Timaru, a fault that could not be rectified on the road. It was decided that Aub's bus, with its passengers still on board, should be towed by another bus slowly down the road until it met the relief one sent out to meet them. Things went well enough as far as Burkes Pass, where Aub's bus was unhooked and allowed to coast down the hill on its own.

The road from the top of Burkes Pass descends fairly rapidly round a series of bends for the first couple of kilometres, then through a series of dips and hollows and more curves until it passes through Burkes Pass village in a left-hand bend. The bus started rolling quietly enough and Aub had no difficulty in controlling it with the handbrake and the mechanical side of the footbrake. However, with the engine out of action there was no help from the servo system, and it was not long before the speed started to increase, and continued to increase until they were careering down the Pass completely out of control.

As Aub approached the bends, he had the option of staying with the road and hoping the vehicle would not roll over, or taking to the gully, which would have been equally disastrous. But luck was with him, and he headed at an estimated 100 to 115km/h for the dips, where he fervently hoped there would be no stray cattle or sheep on the road. By this time the passengers were shouting and yelling, and one woman threw her arms around his neck and completely blinded him, but he managed to fight her off. They shot through the Burkes Pass village still going very fast and went another few kilometres along the flat until at last they rolled to a halt, very much shaken after a wild ride.

One summer Aub was holidaying with a back-country station owner friend of his, Pat Gibson, and was giving him a hand at bringing in the hay. One of the Company's articulated trucks and its driver were being used to bring the bales of hay in from the paddock to the haybarn. The bales, being relatively light, were stacked a considerable height above the ground. Aub watched the driver manoeuvring the unwieldy vehicle backwards and forwards with considerable difficulty in the very confined space, and was rather critical of his technique. The driver welcomed Aub's advice, promptly vacated his seat and suggested that Aub should take over and demonstrate just how it should be done. Full of confidence, Aub jumped in and started to back the vehicle in the direction he thought it should go, but something came unstuck and the next minute, the whole caboosh — hay, trailer, cab and all — had rolled over on its side. I don't know whether Aub considered that this experience qualified him as an experienced articulated-truck driver or not, but he certainly enjoyed telling this story against himself.

Another well-known and popular driver who has been with the Company for about thirty years is Spike Woods. Tall, blond and ruddy complexioned, Spike has driven buses, coach tours and freighters on nearly all the Company's operations and is known throughout the Company for his never-failing cheerfulness and his stutter. This stutter hits him at awkward moments, but when he has been on a tour for a short time one would never know that he had this problem.

Driving a service bus up to Mt Cook one day, he was approaching a point near Holbrook station where Mt Cook can first be seen through a gap in the hills, and he said through the speaker system: "L-l-look to your r-r-right now and you'll see M-M-Mt Cook — oh, it's too bloody l-l-late!'

During busy periods staff were called on to do all sorts of

odds and ends of jobs around the place, and in the days when we owned Eichardts Hotel in Queenstown, drivers were often given the job of helping out behind the bar. Spike was helping out as barman for a week or two, and one day a big rough-looking character came into the bar and asked Spike: 'W-w-w-what t-t-time does the b-b-bus l-l-leave for Cromwell?'

Spike carried on serving drinks and completely ignored the question. The tough character repeated his question more insistently, and finally one of the customers in the bar gave him the information. When he had disappeared a customer asked Spike, 'Why didn't you answer that bloke? You know perfectly well what time the Cromwell bus leaves.'

Spike replied 'D-d-do you think I was wanting a p-poke on the b-b-bloody nose?'

The Hawke's Bay Motor Company has been going as long as, if not longer than, the Mount Cook Company. It started off in the days of the horsedrawn coaches, then moved on to motorcars and later, buses, as these were developed. Under the general managership of J. T. Harvey, new routes were explored and much pioneering work was done under extremely difficult conditions. The full story of the Hawke's Bay Company is told in *Coaches North*, by Len Anderson, and space does not permit it to be repeated here.

Although the country between Napier and Taupo is not as high as the Southern Alps it is, in many ways, much rougher, having steep ridges, frequently intersected by deep gorgy streams. It has none of the wide flat glacial valleys of the South Island, and the early roads had to be cut up one side of a ridge, over the top and down the other side, through a deep stream and up another ridge, for endless kilometres which must have made for tedious travelling — though interspersed by periods of excitement, if the pictures of the early coaches are anything to go by.

The HBMC under Harvey, his daughter Cherry and then Fred Tebay, and later A. R. Giles, kept up with developments, expanded its routes, and operated successfully for many years and is one of the most prestigious of the pioneer companies. It operated only in the North Island, as the Mount Cook Company did in the South, so there was a certain affinity between the two, and they were complementary to each other. It was logical that a merger should take place, which it did in October 1972, and it has been operating to our mutual benefit ever since.

When A. R. Giles retired as general manager his place was taken by A. Jones and later by E. W. Myers. As well as Arthur Giles, two other Hawke's Bay Motor Company directors joined the Mount Cook Company board — G. E. Bisson, a solicitor from Napier, and R. C. Dockery.

The HBMC operates scheduled services from Havelock North and Napier to Gisborne, and from Napier to Taupo, and thence (in conjunction with the NZ Railways) from Taupo to Auckland. It also runs scheduled services from Taupo to the Chateau.

Incorporated in the Hawke's Bay services is the Luxury Landline service which we took over in 1970 and which operates daily each way between Wellington and Auckland. Today it uses the large Mt Cook-Denning coaches built by the Company in Christchurch.

The HBMC also operates four-wheel-drive tourist buses out to the gannet colony at Cape Kidnappers, and operates some 120 rental cars.

12

Hotels

DESPITE its achievements in other fields over the years, the Company's long experience with hotels has not been a very happy one. The first to be acquired, The Hermitage, absorbed much of RLW's time and energy, as well as all the surplus cash generated by the Motor Company, and when the lease finally expired, and The Hermitage was returned to the Government in 1944, he was happy to take a sizeable cheque for compensation for improvements made by the Company and to kiss it goodbye.

It was not long, however, before the Company was to suffer almost as much through lack of control of The Hermitage as it had when it had been in control, and the following notes tell some of the story of our participation in hotels. Parts of it were told to me by RLW and others, and some parts are from my personal recollections.

RLW's idea was to develop a string of hotels and travel offices throughout New Zealand so that tourists coming in at Auckland could be passed from one to the other right down the line to Mt Cook and Queenstown.

The lease of The Hermitage was acquired in 1922, and the White Star Hotel in Queenstown about 1923 or 1924. New wings of firstclass rooms were added to each a year or two after acquisition.

The Government, when the Rt. Hon. Gordon Coates was prime minister, were keen to see the tourist industry developed, and encouraged the Company to build some accommodation at the North Island's main mountain resort in the Tongariro National Park. The original idea was to supplement the Whakapapa Huts and build something fairly cheap and simple along the lines of the motels that evolved in the 1950s, but Gordon Coates preferred something which would give the North Island an international prestigious appeal like that of The Hermitage in the South. He encouraged RLW to develop

grandiose plans for the building, and promised adequate
mortgage money to see the project completed.

Herbert Hall was the architect, and he designed the Chateau
Tongariro along the lines of the Canadian Pacific Railways'
hotels in Canada, such as the Frontenac, the Vancouver, and
others but, of course, on a smaller scale. The hotel was completed in 1929, and it was a magnificent building inside and
outside. Ultra-modern in every way, it was a tremendous acquisition to the New Zealand tourist industry.

Guests entered through large portals and plateglass doors to
the spacious reception area, where they were greeted by girls in
uniform and porters in livery ready to carry away their baggage. Beyond was an imposing lounge with its high ceiling
supported by large columns, with oak parquet flooring and
furnished with luxurious settees and easy chairs. Floor-to-
ceiling plateglass windows gave magnificent views of Mt
Tongariro and Ngauruhoe.

All the bedrooms were right up to date by world standards
and luxuriously fitted with period-style furniture. As well, the
very latest in plumbing — hand-basins with running hot and
cold water — replaced the old china basin-and-ewer and the
mug of lukewarm shaving-water brought around by the
chambermaid at seven in the morning with the tea. The whole
establishment conveyed an impression of luxury and
spaciousness that is found in few hotels built in more recent
decades.

To run the hotel, many staff with overseas experience were
employed, and the chef, always addressed as Mister Brooks, a
very highly qualified English chef of international renown, was
imported at great expense, especially for the purpose. He drew
a salary greater than that of the managing director, RLW.
When on duty, Mr Brooks wore his immaculate white chef's
clothes and hat, but when he went to town, he wore a swal-
low-tailed coat, striped trousers and topper. When the Chateau
company went broke, he moved to The Hermitage, where he
worked for a number of years and taught up-and-coming chefs
their craft, and became known to many of us as a real
character.

The revenue intake of the Chateau started off in a most
encouraging way, but before many months had passed, the
depression had started and the hotel began to run into serious
cash problems. RLW kept on at Gordon Coates to keep to his
word and make mortgage money available, but the prime
minister had his own problems and said, 'Wig, there's a De-

pression on, and in spite of my promises to you, there's no money available, and I simply cannot help you.'

RLW always contended that if the Depression had held off for another six months the hotel would have generated enough cash flow to have survived. He would have worked night and day to ensure this, but in fact the Company had to go into liquidation, and the Government, which held all the main mortgages on it, took it over. Claims were lodged against the Mount Cook Company, and litigation followed. Although the Company won, it was drained of cash and resources and was left in poor shape to survive through the next three or four years of recession.

While the Chateau was being built, the Mount Cook Company took over Brents in Rotorua, but here too the tourist flow had come almost to a standstill. There was insufficient cash to keep up the interest payments, and this hotel too reverted to its previous owners.

About 1936 the Company purchased Eichardts Hotel in Queenstown. By now the tourist flow was starting again, and by running it in conjunction with the White Star Hotel and virtually closing one or other down during the winter, both hotels managed to survive through the war period. The White Star was sold in 1943.

The acquisition and development of these hotels did a lot towards raising standards and providing accommodation more suitable for overseas people, but things never ran smoothly with them. We were continually having problems with staff and management, and the hotels were a continual drain on the cash flow of the transport side of the Company. With the cessation of the war, traffic picked up surprisingly quickly, returned servicemen travelled round on passes provided by the Government, while others, sick and tired of the war, taking their first holiday for years, were travelling round. Petrol was still rationed, so they travelled by bus.

The Company then started reinstating its Landcruises and other tours it had operated before the war, and it was not long before it found that its loss of The Hermitage lease in 1944 was to cause serious problems. The solutions appeared to be to develop another resort in the area as a substitute for The Hermitage, and to step up the development of skiing at Queenstown in the winter; I have told how Coronet Peak was developed, and with what considerable success.

It was also decided to put some accommodation at Lake Ohau, which lies tucked away in the Alps, only sixty-five or seventy kilometres away from The Hermitage as the crow flies. The lake is usually crystal-clear and it is surrounded by high, rugged mountain ranges, covered in many places by a thick carpet of beech forest. It has a charm all of its own, and beautiful alpine views in almost every direction. It provides good trout fishing and boating opportunities, while the snow-filled basins immediately above the lake appeared to offer excellent prospects for the development of skiing.

Wartime building controls were still on, and we could not get permits for new buildings. Neither did we have the resources to build anything on too grand a scale, but a large hydro-electric project, the control dam at Lake Pukaki, had just been finished, and we managed to buy two accommodation wings, each with about sixty bedrooms, from one of the main contractors. These were cut into sections and transported over to the western side of Lake Ohau, where they were re-erected. A new building was constructed alongside to house the lounge, dining-room, kitchen and ablutions and, when completed, it provided accommodation for between fifty and sixty people.

The Company did not have the funds to build anything palatial, but it had a real wealth of experience in its enthusiastic employees who went to Ohau. They lived in tents and worked like beavers carting metal for access roads, digging channels for culverts, carting tanks and pipes for the water supply, and all manner of things to help to get Ohau Lodge established.

Somewhere an old secondhand three-kilowatt generator and turbine had been bought, and this was installed a short distance away from the Lodge. To get pipes to feed it with water, Jack Anderson took a truck down to one of the old goldmining areas south of Queenstown and managed to get enough, about thirty-five centimetres in diameter, to do the job. A dam was built in the creek to put water into the pipe, which ran down the hillside to where the nozzle sent a jet of water in the general direction of the turbine, which wobbled and groaned its way round fast enough to generate the Lodge's needs for lighting and a number of other purposes. It was still wobbling and groaning away and producing power several years later, when the Lodge was linked to the main grid.

Aub Rollinson, Jack Anderson, Keith McGowan, Spike Wood, Noel Cochrane, Jim Simmers and many others worked for long hours for many weeks to provide roading, electricity, water and landscaping, and finally the Lodge opened in time for the summer season of 1951. This broke the deadlock at The Hermitage. The Lodge is still very popular and is used today as an alternative holiday place, and by the tours which cannot get accommodation at The Hermitage, or which require cheaper accommodation.

The old problem of seasonality was still with us, and although the Lodge had excellent occupancy during the summer, it fell away badly during the winter. So here again we had to develop the skiing. The range of mountains behind the Lodge runs up to about 2000 metres, and there are a number of cirques which hold a lot of snow during the winter. The highest one, which is directly above the Lodge, was selected.

A line was surveyed from the Lodge to the cirque, and Murray Mahon a contractor from Geraldine, undertook the job of cutting the road. He and his men did a magnificent job under very difficult conditions and we will always be indebted to Murray for his enthusiasm and determination to get the job completed. It was a much tougher proposition than anyone had expected, particularly in the upper reaches, where a lot of hard rock was encountered, but in three or four years a track had been punched right up to the cirque, allowing us to install some rope tows and buildings for shelter.

It was late in the season when the road had advanced far enough to allow the installation of tows and buildings, and already snow was lying on the ground, hard frosts were occurring, and timber and other materials left lying on the ground overnight would be frozen-in when work started the next day.

Noel Cochrane relates how a building being erected to provide shelter for skiers was hit overnight by a very strong wind when it was only partially completed. When they returned next day it was 15 or 20 degrees out of plumb. Snow had blown into the cracks and had frozen solid, which meant that they had to thaw out each joint with a blowlamp to get it true again. The scorch marks of the blowlamp were on the timber for all to see for several years afterwards.

The ground on the line of the ski-tow was frozen solid, and made digging of holes for the poles extremely difficult. They resorted to blasting to loosen the ground to allow the holes to be dug out but, according to Noel, none of them were really qualified and it is a wonder they did not blow themselves up. They used gelignite, an explosive which becomes highly dangerous to handle if allowed to get too cold, so they carried it round in their shirts to keep it warm.

Jack Anderson can turn his hand to most things, but some of

the gelignite charges he laid failed to go off and, as they would soon become brittle and dangerous in the cold ground, they were not safe to touch. So they would put another charge over the top to detonate the one below, and sometimes succeeded in getting them off. However, by now they were running short of fuses, and were cutting them shorter and shorter, which gave them less and less time to get away from the danger area. Noel Cochrane and his assistant, Ron Allen, were younger and more agile than Jack, and could sprint out of the danger area pretty smartly, but when Jack, lumbering along behind, got caught in a shower of falling rock, they reckoned that they really had made the fuse just a fraction *too* short.

The road was narrow and rough but reasonably safe, and skiers were carried up in Land Rovers and ten-seater minibuses for the greater part of the journey until they were stopped by snow. The basin was reasonably close to the Lodge, and many people walked part or all of the way back in the evenings, taking no more than fifty minutes or so.

The cirque used for skiing is quite large in extent, has large flat areas suitable for beginners, and was popular right from the outset. Jack Anderson was in charge of the skifield and the road, and he did a tremendous job over two or three seasons in getting it established. He managed to keep those temperamental rope-tows going under all sorts of difficulties, and patiently spliced ropes with his bare hands in freezing conditions, time and time again, to let the skiing continue. As with so many other of our staff, Jack's dedication ensured the success of the project. The Lodge not only overcame the deadlock at The Hermitage, but it provided a much needed addition to the accommodation in the Alps and created a new holiday area at the same time.

It is ironical that when The Hermitage was completely burned out in 1956 the Tourist Department called on us to provide accommodation at Ohau for their coach tours, as none was available anywhere else in the area. We were happy to let them have all the accommodation which was not already required for our own tours.

The Eames family took over the Lodge several years later, and have not only improved it enormously but have also cut a new road to the skifield which is wider, straighter, better graded and has less hairpin bends than the old one, and it provides much better access to the skifield.

The development of the Lodge at Ohau put a severe strain on

the Company's financial and other resources; money for tourist projects was not readily available from the banks or anywhere else, as bankers and financiers didn't have much faith in the future of the industry. When an offer was made for Eichardts Hotel in Queenstown the directors decided to accept it, and although this solved our immediate liquidity problems it created problems in the future which were just as complex and no less important than the loss of the lease of The Hermitage.

Already the shortage of accommodation at Queenstown was becoming a problem, and the Company had prepared plans to build a new wing on to Eichardts, but our approaches to Government and other sources of finance for this seemed unlikely to succeed as the Company could not handle the extensions and other expenditure on its own. This strengthened the directors' resolve to get out. An offer of finance to build a new wing came through from the Government only weeks after the sale was completed, which made the sale more than ever a bitter pill to swallow.

Eichardts was sold to the Buckham brothers who in turn sold it to the Tourist Hotel Corporation, who were delighted to get into Queenstown and had all sorts of plans for developing that site and others associated with it. However, there was a hue and cry about the Government competing with private enterprise, and building was deferred until there was a change of Government in 1963. The National Government then decided that Queenstown was for private enterprise only, and that the THC assets should be sold.

These were advertised, and the Company submitted proposals to buy Eichardts and build a new L-shaped wing, which would provide a reasonable increase in the number of rooms, on the land attached to it on Church Street. By making use of the existing Eichardts' kitchen, dining-room, lounge and bars, the cost of the enlarged hotel would be within the Company's ability to finance.

The Company's offer was accepted, and it started the preparation of plans for the new additions in order to get building started as soon as possible, for already the shortage of accommodation was acute.

However, before it could start it found that the Minister of Tourism had undermined our proposals by agreeing to sell the area of land, on which we proposed to build, to the Queenstown Council for a carpark. Even today we cannot understand how the Minister could agree to selling the land to us then sell it to the Council. It is possible that we could have upset the deal by taking legal action, but at a series of meetings the Council explained their planning reasons for wishing to have the carpark in the centre of the town and for the larger hotels to be away from the centre. While we sympathised with this, we were reluctant to move away from the Eichardts site. Other THC land was available for hotel building towards the Government Gardens, but we were reluctant to change because, in the first place, Eichardts was in our opinion a much better site, and in the second, the cost of putting on a new wing on to an existing hotel would obviously cost only a fraction of what a completely new hotel would do.

Finally, and reluctantly, we agreed to go along with the Council's wishes, and prepared plans for a completely new hotel on the site occupied by the old Buckhams Brewery; however, test bores proved that thousands of years of silting of that corner of the bay of Horne Creek had filled it with débris which would have made the construction of a high-rise hotel there difficult and expensive. So again we took the Council's advice and moved our planning to an area of Government land adjoining the Park which had been set aside for the THC to build on. This site was hilly, had a creek running through it, and ensured that the building of a hotel there was going to be expensive. Plans were drawn up, estimates made and it was found that the project was far too big for the Company to handle on its own. The Company had far too many commitments as it was with its air, road and Coronet Peak operations, but there was a desperate shortage of accommodation and so it looked round for partners, and found these in Dominion Breweries and Shaw Savill.

Before building could commence, the Town and Country Planning requirements had to be met and we negotiated these and a subsequent appeal hearing with very little opposition.

Detailed plans and working drawings were then put under way with all speed, and we were within weeks of going to tender, when we were astounded to learn that we had been served with a writ of injunction to prevent us from going ahead. We had assumed that everyone had accepted the decisions of the Town and Country Planning Authority and the Town and Country Appeal Authority, and we did not admire the tactics of a group of objectors who had sat through all the hearings without getting off their seats and offering any opposition or making any comment. They had let us go to very considerable effort and expense without indicating to us that they were attempting to stop us.

The writ was based on the grounds that the licence issued to us by the Lands Department to occupy the area had been incorrectly dated, and was therefore invalid. This unfortunately proved to be correct. We contended that the Lands Department could have rectified the situation immediately by writing out a new licence, but in spite of all our efforts to get it resolved, it was about six months before the Crown Law Office ruled that this procedure was correct and it took about another six months for the Lands Department to write out another licence. By this time all the dogs in the country were barking and the politicians, reverting to type, froze up.

In due course a new licence was issued but, instead of being made out in a way which would have validated all the previous Town and Country Planning Board and Appeal Authority hearings, it forced us to go through all those time-consuming procedures again. As with the previous hearings, all the decisions were given in our favour and the matter finally reached the Supreme Court, which also decided in our favour. We had seven wins in all, and not one loss, but before we could go ahead with the hotel we had to get the consents of the Minister of Finance, the Minister of Lands, and the Minister of Tourism.

We approached the first minister with the evidence that we had all the consents necessary, had completed all other formalities and had arranged finance, and he said: 'Fine, I'll give you my consent when you have got the consent of the other ministers.'

The next minister said the same, so we went on to the third, and he said the same, so we finished up back with the first one! It seemed impossible to get any finality, with every politician passing the buck.

We and our partners were getting heartily sick of the whole business, and the cost had risen to an almost impossible level, so when there was a change in Government and the Labour Government offered to buy us out, we accepted, even though it spelt the end of our interest in hotels, and a considerable financial loss to the three companies involved.

The exercise, which had lasted for nearly nine years, wasted a tremendous amount of Mike Corner's and my time and had cost many thousands of dollars. It was a classic example of politicians lacking the guts to make decisions, bumbling on the part of the bureaucrats, and the devious actions of so-called conservationists — some of whom turned out to be land-developers who have done far more damage to the environment in the vicinity of Queenstown than ever would have been done by the hotel and who would not accept the rulings of the Government-appointed authorities, nor even those of the Supreme Court.

The warning 'Put not thy faith in princes' was written a long time ago, but it still applies.

13

Aviation Ahead of Its Time

FROM ITS VERY EARLIEST DAYS, flying had fascinated RLW. Opuha station, where he had been brought up, was only a short distance from Waitohi, where inventor-aviator Richard Pearse was experimenting in the early 1900s and achieved a powered takeoff in the autumn of 1903. It seems unlikely that RLW knew what the secretive Pearse was up to — he would almost certainly have offered to share his engineering knowledge and workshop equipment with the self-educated and impoverished inventor, though it is not so certain that Pearse, independent and suspicious, would have accepted the offer.

If RLW had been young enough to join the armed services in World War I he would have volunteered for the Royal Flying Corps, but the end of that war brought him the opportunity of adding aviation to his many interests. When the firing stopped, the British Government had thousands of surplus military aircraft on its hands, and in 1919 it offered each Dominion 100 aeroplanes as a free gift and as a basis for encouraging air-mindedness within the Empire.

After some hesitation New Zealand agreed to accept forty of these aircraft, mostly Avro 504K trainers, two-seater Bristol Fighters, and de Havilland 4 and 9 single-engined bombers. About half of these machines were assigned to the embryo military-aviation base at Sockburn (now Wigram) at Christchurch, and the rest were put on offer to any individual or organisation prepared to make some serious attempt at developing civil aviation.

Ten of these aircraft were taken over by the Canterbury Aviation Co. of Sockburn, who flew them round Canterbury, mostly on 'joyriding' — i.e. taking passengers for a quick takeoff, circuit and landing for five shillings a head — a monotonous but quite lucrative activity, for at that time few people had ever seen an aeroplane at close quarters, let alone having enjoyed the thrill of flying in one.

RLW's first idea was to co-operate with the CAC to achieve his dominant aim of bringing Mt Cook even closer to the mainstream of population, and in 1920 a CAC aircraft piloted by Captain Euan Dickson flew RLW and T. D. Burnett of Mount Cook station from Fairlie up towards The Hermitage. There was a heavy nor'wester blowing, and although they climbed to 13,000 feet, the considerable turbulence decided Captain Dickson to turn back. On his return to Christchurch he recommended to the CAC that they should have nothing to do with the project — the days on which the weather would be suitable would be so few that the service could never pay its way; and, in any case, the aircraft would have to fly very high, and English experience had proved that only a small percentage of passengers could tolerate an altitude of 10,000 feet or more.

At this point it may be noted that in those days flying among mountains was not at all a popular pastime with even experienced pilots. What were still being respectfully called 'air-pockets' could be alarming in low-powered and rather fragile aircraft, and most pilots liked to be able to see at all times, within gliding-distance, flat country that offered some prospect of an uneventful forced landing in case of engine failure.

RLW had built high hopes on a favourable report from the CAC. He had organised a celebratory luncheon at Fairlie to which MPs and local VIPs had been invited, and had gone so far as to print the optimistic souvenir-card produced in this book. He was bitterly disappointed.

However, he was never one to accept defeat lying down. The Government still had unwanted aircraft to dispose of, and their allocation was in the hands of the Air Board, which consisted of Captain T. M. Wilkes, later a popular and respected Director of Civil Aviation, and Captain L. M. Isitt, who was appointed Chief of Air Staff during World War II.

So RLW set off for Wellington with a vague hope that he might be able to talk them into letting him have an aeroplane, and that he would be able to think up some use for it.

Rather to his surprise they took him quite seriously. What were his plans for developing civil aviation? On the spur of the moment he said that he would organise a weekly air service between Invercargill and Wellington, but that it would not trespass on the current activities of the Canterbury Aviation Company.

'And how many aeroplanes would you need?'

This question so rocked RLW, who had hardly reckoned on

getting a single aircraft, let alone a fleet of them, that he had to ask for time to formulate a considered reply, which eventually took the form of a letter dated 13 August 1920:

It is the intention of the Company to establish services in the southern and western portions of the South Island utilising large, high-powered machines with big capacity for carrying both passengers and cargo.

It is desired that the following, two Avros and three DH9s with spares, be handed over to the Company, which will undertake the care of and maintain them.

Pioneer work will be carried out, and subsequently larger and more up-to-date aeroplanes will be purchased which will be more suitable for our work and will be an asset to the country should they be required for war purposes. . .

The Air Board, no doubt delighted to find an outlet for aircraft that would otherwise rot in their packing-cases, promptly gave RLW a full written agreement to his application.

The CAC reacted sharply. The Board, they complained, had no authority to give away aircraft that were Government property; RLW's airline would compete unfairly with their own proposed Christchurch/Blenheim service; they might perhaps tolerate a rival firm based as far away as Dunedin, but a Timaru firm would be altogether too close — it would split the Canterbury market, it could not succeed, yet it would imperil the survival of the CAC.

Their anxiety was understandable. It caused some repercussions at Cabinet level; certain Ministers of the Crown ducked for cover, RLW was asked to 'keep to himself' the Air Board's letter of agreement, and there were sharp altercations in the columns of the Christchurch (pro-CAC) papers and the *Timaru Herald* (pro-RLW).

Although an air service into and out of the Mt Cook area had not been mentioned in the RLW/Air Board correspondence, it must have come up in conversation, for at this stage the Board decided they had better take a look at its possibilities. On 21 September 1920 they flew a military DH4 (similar to the DH9 but with a 375hp Rolls Royce engine instead of a 250hp Siddeley Puma) from Washdyke, taking off at 10am. They reconnoitred around The Hermitage and were back in Timaru in good time for lunch at the Grosvenor Hotel. The outward flight had taken them sixty-eight minutes; with a brisk wind under their tails the return flight took a mere twenty-seven minutes, and this sent the *Timaru Herald* into ecstasies — as well it might, in the days when the Timaru/

Hermitage road trip meant a long hard day's motoring.

By 2 November the suspense was over. Cabinet endorsed the Air Board's original decision. RLW was now in the aviation business, and the New Zealand Aero Transport Company came into being.

RLW's stated intention had been to fly a weekly service between Invercargill and Wellington. The basic question of whether such a service could generate enough passenger and freight traffic to become even modestly profitable does not seem to have bothered him. Characteristically, he was preoccupied with the many physical problems of getting a scheduled service into reliable operation; if that were achieved, the economics would somehow look after themselves.

There was no problem about selecting suitable aircraft, as only the two types were available. The Avros had low speed, low power, short range and a low payload; the pilot sat up front, and behind him two passengers could be crammed into a seat originally designed to carry a single military observer or pupil-pilot. They were suitable only for joyriding and various short-haul jobs.

The DH9s were nearer the mark for serious airline work. The Puma engines were very reliable for those days and could bring the aircraft along at a cruising speed of 180-200km/h with fuel enough for relatively long hops. The airframe had been designed for a pilot and three others, all in open cockpits, but Bert Mercer and his staff adapted the passenger accommodation into a covered cabin holding four seats, most of the work being done by Hughie Mayo, a cabinetmaker of the old school of perfectionists.

But if the aircraft had more or less selected themselves, there were many other headaches. The proposed Invercargill-Wellington route had to be surveyed and decided upon. Landing-grounds had to be selected, negotiated for, and cleared of fences and ditches. Some sort of publicity and booking arrangements had to be provided. All this entailed much exploratory flying and discussion, and provided some memorable moments.

In December 1920 Maurice Buckley, with RLW and Bert Mercer as passengers, had flown to Dunedin and they were continuing on to examine the possibilities at Invercargill. As was the practice with those early flights, arrangements had been made with the postmasters along the route to send telegrams back to the Timaru office when the aircraft passed overhead. On this occasion, the postmaster at Gore duly reported a sighting at 9.22am, but then came silence.

Back at Timaru, uneasiness deepened into anxiety, and anxiety into real alarm. If the aircraft had forced-landed anywhere along that closely-settled route, it was absolutely certain that a local farmer and his family would have dashed out to investigate this unheard-of phenomenon and would gladly have passed a message back to Timaru. Timaru manager Jim Richards and his town staff regarded long-distance flying with apprehension, and so did my mother. All day long Jim kept ringing her up to report that no message had yet come through, and imploring her not to worry and, naturally, after each ring her worries moved up another peg. When, late that night, the All's Well message at last came through, the relief was indescribable.

What had happened was that after passing Gore the aircraft had run into increasingly strengthening head winds, to the extent that the party had decided to give it away and park down on some suitable paddock until they could set off again. They landed according to plan, but by the time they had rolled to a standstill they realised that all three of them would have to leap out and throw themselves on to the aircraft to stop it being blown across the paddock and into the nearest fence or other obstacle.

They hung on like grim death, momentarily expecting to be helped out by the usual onrush of excited sightseers. What they didn't know was that this particular day happened to be the local annual Agricultural & Pastoral Show day, and that every man, woman and child in the district was away at the showgrounds admiring prizewinning stock or having a go at the coconuts. By the time that the wind had dropped and RLW could seek out the nearest telephone, the local telephone exchange had closed for the night, and it had taken a long time to locate a phone that was still in contact with the outside world.

At the Wellington end of the proposed route the NZAT Company was the first commercial concern to use the land at Lyall Bay, now the site of Rongotai airport. The hangar they constructed there in 1921 has been moved and rebuilt several times, and at the time of writing it is still in use, I am told, and now occupied by Mantell Motors.

The Cook Strait crossing was treated with respect by pilots whose engines were inclined to be temperamental. The DH9s' Pumas could usually be relied on, but the Avros were hauled along by 110hp rotary engines in which the crankshaft remained stationary while all the rest of the motor with the propellor nailed on to it whizzed round at some 1000 revolutions per minute. Carburation was highly inefficient, plugs were prone to oil up during flight, and it was by no means unknown for one of the nine cylinders to forsake the rest of the engine, zip through the cowling and head off into outer space.

In November 1921 Bill Park's Avro struck engine trouble while crossing the Strait. In company with another NZAT Avro he had left Blenheim for Wellington, but both aircraft had had to put back to correct engine faults. At the second attempt the other Avro was able to carry on to land at Lyall Bay, but Bill had to go back to Blenheim again for further adjustments. By tradition, his third attempt should have been lucky, and in fact all went well until he was some eight kilometres off Tarawhiti Point, but here he ran into one of Wellington's choicer gales. Bill's top speed was some 120km/h, but he was now flying against a wind of almost the same speed, so was making very little headway. At this juncture his engine started to wilt again, and he began to lose height so fast that the best he could hope for was to greet the shingle beach at Red Rocks Bay.

His wheels actually touched the breakers before they rolled along the shingle in what would have been a perfect landing — if the gale hadn't then bowled the Avro back into the sea. Luckily, weekend holidaymakers nearby rushed to his rescue and salvaged the aircraft virtually undamaged.

Despite this and other near-misses, RLW judged that the time was ripe for a demonstration of reliable flying that would capture the public imagination and promote confidence in the practicability of commercial aviation.

It seemed perfectly feasible for a DH9 to be flown through from Invercargill to Auckland in a single day, given average good weather along the route. A sponsor would be needed to finance the venture, and Herbert Fleming, managing director of the firm manufacturing Creamoata, a popular breakfast cereal, was game to lend the necessary hand.

The aircraft was painted in flamboyant stripes of red and yellow and CREAMOATA was displayed in huge lettering on the undersides of the lower wings. To emphasise the slogan 'Eat it with a Silver Spoon', hundreds of Creamoata spoons were fitted with tiny parachutes to be thrown out as the aircraft passed over towns of any size.

The date was 24 October 1921, Bert Mercer was the pilot,

RLW and Herbert Fleming of Creamoata were the passengers. From Invercargill to Timaru all went according to plan, but here they had to stop for twenty-four hours to let a cold front pass through.

They took off again at precisely the hour originally planned, flying over Ashburton at 8.29, Christchurch at 8.58, and landing at Kaikoura to refuel at 9.55, taking off again at 11.15. They passed over Wellington at 12.15pm, landing at Trentham at 12.25.

Here, when the engine was being started up again, there was a sad mishap. In those days there were no self-starters, and an engine had to be started by one or more men swinging the propellor by hand — always a risky procedure, even when the prescribed drill was observed.

One of the NZAT's pilots, S. V. Mallard, who had been sent ahead to help with refuelling, was swinging the propellor when the engine fired prematurely and broke his shoulder.

The takeoff from Trentham was made at 1.52pm, they landed at Hawera at 3.25 to refuel, and set off on the final leg to Auckland at 4.05. At 5.45 they were over Waikato Heads, at 6.00 over Onehunga, then circled above Auckland while a smudge-fire was lit at Cornwall Park to show them the wind-direction for landing. They landed at 6.08, saw that the DH9 was safely pegged down and a night-watchman put on duty, then went off to celebrate.

The total flying-time was 8 hours 53 minutes. RLW had proved his point, newspapers throughout the country gave the achievement a blaze of publicity and, it is to be hoped, the sales of Creamoata too became airborne.

RLW was years ahead of his time in his understanding of the vital importance of capturing publicity and confidence in his ventures, and he was not so wrapped up in them that he overlooked the need for essential profitability. In his time, the approach to new projects via cautious feasibility studies was hardly thought of, but he well understood that NZAT must somehow pay its way while its hopefully-profitable airline activities were being built up.

The Invercargill-Auckland flight had won invaluable short-term publicity, but it was equally necessary to promote longer-term enthusiasm and confidence by letting people watch flying at close quarters and even experience the novelty of seeing their hometowns from an unfamiliar angle. So joy-riding, profitable both in cash return and in making people

The first attempted flight to Mt Cook. *From left*, RLW, R.L. Banks, and Capt. Euan Dickson with the Avro 504K.

The first successful flight to Mt Cook. Captains L.M. Isitt and T.M. Wilkes with the DH4.

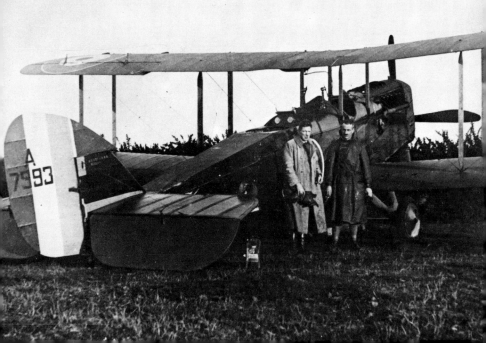

The airline killed by official neglect: NZ Aero Transport DH9, 1920. It was in this type that the first Invercargill-Auckland flight was made, in a single day's flying time. *Below*, the DH9 at One Tree Hill, Auckland, after its inaugural flight.

A.G. Wigley, RLW and Harry Wigley, 1 August 1937, the day that RLW took his pilot's certificate.

Executive transport, pioneered by RLW in his BA Swallow. John Kilian and Harry Wigley in the cockpits; on the ground, Capt. J. Busch, later manager of National Airways, RLW, and Norrie Coxhead.

A fairly sophisticated passenger aircraft of the late 1930s: the Waco.

The Waco with a 1hp power-unit after a forced landing in the Lindis Pass.

Miles Whitney Straight, bought in 1950 for communication work.

The original working model of the retractable ski/wheel undercarriage whose development has brought 'ski-plane adventure' to tens of thousands of visitors to Mt Cook.

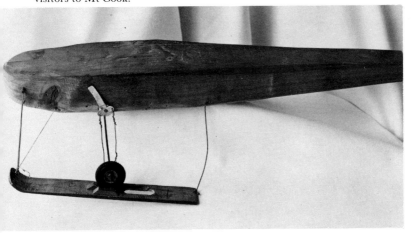

The ski-plane undercarriage. *Above*, wheels for hard surfaces. *Below*, skis for snow.

Alan McWhirter photographed by Harry Wigley after the first landing on the Tasman Glacier.

First landing on the Ball Pass: Brian Wigley and John Evans.

Top, first landing of the Company's DC3 on the Mt Cook airstrip, 1 November 1961. *Middle*, two of the Company's HS748s at Queenstown. *Bottom*, Sonia Mee, the Hon. H.J. Walker (then Minister of Tourism), Isla and Harry Wigley, on the occasion of the first HS748 landing at Mt Cook.

airminded, was the interim answer.

Townspeople in Auckland, Christchurch and Timaru enjoyed permanent local flying opportunities but, over the rest of the country, aviation had to be brought to the district. The procedure was simple. A suitable paddock was located, its owner talked into allowing it to be used, advertisements were inserted in the local paper and reinforced by the sight of the arriving aircraft circling overhead.

The results were satisfying. The locals turned out in droves to see the fun, people formed up into long queues to pay their shillings or pounds for shorter or longer flights, and RLW used to recall that on many occasions business was so brisk that the staff had difficulty in finding a safe place in which to stow the cash away, and had to walk around with their pockets stuffed so full of money that notes of all denominations were sticking out in all directions.

But inevitably, and as foreseen by the Canterbury Aviation Company in 1920, CAC and NZAT came into hot rivalry to be first into each district to clean up all its loose cash and hurry on to the next area before the opposition could move in. For example, the *Timaru Herald* reported on 21 January 1921:

> A short time ago the Christchurch machine was advertised to give flights at Geraldine, but on the date shown and from the paddock advertised by the company, it was a Timaru machine that gave the many enthusiasts trips to the clouds.
>
> Also, the Christchurch machines were advertised to give flights from Mosgiel on a certain date, but the Timaru company had a machine plying for hire from Andersons Bay foreshore in the heart of Dunedin, a day in advance of the Christchurch men's advertisement. The Timaru men did a surprising amount of business before the northern men reached Mosgiel, nearly killing a cow and rendering their machine unserviceable . . . The animal, by the way, was not hurt but continued to graze peacefully.

In this instance the two companies resolved their differences by conferring with the local harbour board, with the result that they agreed to share the use of the Andersons Bay 'aerodrome'.

If the pilots and mechanics of the joyriding barnstormers were idolised by an admiring public, the local publicans regarded them with mixed feelings. Sure, they kept the bar cash-registers very busy, but the bedrooms were not improved by being used as makeshift workshops for essential maintenance jobs during the evenings. Flying-wires were often spliced

by being stretched over the brass knobs of the old-fashioned
bedsteads, with disastrous results to the paint; engine components were dismantled and their oily parts strewn all over
the floors and carpets; hotel towels were not easy to launder
after being used to wipe greasy hands and mop up the general
mess.

Nor were serious churchgoers gratified by flying on the
Sabbath:

THE CLOUD-RIDERS: PROTEST BY PRESBYTERIANS

The Session of Knox Church, Waimate, protests against the
exhibition of aeroplane joyriding which took place all day
on a recent Sunday. Not only do they consider such exhibitions to be in the interests of none but thoughtless and
grasping proprietors, but in this case the machine was directed so low over the town that worshippers in Church and
Sunday School were greatly disturbed; indeed, the services
were completely interrupted. The Session respectfully asks
those in authority that worshippers on the Sabbath are not
harassed in such ways.

They had a point. But it is only fair to add that the low-
powered, low-compression, slow-revving rotary engines of
those days were far less noisy than those used in the light
aircraft of today. They made, in fact, a low-pitched sort of
drone, neither piercing nor offensive.

The joyriders could also fall foul of the Law on occasions:

AVIATORS IN COURT

The SM yesterday read a considered decision on the charges
against Captains M. W. Buckley and P. K. Fowler for
breaches of the Aviation Act. His Worship's decision was as
follows:

The defendants are charged with that on 4 September
1921 at Timaru they did carry out trick flying — to wit,
nosediving in an aircraft over a town, to wit, Timaru, contrary to the provisions of the Aviation Act (1918), and the
regulations made thereunder and published in the *New
Zealand Gazette* of 18 March 1921. And also that they did
contrary to the said Act carry out flying by aircraft which by
reason of low altitude and proximity to the dwellings was
dangerous to the public safety.

His Worship then admitted that nobody knew how 'trick flying' should be defined, but he made a gallant shot at this. He
accepted the defendants' evidence that the alleged 'nosedive'
had been merely a steep turn made in the course of ordinary

aerial navigation, and dismissed that charge. But he found them guilty of low flying (they had been gliding fairly low over Caroline Bay to see whether it was usable as an aerodrome — or so they said). He pointed out that this offence could carry a fine of £100, but contented his conscience by awarding a fine of only twenty shillings each, with costs.

On another occasion the Company was accused by the South Canterbury Acclimatisation Society of deliberate low flying over the Washdyke wildlife sanctuary on the opening morning of the duckshooting season. It was alleged that this had been done at the request of certain shooting enthusiasts to scare the duck out of the sanctuary, and that the Company had been paid £10 for doing it.

The case — if there had been one in law — never reached court. RLW met the Society's committee and demolished the charge. Yes, two NZAT aircraft had been flying on the morning in question, but they had never gone within 400 metres of the sanctuary. And yes, certain individuals had suggested to him that aircraft should disturb the duck on that day, but he had at once turned them down and instructed the Company's manager that nothing of the kind was to be attempted; this instruction had been strictly adhered to. The Company had never been offered money for such activities, and he moved that the allegations be brought into court so that they could be publicly refuted and discredited.

However, the meeting decided not to prosecute the Company, the chairman adding the cryptic advice, 'Don't do it again!'

Air Board statistics for November 1921 show that civil aviation had made a promising start. The Walsh brothers at Kohimarama, Auckland, had carried 220 passengers, Henry Wigram's men at Sockburn had carried 236, NZAT at Timaru had carried 488. The figures for the preceding months of 1921 were in very much the same ratio. That the company operating from the smallest of the three centres should be doing double the business of either of the other two gives a fair indication of the drive and enthusiasm of RLW and his team at NZAT.

Operationally speaking, all three firms were making a success of the job, but financially all three were sinking for one reason or another. By 1923 all three were going into liquidation.

In the case of RLW there was an especially cogent reason for his having to give up his interest in aviation. His fellow-directors of the Mount Cook Motor Company had never shared his enthusiasm for flying and were apprehensive lest their company, which was earning satisfactory revenue, should be pulled under by the unprofitable NZAT. They felt that not only was RLW neglecting Mt Cook but that he was also endangering his life; it was time he came back to earth and applied all his energies to being fulltime managing director of the more important company.

So NZAT was put into liquidation. The aircraft and spares were returned to the Air Board, the pilots and engineers had to disperse and await the regeneration of civil flying that took place in the later 1920s.

The last flight made by an NZAT aircraft was memorable. In the closing days RLW, despite the explicit disapproval of the Mount Cook Motor Company's board, had been taking a few flying lessons from Bill Park. He went out to Washdyke one day for some more dual, discovered that Bill was away somewhere and, characteristically, ordered one of the Avros to be wheeled out of the hangar.

'But what do you want us to do that for?' asked one of the engineers.

'I'm going to fly it.'

'But — but — you've only had a couple of hours' dual.'

'That's plenty,' says RLW. 'Anyone like to come for a ride?'

Not many people would have had the nerve to fly with a middle-aged pilot on his first solo, particularly if he had only a couple of hours' dual in his logbook, but Bill Burrows, a hangar apprentice, clambered happily into the spare seat. The engine was started, RLW taxied confidently down to the airfield boundary, turned into wind, and got safely airborne.

He did an admirable circuit round the airfield, cut the engine, and glided in to land. As he made his final approach he remembered that Bill Park had warned him that he was tending to glide too fast, so he reduced speed — and overdid it.

The Avro stalled and nosed into the ground, the undercarriage collapsed, and the propellor gave up the ghost. RLW and an astonished Bill Burrows stepped out and down to the ground, which was appreciably closer than it had been when they took off, and trudged back to the hangar.

That was RLW's first solo, and the swansong of NZAT. But RLW lived to fly again another day. His second solo came some sixteen years later, by which time he was nearly sixty years of age.

14

Aviation Comes of Age

In *Ski-plane Adventure* I outlined the events which led up to the
Mount Cook Company's second adventure into civil aviation.
To summarise: the first era of commercial flying ended about
1922, and civil aviation in New Zealand came virtually to a
standstill until the introduction of the famous Gypsy 1 Moth
and the similar Avro Avian and Simmonds Spartan biplanes of
the late 1920s. These safe, easy-to-fly little aircraft were inex-
pensive to operate and did more to popularise aviation among
the masses than anything else that had preceded them. Charles
Lindbergh's solo flight from New York to Paris and, closer to
home, the trans-Pacific and Tasman flights of Kingsford-
Smith, also maintained and stimulated interest in aviation.

A firm called New Zealand Airways operated Simmonds
Spartans out of the Saltwater Creek airfield south of Timaru in
the early 1930s, its chief pilot and chief instructor being Tiny
White, a World War I pilot and aviation enthusiast. From time
to time during flying field days and pageants, Tiny's visits to
Mt Cook and Queenstown, I would help him out by refuelling
his aircraft, manhandling it on the ground, selling tickets, and
in various other ways, and it was not long before I started
taking the odd flying lesson.

I had discussed this with RLW but he was disapproving and
told me not to waste my very limited pay on flying. In spite of
this I used to save up a few pounds and sneak down to see Tiny
to buy twenty or thirty minutes of dual instruction.

Years later, when Tiny was station commander at RNZAF
Levin, where I spent some weeks marching round the barrack
square at the beginning of World War II, he told me how RLW
had been surreptitiously taking flying lessons while I was, and
had sworn him to secrecy. Tiny's biggest problem had been to
ensure that RLW and I did not meet each other at the airfield.

A year or so after those first lessons I decided to go ahead and
get a private pilot's licence. I went to Christchurch for a week

or ten days and learned to fly with the Canterbury Aero Club. My brother Sandy qualified at about the same time. At home he and I talked of ways and means of building up enough hours and experience to qualify for our commercial licences, and discussed the pros and cons of owning our own aeroplane. We sent away for brochures on the various types available, and used to discuss the merits of each one at great length. One evening at home when we were close to making a final decision, we were intrigued to notice that RLW, still disapproving in principle, sat near us for about two hours without saying a word — but reading his newspaper upside down!

After this we reckoned it was only a matter of time before he came down on the side of the enthusiasts, and sure enough he did, by buying the aeroplane for us. Soon afterwards he began taking flying lessons again, did his second solo, and eventually got his private pilot's licence.

The aeroplane he bought was a little two-seater low-wing monoplane, the BA Swallow, which would take off or land on the smallest paddocks and was a sheer delight to fly. We all used it for communication purposes, but it was the special joy of RLW, who would push it out whenever the weather was fine and go flying to Mt Cook or Queenstown or other parts of the country just for the sheer joy of flying.

He was so keen on flying that he thought everyone else should be too, and he would always offer members of The Mount Cook Company staff or any of his friends the chance to go along with him. Some of his passengers were not at all enthusiastic, and feared the worst every time they went up. Aub Rollinson, later the Company's general manager, was one of these, but one nice sunny afternoon he was talked into going along.

They flew around the countryside looking at this and that, and then returned to the airfield, where RLW intended to do some practice on 'touch-and-go' landings. (You do a normal circuit and approach, land, and then, before the aircraft comes to a stop, you open the throttle and take off on another circuit.)

After half a dozen of these, Aub yelled over the speaker tubes: 'I would like to land and get out.'

RLW yelled back 'What the hell do you think I'm trying to do!'

RLW used to tell another story against himself and a reluctant passenger. As soon as the throttle was opened, this character slumped down in the front cockpit and his head disappeared from view. As they cruised round, the head emerged — until they hit a small bump, and then it would disappear again. After a while, the head was in full view, and RLW called through the phones, 'Can you see the Port Hills?' A voice came back, 'They all look the bloody same to me.'

They returned to the airfield with the head fully extruded, and the passenger apparently taking an intelligent interest in his surroundings. When the throttle was closed to make the approach, the head popped down and stayed down — until RLW made one of his worse-than-usual landings, when he was startled out of his wits by a bloodcurdling scream from the front cockpit. The passenger had imagined that the plane would drop like a stone as soon as the throttle was closed, and thought they had crashed.

After a year or two I had built up enough hours and experience to get a commercial flying licence, and we formed Queenstown-Mount Cook Airways with the idea of doing scenic and charter flights and, eventually, scheduled services. We intended to base the operation on Queenstown, and a rough but serviceable hangar was built in the shelter of the trees at one end of the newly completed airfield.

We bought an American Waco aircraft from the Otago Aero Club, who did not have enough commercial work to justify its existence. It was a biplane capable of carrying a pilot and four passengers, and was better appointed than the average aircraft of that era, with nicely upholstered seats, wind-down windows, ashtrays and other fittings, but its radial motor of about 170hp was so close to the pilot that the noise was deafening and, of course, it made the cabin very hot.

Two engineers, Bill Dini and Alf Henry, were employed to keep it serviceable, and they earned their keep, for when the weather was suitable we flew from daylight till dark. We flew scenic flights from Queenstown, over Milford Sound, and from The Hermitage round Mt Cook and the glaciers, while charter trips took us all over the South Island. In the two or so years until World War II put an end to the venture, we did a lot of flying, and the business was building up very satisfactorily. We had learned a lot about the problems of flying in the Alps, and about the demand for air services of various kinds, and had got to the stage where we needed newer and more suitable aircraft, and more pilots to fly them. We had proved that it was perfectly feasible to run a commercial flying operation in the Alps and, contrary to the opinions of many people, safely.

Several pilots had flown from these mountain places for brief

periods when the weather was good, but packed up and got out
as soon as it looked like deteriorating. Many of them spoke in
awed tones of the dreadful things which would happen to an
aeroplane striking an 'airpocket'. They said it would drop
thousands of feet like a stone, and the pilot would completely
lose control. They told all sorts of hair-raising stories of how
they had escaped death by inches.

I had listened to these stories with some scepticism, for on
skiing, climbing and shooting trips in the Alps I had studied
the movements of the air currents by watching the drift of
clouds in the valleys and over the valleys, and the movement of
dust and snow blown on the hillsides, and also the movement
of snow-tussock and trees. I believed that the air moved in
certain patterns, and that if these were understood it should be
possible to fly perfectly safely in the Alps under all but the most
adverse conditions, even though, as would be expected, the
turbulence would become severe on occasions.

The more I flew in the Alps, the more I learned about and
came to understand the air currents, and the more I felt at
home there. I was convinced that sooner or later scheduled
services and other types of alpine flying would be accepted as
safe and normal operations. In two years or so I did many
charter trips and scenic flights and carried many passengers,
and the old Waco proved that flying in the Alps and fiords was
feasible, even though the engine let us down rather badly on
two or three occasions.

On one of these trips I was flying a party of skiers above the
clouds, at about 2700 metres from Queenstown to Timaru
when the engine flew to bits, making a most ungodly din and
vibrating horribly. There was nowhere to go except down,
which was a bit unnerving when we knew that the tops of
various mountain ranges in the vicinity were hidden in the
cloud below us. Fortunately we broke into the clear above a
valley, where we glided down and made an uneventful forced
landing in a paddock of young oats.

On another occasion the engine stopped dead when, with a
full load of passengers, I was flying over Lake Wakatipu near
Queenstown. After I had pulled and pushed all the knobs on
the dashboard and invoked the deity who looks after airmen
who suffer from unreliable engines, it started on one cylinder,
then on a second, and finally enough of them joined in to get us
clear of the water with only a metre or so to spare.

That aircraft frightened the daylights out of me on several
occasions. It was finally commandeered by the Air Force at the

outbreak of the war and, when it turned on its favourite act over Cook Strait with a senior engineering officer on board, it was once too often: when they got back to Rongotai he ordered the brute to be chopped up.

But it had proved that flying in the Alps had definite possibilities. Business had reached the stage when there was more flying than one aeroplane and one pilot could handle and, but for the war, the fleet and the staff would have been increased from then onwards.

When the war began it was impossible to say how long it would last and how it would finish, and there was no point in keeping Queenstown-Mount Cook Airways going any longer than necessary. I flew hard through that last summer season and carried more tourists than ever before, but then the peacetime stream of traffic started to dry up, so in mid-February 1940 I marched off to the war. Or, to be more precise, I joined the Royal New Zealand Air Force and was posted to the School for Flying Instructors at Mangere, Auckland.

The Second World War, like the first one, gave a tremendous stimulus to aviation. Money was spent on research and development which could not possibly have been afforded in peacetime. Those of us who survived received the benefit of Air Force training in flying and navigation and logged up thousands of hours on training and operations. The six and a half years which I spent with the service provided experience in many sectors, some pleasant, some unpleasant, and by the end of the war my enthusiasm for aeroplanes was gone and I didn't care if I never saw another.

However, it was not long before the Company bought a war-surplus Tiger Moth for use as a communications aeroplane to get more quickly round its various branches. The roads were bad, mostly unsealed, and the Tiger Moth could get us to Queenstown, Mt Cook and other places and back in a day or less, when the equivalent journey by road would take two or three days. Later the Tiger was sold and we replaced it with a Miles Whitney Straight, a delightful little cabin two-seater low-wing monoplane with a cruising speed of 200km/h or more. This served us well and kept us in touch with civil aviation which, as was to be expected, developed rapidly after the end of the war.

It seemed that we ought to be moving into civil aviation again, as one operator had already jumped our claim on Queenstown and others were operating spasmodically from Mt

Cook, but all our time and financial resources had to be totally committed to rehabilitating the coach service. However, by 1953 it was clear that we could not defer our involvement in commercial aviation any longer, and we applied to the Air Services Licensing Authority for passenger, freight and top-dressing rights in the Mackenzie Country, including Mt Cook.

The Auster aircraft, a four-seater cabin high-wing mono-plane was about the cheapest aeroplane we could buy which would serve the purpose, so we ordered two of these to get the operation under way. In *Ski-plane Adventure* I have covered the Company's development of commercial flying, and I will not repeat it here.

Struan Robertson, who had been flying Wellingtons for the RAF over Europe until he was shot down and spent the rest of the war as a prisoner, joined us in 1953. After sampling various civilian jobs he had drifted into agricultural flying on rabbit poisoning and topdressing, and joined us with considerable experience in this work.

A genial character, popular with the farming community amongst whom he worked, and a packet of energy, Struan would never walk anywhere where he could run, and over the years he did a tremendous job for the Company in getting the aerial work and the passenger side soundly established. The first two years or so the passenger work was hard slogging, for the people visiting the resorts that we served — Mt Cook, Ohau and Wanaka — did not seem to have much money to spend on such luxuries as flying. However, growth was steady and encouraging.

On many occasions when Struan could not cope on his own, I would fly up from Timaru to Mt Cook to help him out. Looking down on the vast snowfields at the heads of the big glaciers, the Tasman, Fox, Franz Josef and others, I wondered, as I had before the war, how we could possibly make use of them. Several I had traversed while touring on skis, and I knew that they extended flat and smooth as a billiard table for many kilometres.

The scenery surrounding these glaciers was magnificent: they flowed down the mountainsides like wet icing on a cake, becoming tortured and broken into all sorts of weird shapes, crevasses overhung by seracs, spires, and all sorts of futuristic designs. But only hardy climbers and skiers could enjoy them. What a tremendous thing it would be to be able to fly our visitors round such areas and land them on the snow in this fantastic fairyland of black-and-white!

Fitting the aircraft with skis, as had been done in Canada and Scandinavia, was the obvious answer, but unfortunately the Hermitage airfield was covered in snow for only a few short weeks each year and then very few people visited the area. I had a talk with Mr Carpenter, head of the Airworthiness Division of the Civil Aviation Department in Wellington. Carp, as he was known, told me that he had been a bush pilot in Canada and had had considerable experience in flying ski-equipped aircraft. He said it represented no great operational problems, and he promised to help us in any way he could in getting skis fitted to the Austers.

We made enquiries all round the world, but we could not locate skis suitable for the Auster, so Carp encouraged us to go ahead and build our own. Keen as we were to try out an aircraft on skis, we soon saw that it would be a waste of time unless the skis were made retractable and auxiliary to the normal wheeled undercarriage, so that we could land either on grass or snow, as required. But no such dual-purpose landing-gear had as yet been invented for the Auster, and if we wanted it we would have to start from scratch and develop it.

I had a reasonably well equipped workshop at home, as I had always been keen on woodwork and metalwork, and after dreaming up a design I started building retractable models. Some worked and some didn't, some would work this way, but wouldn't work that. Some showed a glimmer of hope. We persevered with the one that showed most promise, altering and testing it until we had a design which worked well on the model and which ought to work just as well when fitted full-scale to an aircraft. This successful model is still in my office, and it still works.

Next, I drew up a set of plans to scale and sent them to Carp, who suggested that we should go ahead and build a full scale set and told us how to go about testing it for strength.

Wooden skis made of laminated oregon were built by Arnold France Ltd. of Christchurch, and the tubular steel gear was knocked up in the Company's Timaru garage by Hughie Fergusson, who had become a specialist welder at the expense of the Air Force during the war. When the skis and the retraction gear were completed we applied load tests to them. Blocks were placed at each end of the ski and a heavy weight in the form of a bus was lowered by hydraulic jack on to scales placed on the centre until the required loading was reached. The ski bent, creaked, and looked perfectly horrible, but it took the load and with plenty to spare.

The next test was on the retracting gear, and this was done by putting one wheel in the snow position on the ski, which had been anchored to the ground. The tail was then put up on a trestle and a spring balance with a block and tackle attached, applied laterally to the tailwheel. Pressure was applied sideways until the required number of foot/pounds of torque were measured. In this process the steel undercarriage and the ski gear attached were twisted and distorted into all sorts of excruciating angles, but successfully passed the test. Shortly afterwards we increased the pressure just to see to what degree the strength of the gear exceeded the requirement, and eventually it fractured with a deafening bang.

By now we had been working on the ski-plane project for eighteen months or more, and the tests had brought us very close to the stage when we could put theory into practice. When all the tests were completed to Carp's satisfaction, we were given permission to do aerodynamic flying tests to make sure that the skis did not upset the trim of the aircraft, nor start flapping uncontrollably around in the wind. These tests were quite satisfactory, and we also found that it was relatively easy when in the air to put one's hand out of the window and move the lever which controlled the skis backwards and forwards from the land position to the snow position.

By the time all these tests were completed we felt a bit like George Washington and his little axe, or a kid with a new toy. We were impatient to take the aircraft out on to the snow, but for days on end the weather in the Mt Cook region stayed bad, with high turbulent winds and rain, and we had to wait in Timaru for it to clear. At last we received a message to say that a cold front was moving through with a light fall of snow and the weather was expected to clear on the following day.

Squib McWhirter had had a considerable amount to do with the construction of the retractable ski gear in the garage, and he joined me as passenger when I left for The Hermitage soon after daylight on 22 September 1955. Harry Ayres, Murray Douglas, Sir Edmund Hillary, and a number of others were on the airfield to greet us when we arrived, for they were all agog to see the outcome of our experiments.

We were completely confident that we had thought of every eventuality and that nothing could possibly go wrong. Others had their doubts, and insisted that a ground party should go into the head of the Tasman Glacier, where we intended to land, to mark out the snow and to be on hand in case the aircraft rolled over on to its back, or got stuck. We agreed that this idea had some merit, for the glacier was a complete wilderness area, and the nearest living soul was some fifty kilometres away. But such a ground party would have taken four or five hours to scramble over the rocky moraine and rough ice of the lower Tasman Glacier, and we were not only impatient to get cracking, but were concerned that the weather would not last, so we decided to press on regardless. We expected no trouble, but we carried ice-axes and climbing boots, warm clothing and some food in case we had to walk our way out.

The vast expanse of the glacier would be completely untracked after the new fall of snow, and we were a little worried whether we could judge our height above the snow during landing, so we took with us some lumps of foliage about half a metre long which we could throw out to act as markers on the snow.

When everything was complete, Squib and I climbed on board, the motor was started and we took off and headed up the glacier, climbing steadily. Southerly cloud still hung over the valley, but when we were level with the Hochstetter Icefall we broke clear of it into brilliant sunshine, with the glacier below us and the surrounding peaks glistening white under a light coating of new snow. On reaching the Malte Brun Hut, we saw below us the perfectly smooth flat expanse of snow extending six to eight kilometres to the head of the valley and the best part of three kilometres wide, an ideal airfield.

We circled over it, trying to pick out some drifted snow or something which would give us an idea of our height above it, but snow must have fallen the previous night under flat calm conditions, for it was an unbroken white in every direction. Finally, we reduced height to about 100 metres above the snow, reduced power, put on quarter flaps and flew straight down the glacier with Squib throwing out lumps of foliage every fifty or sixty metres.

I opened the throttle, climbed in a wide circle, and came back on a reciprocal course to pick up the line of the markers, but the glacier was so large an area that, as we found later, even a human being is dwarfed by the magnitude of the landscape and is difficult to pick up. However, as we got closer to the snow the foliage began to show up as tiny specks, and finally it gave sufficient lead to allow me to attempt a landing.

I took the Auster in with quite a bit of power on so as to land at a minimum speed and to hold the tail down should there be more drag on the skis than we expected. However, the landing was so smooth and so effortless on the soft snow that it was almost impossible to tell when we had touched down. So smooth that it was almost an anti-climax.

The landing was far simpler than even we had expected, but the aircraft did come to a stop rather rapidly, and this suggested that take-offs might be our problem. I turned the aircraft downhill and opened the throttle to find out and, sure enough, the skis ploughed through the snow, throwing clouds of it into the air, the aircraft rolled from one side to the other and refused to get more than about 25km/h. After wallowing round for two kilometres or more, we struck a bump which tossed us into the air for just long enough to stay airborne, and so we climbed away, pondering the fact that take-offs were likely to be the most difficult part of the operation.

But if we had landed and taken off once we could do it again, so we went in for a second landing and found it even easier this time, as we had our previous tracks to land on. The second take-off was also much easier on the tracks of the previous take-off.

This was the culmination of several years of dreaming, planning and hard work, a day of fulfilment and excitement that was shared by many friends at Mt Cook. After taking some photographs and walking round for a while, we returned to The Hermitage and made several more trips on to the snow, carrying as passengers, Sir Edmund Hillary, the conqueror of Everest, the well-known guide, Harry Ayres, and Murray Douglas, Doug Drake and Hap Ashurst.

That day marked the beginning of one of the most successful aviation projects in which the Company has embarked. It has developed from that first landing with the Auster to where today a fleet of fourteen six-seater Cessna 185s with 300hp motors, give annually some 50,000 people, including the halt, the lame and even the blind, the unforgettable joy of landing on snow in the very heart of the Southern Alps.

The ski-plane's first landing on the snow caught the public's imagination immediately, but we had a long way to go before it could become a commercial proposition. We flew into the snowfields as often as the weather permitted to test out the ski gear, to learn techniques for handling the aircraft on snow, and to explore more and more snowfields in the areas attainable from The Hermitage.

Until we perfected the techniques we frequently bogged down with one ski buried deep and a wingtip resting in the snow, the aeroplane at a most undignified and alarming angle. We learned how to overcome this, but then the aircraft would become obstinate and refuse to get airborne, even after chugging down the glacier for a couple of kilometres or more. We overcame this to a large extent by fitting a teflon running-surface to the skis.

Although many incidents occurred during this testing period, very little damage occurred to the aircraft and none at all to pilots or passengers. Some people have pointedly asked me why one incident in which I was involved, to my embarrassment, was not reported in *Ski-plane Adventure*. The first answer was obvious, and the second was that the ski-plane had not yet proved itself to our complete satisfaction and we felt that reports which were likely to frighten prospective passengers should be left out.

Some months after the first landing on the snow, I had done a morning's testing in the Auster, flying around the various glaciers, and had landed briefly at the Birch Hill airstrip near The Hermitage to let John Hunter-Weston, the other pilot flying the ski-planes, pick up his suitcase from The Hermitage and fly with me to Timaru. John was away much longer than he should have been and, as the telephone to the airstrip was not working, I took off and circled The Hermitage a few times to give him the hurry-up. After a while I noticed him walking down towards a shingle airstrip we had built immediately below The Hermitage, and to save time I decided to land there, although we did not normally use it with the skis on.

I did a short approach and then, as I was holding off with the tail well down, I heard a clicking sound on the heels of the skis. It flashed through my mind that I was landing with the skis down, but before I could do anything about it the aircraft landed firmly and ground rapidly to a halt, the skis making an almighty noise on the shingle. As we slowed up, the tail rose higher and higher until the Auster was standing on the tips of its skis like a ballerina, then flipped over on its back. A cloud of fumes rose and there was a hissing noise mighty like the sound of escaping petrol, so my passenger and I, hanging upside down on the straps, had to attempt an exceedingly speedy departure. Neither of us was injured in the prang, but my passenger had neglected to take the precaution of supporting himself before pulling the pin out of his safety belt and landed heavily on his head on the cabin roof; even so, he was still out of the aircraft before I was.

It was a piece of carelessness on my part, I probably hadn't

paid enough attention to retracting the skis, as we had landed
on the grass of the Birch Hill airfield on two or three occasions
with the skis down when the ski gear had been damaged and
jammed, and they had slid over the grass so easily that there
had been no danger of the aircraft nosing over.

Before long a crowd of people from The Hermitage had
gathered round to see the aeroplane lying flat on its back with
its skis in the air, and as it was the type of publicity that we did
not particularly welcome at that stage, we made use of all the
available labour to get the aircraft back on its wheels again as
quickly as possible. The skis were removed, a rope was attached
to the tail, and with half a dozen people pulling on it and
another half dozen lifting, it was manhandled back the way it
had come until it was back on its wheels again.

The windshield was broken and there was some superficial
damage to the wings and the rudder, but apart from that the
aircraft was quite airworthy and we flew it back to Timaru,
where Dave Graham repaired it with his usual efficiency.

After we had made many landings on the snow, modified the
ski gear, and learned just how to fly in and out of the snowfields, the Civil Aviation Department gave us approval to go
ahead with commercial operations. Three Austers were fitted
with skis and they did an excellent job in getting the operation
established, as they had a very low landing speed, were very
safe, and reasonably light to dig out when they become stuck.
However, their takeoff and climb performance with an engine
of 145hp was inadequate and the cabin was too small and too
crude for a pilot and three passengers, so we adopted the
Cessna 180s with 230hp, in due course changing over to the
six-seater Cessna 185s with 300hp motors.

The Cessna 185 has been used very successfully for a number
of years, and has given thousands of passengers their first
experience of real alpine country and often their first walk on
the snow. At present, experiments are being carried out with
twin-engined Britten-Norman Islanders on skis, and this aircraft shows promise as a replacement for the Cessna. However,
it will be some time yet, and many trial landings on the snow
will be needed, before it can be decided whether this aircraft is
suitable for full-scale commercial operations on skis.

The development of the ski-plane was fully supported by the
Tourist Hotel Corporation, and particularly by Lawrie and
Pat Dennis, who were managing The Hermitage at that time
and who recognised it as a major attraction which would allow
guests to penetrate right into the heart of the Alps and enjoy

what only the climbers and ski tourers had enjoyed hitherto. The Mount Cook Parks Board also gave its wholehearted support for this reason and, as well, for its importance in alpine rescue, for transporting materials for the building of alpine huts and, later, their supplies of food and fuel. It was also a boon to climbers, who used it to fly into the high-altitude huts to begin climbing and exploring immediately instead of having to waste precious days of fine weather in climbing in with heavy packs on their backs.

As a tourist attraction it was unique, for it was the only one of its kind capable of operating for twelve months of the year. It was soon getting worldwide publicity, with people coming to New Zealand solely to do a ski-plane trip. As traffic built up and ski-planes were introduced to the West Coast at the Fox and Franz Josef Glaciers, hangars had to be built to shelter and service the aircraft, houses built for pilots, engineers and drivers, as well as other facilities to service passengers. On fine days the bases at Mt Cook, Franz Josef and the Fox are hives of activity. It is now quite a large operation employing fifteen pilots, eighteen engineers and ground staff, and is an established part of the New Zealand tourist scene.

When the weather is fine and snow conditions are good there is a heavy demand for the services of the ski-planes, and in recent years some 50,000 people have been landed on the snow in each year. As is to be expected with this amount of flying, a few incidents and accidents have occurred, but to date the only passengers to suffer were hurt not on a deliberate landing on the snow but when a pilot, searching for some lost climbers at a high altitude, flew too low and too slow and got caught in a downdraught which caused him to stall heavily on to the snow and injure three of his passengers, two quite seriously. Fortunately some occupants of the nearby Alma Hut were quickly on the scene to help the injured people, and in within a very short time two other ski-planes landed close by, took the injured on board, and flew them to the Hokitika airport where an ambulance was waiting.

The huge size of the snowfields and the ease of taking an aircraft off and landing it on the snow have made it a very safe operation, as the record has proved, while the ability of other radio-equipped aircraft to come quickly to the aid of others stuck or damaged has prevented people from being marooned overnight on an alpine snowfield. Aircraft have occasionally been caught on a snowfield by bad weather and the passengers forced to overnight there, but they have been flown out next day not much the worse for their experience. The aircraft are equipped with emergency rations and survival gear and, provided that the passengers stay with the aircraft and do not expose themselves to dangers of the weather or getting lost in the snowfields, they are perfectly safe.

When flying a ski-plane from the Fox Glacier, John Stokes became the first of our pilots to overnight on a high-altitude snowfield. In marginal weather, accompanied by a doctor, he flew into the névé at the head of the Fox to pick up an injured climber, and before he could become airborne again the weather closed in, reducing visibility to a few metres. They sat in the aircraft waiting for it to break enough to take off, but they were still waiting at dark and had to overnight in the aircraft. Conditions were very cold, but John kept his passengers warm by starting the motor at frequent intervals and turning on the aircraft's heater, which is very efficient. The weather cleared next morning and they took off without delay to fly the injured climber to hospital.

Several years later another incident occurred involving several aircraft, and this had its comic side. The aircraft had been flying from The Hermitage to the head of the Tasman Glacier all day, shuttling backwards and forwards and carrying a large number of passengers. Late in the afternoon a cloud developed very suddenly over the head of the valley, and almost immediately three aircraft on the snow were engulfed in a snowstorm which reduced visibility to a few metres. The pilots did their best to keep their passengers amused and warm, and prepared to take off the instant visibility was adequate, but when darkness fell they were still weatherbound.

They kept their passengers warm in the cabins of the aircraft, gave them hot soup and emergency rations and did their best to prevent them from becoming bored by telling them stories of the Alps and their flying adventures. The weather cleared marginally in the morning, but they were unable to take off as snow was plastered heavily all over the aircraft.

Bill Davies, the manager of the Light Aircraft Division had reported to me the previous evening that the three aircraft were marooned on the glacier, and he outlined the arrangements made to care for the passengers. He rang again in the morning saying that they had survived the night in reasonable comfort and that two relief planes were on their way to pick them up as soon as the weather cleared, so his worries would soon be over. An hour later he rang again to say that the relief planes had landed, but before they could take off, the weather had closed in again and he now had *five* aircraft marooned on the glacier. I said: 'Congratulations, you're getting better at it!' — but he didn't seem to appreciate my remarks.

Soon after this the weather finally cleared and all passengers and aircraft returned to The Hermitage, none the worse for their experience. Throughout the emergency the aircraft maintained contact with each other and The Hermitage by radio, so it was not long before the word had leaked out and reporters from the various media became alerted to what they expected to be a major calamity. They converged on The Hermitage later in the day after the aircraft had been flown out, but were disappointed to find practically nothing to report — thanks to Dave Wilkes.

Dave was manager of the ski-plane operation at the time and one of the most efficient up-and-coming members of our staff. He was forthright and independent in his thinking and had, to say the least, a fairly resistant attitude to the media. Knowing that reporters would be flocking into the area he loaded all but two of the ski-plane passengers on to the first 748 through Mt Cook, to allow them to catch up on their itineraries, and the remaining two he had filled so full of rum to restore their shattered nerves that they were incapable of talking to anyone.

Dave Wilkes lost his life in an aerial topdressing accident shortly after this. He had been very popular with his flying colleagues and the tourists whom he looked after so pleasantly and efficiently; his loss was a great blow to us all.

15

The Airline

THE TREMENDOUS DRAWCARD of the ski-planes attracted into the South Island and the Mt Cook region many overseas visitors who would previously have arrived in Auckland, taken a look at Rotorua and then departed from Auckland having 'done' New Zealand.

They stimulated traffic to the South Island, but they could not solve the problem that RLW and so many others had been studying over the years back to the turn of the century: the relative inaccessibility of the South Island. The problem was still there, but now more insistent than ever before, as the international air age had arrived. People were coming to the South Pacific in increasingly greater numbers, and wanting to explore further afield.

Several American tour operators tried to bridge the Cook Strait gap by using light aircraft, but this was an untidy operation that highlighted the problem without curing it. On one occasion Hemphill World Tours engaged us to fly a group of passengers in five or six light aircraft to Mt Cook, Queenstown, Te Anau and back to Christchurch. As we were short of pilots, I piloted one of the aeroplanes.

The weather was patchy, to say the least, and on the return flight it deteriorated to the extent that most of the passes were under cloud and it was raining heavily. We should have stayed on the ground, but connections had to be made with international flights so we boxed on, up and down the valleys and through the passes with very little room to spare. Finally I landed at Omarama and waited to see where all the other aircraft had scattered themselves. One by one they came in and landed safely, to my great relief.

This effort brought us in a few dollars in revenue, but it proved to me quite conclusively that flying American tourists round in light aircraft was simply not on — we would have to go back to RLW's theme of the 1920's and start thinking in terms of a properly constituted airline.

But where should we start? There were no airfields to take even the smallest of airliners, there were no radio or navigational aids, there were none of the other essential facilities. Assuming that we would somehow manage to provide our own airfields and other facilities in due course, and tailor them to our requirements, the first and most important task was to select a suitable aircraft.

We considered the various types then available, but had to reach the conclusion that the only one which had any real hope of success was the trusty old DC3. It carried a big enough load — twenty-eight passengers — to be worth while promoting; it could handle most groups which were then passing through the country; it had a good radio and sufficient radio nagivational aids to do a considerable amount of bad-weather flying on instruments. It was readily available, and large stocks of spares were carried by NAC (now Air New Zealand). Many pilots had been trained to fly it, and many engineers to service it. It was a real airliner, proved in service even before the war and during the war, and one in which the travelling public had confidence.

Its two drawbacks were, first, that it might be too large for our traffic potential and might cost us a lot more money than the traffic would justify; and secondly, that it was too large for the existing airfields on our routes, whereas a smaller aircraft would be able to use them

Satisfied that we could put sufficient effort into our marketing to fill the seats up to about the break-even situation, we turned our attention to the airfields. A completely new airfield would be required in the vicinity of Mt Cook, right in the mountains, which would be used when the weather was good and when it was not covered in snow; and another one was required forty to eighty kilometres away, out in the Mackenzie Plains, where the weather was very much better, as an alternative.

The airfield at Queenstown required lengthening, but it was controlled by the local airport authority which, although keen to see an airline established there, was short of the necessary funds and not likely to move quickly, if at all. The alternative was Cromwell, about sixty kilometres away, where a completely new airfield would have to be constructed.

In the Te Anau-Manapouri area the only airfield was far too

small and there were no prospects of extending it; here again, a completely new airstrip would be required.

All the airfields would need to be over 1600 metres long, and although situated on flat shingly country would require greater or lesser amounts of work to be done on them. Surveys were made, estimates of the cost obtained, and plans submitted to Air Department for its approval. The Department was fully co-operative and provided a lot of assistance, and in due course work was begun on the airfields at Mt Cook, at Glencairn, just south of Pukaki, at Cromwell, and at Manapouri, with a completion date fixed for the spring of 1961.

Negotiations were carried out with NAC over the purchasing or hire of an aircraft, the secondment of crews, and the use of maintenance facilities. Our old friends, Sir Leonard Isitt and general managers Captain Jack Bush and later Doug Patterson, were fully co-operative, and sold us a DC3 on terms and conditions which were very favourable and would allow us to retire gracefully from the scene if our minimum traffic requirements did not materialise.

Considerable selling had been done in the States, where we expected most of our traffic to originate, and the Government Tourist Department and other agencies gave full support to promoting the service. It got away to a reasonably good start on 1 November 1961 and the loadings were sufficient to cover at least most of our direct operating costs. When the service was suspended, as planned, at the end of the summer season, we took stock of the situation and in the light of experience, tried to assess its future potential.

Certain things stood out. One was that a reasonably high degree of regularity could be maintained. The aircraft could fly down the central areas of the South Island where there was a low rainfall and normally clear skies, and then fly up the wide flat valleys running into the mountains and land at places like the Mt Cook airstrip, in the heart of the Alps, in perfect safety. A second point was the aircraft's ability to fly low down alpine valleys such as the Tasman, when the weather was good, and to weave from side to side to give the passengers such outstanding views of that spectacular country that they had dubbed it 'the world's most scenic airline'.

As well as the highly experienced and competent pilots manning the DC3s, we carried pursers whose job it was to do the documentation, help with loading and unloading the aircraft at wayside points, and generally to look after the passengers in the air. These pursers were put through a training school where, among many other things, they were taught that if passengers were having trouble with their ears during descent, they should tell them to hold their noses and blow as hard as ever they could to clear the eustachian tubes — those small ducts in the inner ear. On one flight, one of the captains was going down the cabin talking to the passengers when he was somewhat startled to hear a purser explain to one of the passengers: 'Madam, if you are having trouble clearing your ears, hold your nose and blow as hard as ever you can, and it will clear your fallopian tubes.'

The old DC3 was ideal for its purpose; it rumbled its way down through the mountains or over their tops in a surprisingly short time, yet it was slow enough and manoeuverable enough to fly low and to follow the valleys when the weather was bad. The airline distances were much shorter than the road distances — 204 kilometres by air as against 349 kilometres by road between Christchurch and Mt Cook, for instance, an air journey of about forty-five minutes as against a bus journey of about six hours. The airline was definitely showing promise, and we decided to continue for another season.

For the next few years traffic growth was spectacular, ranging from approximately 40 per cent to 110 per cent a year, until by 1968 we were operating three DC3s of our own and had to charter another from NAC for quite a bit of the season.

The DC3 had served us faithfully and well, but it was too slow on its cruise and its climb and it lacked a pressurised cabin, so we decided to replace it with a modern turbo-prop aircraft. The Hawker Siddeley 748 was chosen, and the first one, with fifty-two seats, a pressurised cabin, retractable stairs, radar, and many other modern features went into service on 1 November 1967. The financing and purchasing of this aircraft, with a spare engine and other spares costing over $800,000, was in every way a bigger hurdle than the launching of the DC3 service, and it stretched the Company's resources to the utmost limit. Fortunately, traffic continued to expand and the aircraft, which proved particularly suitably for our routes, was soon operating during the summer season almost to capacity. Within three years we realised that a second one would have to be purchased.

In operation, the 748 was found to need only one alteration: it was too crowded as a fifty-two-seater, and was reduced to forty-eight seats, and to forty-four in the winter, when a large number of skis have to be carried.

When the DC3 service was first started we used, as an

alternative to the Mt Cook strip, a strip at Glencairn about twenty kilometres south-east of Pukaki. It was laid out on a long, perfectly flat river-terrace on the banks of the Ohau and was devoid of every facility except for windsock and markers.

Geoff Williams was diverted to Glencairn one day during the early part of the winter when the surface of the ground was frozen, but soft underneath, and which would hold the aircraft or a bus perfectly safely as long as no sharp turns were made or brakes applied too rapidly. Barney Lang, one of our stalwart drivers, was there to meet him, but unfortunately he got his bus badly stuck on the edge of the runway, to Geoff's great annoyance.

Geoff told Barney in no uncertain terms what he thought about his driving and suggested that he should get some driving lessons — and, when entering areas where he was likely to get stuck, should have the sense to use chains.

The bus was dug out and removed from the runway, where it proceeded with its passengers to The Hermitage, while Geoff flew on to Queenstown. On the return from Queenstown, he landed again at Glencairn but unfortunately struck a soft spot and got stuck, with one wheel going down and one wing sticking up in the air at a most undignified angle. Geoff climbed out, made a tour of inspection, and then got on to the radio in the aircraft and called to The Hermitage to send down some manpower, shovels and other equipment to get the aircraft out.

It so happened that Barney Lang was standing next to the radio at The Hermitage and listening, with ill-concealed glee. In due course he asked if he could speak on the radio. He said: 'Bravo Kilo Delta, this is Barney. Have you tried using chains?' There appears to be no record of Geoff's reply.

The HS748 could weave its way down the glaciers as easily as the DC3, as the following comment from the *Christchurch Press* relates:

New Zealand pilots certainly provide their share of thrills for tourists — especially the aerobatics put on as planes approach Mount Cook airport. On a recent flight the Southern Alps were covered in cloud, with only the tops of the peaks poking through.

As the Mount Cook Airlines Hawker Siddeley came in under the cloud to head up the Tasman Valley, one American tourist was impressed with the sheer rock face slipping past, seemingly a few yards away from the port wing. She was advised to look out the starboard side where the opposite cliffs seemed even closer.

'Goodness,' she exclaimed, 'the pilots must be very good. I even have trouble putting the car away.'

Flying out a few days later, another pilot had a gaggle of Japanese agog as he winged over the Tasman glacier and past Mt Cook and Mt Tasman. Miles of film were expended as the plane passed the peaks — close enough, it seemed, for the passengers to be able to reach out and pluck one of the lilies the airline uses as its symbol.

After the 'Fasten Seat Belts' sign went out, our Oriental visitors chattered from side to side, window to window, as the snowcapped peaks slid underneath. One did not know what they were saying but, judging by the smiles, it seems as though they really did have something to tell the folks back home in Yokohama.

Although the airline had the effect of speeding up and increasing the flow of traffic into the South Island resorts, there was still far too great a loss of time between the two major resorts of Rotorua and Mt Cook, and we decided to apply for a licence to fly direct. This was granted and the service began late in 1972, and a year or so later, NAC passed to the Company their licence to operate a direct flight between Rotorua and Christchurch. These two services of nearly 800 kilometres had not only given us much better utilisation of the aircraft, but two much more economic stage-lengths than the very short ones further south. The service was later extended from Rotorua to Auckland, making it possible to leave Auckland at 8am and be at Mt Cook at 10.30, and Queenstown at 11.30, thus achieving what RLW had set out to do in 1921.

Northland and the Bay of Islands are subtropical areas of clear blue seas, sandy beaches, rocky cliffs and bush-covered islands, and have always been popular holiday areas for big-game and other fishing, swimming, yachting, boating, waterskiing and just lazing around enjoying the sun. But the winding roads and lack of good air services have left them comparatively isolated.

With the growing demand from overseas visitors to see more of New Zealand, increased tourist development has been taking place. Spectacular bus trips travel to the extreme north to Cape Reinga, and back along Ninety Mile Beach. Many launch trips are available, and there is a tremendous number of historically interesting places to visit. More and more accommodation has been built each year in the way of motels, and the Tourist Hotel Corporation has an excellent hotel at Waitangi.

A service was operated by the fourteen-seater Grumman Goose for a two-year period, and a test of the market had shown that there would be appreciable demand for a service operated on a proper airline basis with aircraft such as the 748. As well, the local bodies, the local business interests and the local people were keen to see an airline service established into the area, so it was decided that the Company extend its air services from Auckland to the Bay of Islands.

No suitable airfield was available, and a request to the Government to build one was declined on the grounds that it was not prepared to build one for a private operator. This rather contrasted with the Government proposals to take over the strips we had built at Mt Cook and other places in the South Island and, after months of negotiating, we came to the conclusion that if we wanted an airstrip we would have to build it ourselves.

Thanks to the efforts of the Minister of Civil Aviation, the Hon. C. C. A. McLachlan, in response to Mr Corner's persistent negotiating, the Government did, however, agree to lease us land on which the Kerikeri airstrip was to be built, for a period of twenty years, and agreed to take the airport over and pay compensation at the expiry of the lease. This arrangement, which appeared satisfactory to all parties, allowed the strip to be built, and the service began with the HS748s in late 1977, linking the Bay of Islands with Auckland, Rotorua, and all the main tourist resorts of the South Island.

Linking the main tourist and holiday areas of New Zealand, the airline caters to a very large extent for this traffic and is complementary to the trunk services operated by Air New Zealand, with whom we have a good working arrangement to share facilities and the surplus capacity at certain times of the year.

The airline has done a lot to put the isolated South Island resorts — Mt Cook, the Southern Lakes, Fiordland — on the tourist map, and has achieved what RLW set out to do over fifty years ago. It is now an established airline, and its blue-and-white livery, the large mountain lily painted on fins and rudders, are known throughout the world.

Coronet Peak proved its worth in attracting traffic to the airline during the winter, and Ski-Hi package tours were organised to encourage North Islanders particularly, and Australians, to ski there. It was possible for an Aucklander to leave home in the morning, and be on the snow at Coronet Peak soon after 1pm and to enjoy a full afternoon's skiing; on his return next day he could ski hard all morning and be home that night. The number of skiers taking advantage of these packages has increased very rapidly each year, and now the airline is almost fully occupied carrying skiers to Queenstown during July, August and September, carrying traffic without which it could not survive. The number of Ski-Hi passengers during 1977 numbered 4000.

From 1967 onwards traffic continued to grow and a second Hawker Siddeley 748 was purchased, later a third one, and finally a fourth. Each aircraft was flown from England to New Zealand by Company pilots, assisted by a navigator from Hawker Siddeley, and some amusing incidents can be recounted.

On one trip, on arrival at Delhi, Geoff Williams was pleased to be on the ground and was shaking any hands which were proffered until he came across an incredibly ugly character whom he discovered later to be the Agricultural representative. This Ag. rep. was not disposed towards ceasing this hand-shaking, much to the visible and increasing discomfort of Geoff. The Hawker Siddeley navigator could no longer resist the impulse, so he brushed past the enclutched couple, saying, 'Put him down Geoffrey, you don't know where he's been.'

On a later flight commanded by Captain Alistair McLeod with Captain John Thompson, an attempt was made to set a new nonstop record of 1800 statute miles for HS748 aircraft when they flew direct from Darwin to Brisbane. Tension was running high on the flight deck as calculation after recalculation was made to see whether a refuelling stop or a record would be made.

A formal position call to an Australian outback control centre went something like this: 'Long Reach Tower, this is Mt Cook Mike Charlie Alpha.'

No answer.

'Long Reach Tower, this is Mt Cook Mike Charlie Alpha.'

'Mike Charlie Alpha Long Reach ... 'Ang on a minute mate, I'm makin' the tea.'

The thought of some chap having his priorities sorted out relaxed the whole crew.

Some characters flying with the crews of the 748s are typical of tourist people from all over the world and they are often

prone to do a little quiet legpulling — often, unfortunately, to
the discomfiture of their passengers.

One of the pursers about whom many stories have yet to be
told was Davey Bryson, a Welshman. One magnificently fine
day when the aircraft was on its descent to Mt Cook via the
Tasman Glacier, the captain had made his usual spiel about
the age and size of the glaciers and permanent snowfields.
Davey was moving down the aisle assisting passengers to
identify prominent features when his attention was attracted
by an elderly American couple: 'Say, son, is there any wildlife
on this here glacier?'

'Yes, sir,' Dave answered speedily but inaccurately. 'If you
look out there now you can see the Climbers Col, beyond that is
the Franz Josef Glacier, and the Tasman Sea. The polar bears
from Antarctica swim 3000 miles north to the Franz and cross
the Climbers Col to their mating-ground on the Tasman
Glacier below us.'

He left them and continued his progress through the cabin,
no doubt distributing further gems of information. The following day, a ski-plane pilot brought his aircraft and five
passengers to rest on the upper névé of the Tasman Glacier,
and all but two passengers speedily disembarked in order to
savour the splendid views.

When the pilot attempted to extract the elderly American
couple from their seats, he was told firmly: 'No thanks, son, we
can see very well from here. Anyway, we know about bears
back home, and they can be dangerous. But we did bring a bag
of cookies for you to feed them.'

The aircraft have a flexibility to shuttle backwards and
forwards at frequent intervals in the course of a day; they visit
many destinations and carry a large number of people. Typical
was a day in February last, when three HS748s landed at Mt
Cook on scheduled flights from Christchurch or Rotorua, three
from Queenstown, and an additional fifteen flights were made
to Mt Cook with independent parties.

An organisation based in Queenstown with quite wide
ramifications was Tourist Air Travel, the firm resulting from
the merging of Tourist Air Travel of Auckland, West Coast
Airways of the west coast of the South Island, Southern Scenic
Air Services of Queenstown, Ritchie's Air Service of Te Anau,
and Amphibious Airways of Invercargill — all small firms built
up by entrepreneurs who had worked hard to establish their
own specialised types of operation.

Captain Fred Ladd headed Tourist Air Travel in Auckland, a company which operated four five-seater Grumman Widgeon amphibian aircraft from the old TEAL base at Mechanics Bay in Auckland. They serviced the outlying islands of the Hauraki Gulf, did rescue and ambulance work and scenic flights over Auckland, and Fred became a well-known figure around the city and the Gulf. At the other end of the country Jim Monck was operating Amphibian Airways from Invercargill to Stewart Island, servicing lighthouses in Fiordland and carrying a lot of crayfish tails for the many fishing boats operating there.

Ian Ritchie, well known for his aerial-topdressing activities, operated at Te Anau with an eight-seater Dominie aircraft and Cessna 185s, both landplanes and floatplanes. He also did a lot of local flying in Milford Sound and round the fiords, using his floatplanes to carry crayfish tails from Doubtful and other Sounds.

At Queenstown, Southern Scenic Air Services was headed by that well-known character Popeye Lucas, veteran of Bomber Command of the RAF, where he served two tours of duty flying Wellingtons and was awarded the DFC and bar. His story is told in his book *Popeye Lucas*. Southern Scenic operated Dominies on scenic flights to Milford Sound and a scheduled service to Dunedin, as well as carting whitebait out from Big Bay and Martins Bay, and doing a considerable amount of aerial topdressing and rabbit poisoning.

The headquarters of Tourist Air Travel were in Queenstown and were managed by the late Bill Davies. After protracted negotiations which caused some bitterness, TAT was merged with the Mount Cook Company on 31 March 1968.

TAT had five eight-seater DH Dominie biplanes which were getting on in years, the oldest of them having been built about 1935. Made of wood and fabric and with Gypsy Six engines, they were expensive to maintain and, as was to be expected, they did not perform as well as modern aircraft. After the merger they were replaced by Britten-Norman Islanders, high-wing monoplanes carrying nine passengers and equipped with modern engines, constant-speed propellors, and other improvements of the age. Also bought was a twenty-seater turbo-prop Twin Otter to allow us to fly over to Milford Sound on instruments, but this proved a disappointing investment as people would not fly if they could not see and, as we could not get economic utilisation out of it, it was sold.

At Auckland it was intended to replace the five-seater

Widgeons with the fourteen-seater Grumman Goose, which was much more economic, and one was put into service and operated scheduled services to the Bay of Islands, Kawau, Waiheke Island and other places in the Gulf successfully; its economics looked promising.

A second Goose was bought in Miami and, like the first one, it embarked on a delivery flight which was to take it through the USA, to Canada, Iceland, England, Europe, the Middle East, Australia and so to New Zealand. This was a very long flight, and it was necessary to install extra tanks to get it over some of the long ocean crossings. Unfortunately a delivery pilot taking the heavily-laden aircraft off from Wichita Airport in the States stalled it and flew it through some trees, successfully removing the wings, engines and other appendages, and so prematurely ended the delivery.

As we were unable to get another suitable Goose, only a limited number having been built before the war, and as we were losing money on the Widgeons, it was decided that our capital and energies could be more usefully employed elsewhere, and the operation was sold. The aircraft, built of aluminium alloy, were particularly susceptible to corrosion by salt water, making it necessary to rebuild large sections at great expense; this took it out of the air for long periods every year and so seriously reduced its earning capacity.

The amphibian operation was an extremely attractive one, and gave thousands of people the exciting experience of taking off and landing on water. It also provided an excellent service to the people living on the islands and bays in remote districts, where the aircraft could land on water, taxi up on to the beach and disembark its passengers on dry land. We regretted having to sell it.

The operation's new owners are running it in the only possible way for it to survive, as an owner/driver operation, and we wish them every success in their venture.

I have endeavoured to put together an interesting account of the Company's growth and development since that first trip to Mt Cook in the two De Dions in 1906, and I have put the emphasis on the first fifty years or so. The last twenty years have been full of change, mergers and development too, but the Company is now so complex that it would be difficult to crystallise the recent salient points which will, in years to come, achieve historical interest. So I have sketched over these more briefly and will leave it to others who should have a clearer perception of them perhaps thirty years hence, when the organisation will have been going for a hundred years, to cover.

Over the years the Company has employed many people, and space permits us to mention only a few; — those who have stood out because of their special qualities or because they have figured in certain incidents. Inevitably, there are many others whose contribution has been as great but whom we have had to leave out.

The directors have also played an important role in the Company's development. On many occasions they have taken considerable risks in supporting projects that my father ('RLW') or I have put up to them, often without a shred of evidence to say they were viable, and with nothing more than a 'flying by the seat of the pants' feeling that they were right.

Typically, RLW treated a board of directors as a necessary evil forced on him by the Companies Act, and he tended to act first and then, at one of his infrequent board meetings, advise the other directors what he had done. He liked to fill the board with Company executives, relatives or close associates whom he knew would go along with his schemes, but also he did receive a lot of help over the years from people such as J. W. Grant, a brother of my mother's, a member of the Tongariro Hotel Company, and a member of the Mount Cook Board until he retired in 1952.

During its first seventy years the Company has been involved in a wide range of activities that have included: hotel design, construction, ownership and management; skifield development, including the construction and operation of tows and lifts; the carriage of passengers and freight on scheduled motor services; group tours; the inauguration of a rental-car business; the design and construction of undercarriages for ski-planes; scenic flying; and the formation of an airline, flying scheduled and charter services.

Ideally, the history of the Company should be written on a chronological basis; but its activities have been so varied and so complex that the book has had to be divided into five main sections: the Hermitage and Mt Cook area generally; the development of the Coronet Peak skifield; passenger and freight road services, and rental cars; the Company's involvement in hotel enterprises; and finally aviation in three phases — the bold but premature venture of the early 1920s, the renascence of the late 1930s aborted by World War II, and the postwar phase.

To some extent I have had to repeat, but in very condensed form, some of the material given in my earlier book *Ski-plane Adventure*. The present book would have been incomplete without it, and I trust that those who have read the first book will not mind going over the same ground with me again in this one.

To give an indication of the size of the Company today, and as a reference point for future writers, the main statistics are set out below, and the map shows the routes traversed by the Company's coaches and scheduled airlines. Today the Company operates: coaches, trucks, Hawker Siddeley 748 aircraft, topdressing aircraft, ski-planes and rental cars.

Capital $2,438,962
Shareholders' funds $7,169,830
Assets
No. of coaches. . . . . South Island 58, North Island 92
No. of aircraft. . . . . 40 operational
No. of trucks 108
No. of rental cars . . . . . . 107 — Napier
No. of travel offices . . . . New Zealand 12, USA 1
                                         (Los Angeles)
No. of employees 720

By the time this book is published, I expect I shall be retiring from actively managing the Company which I joined nearly fifty years ago. They have been exciting years of change and challenge, years in which more development has taken place in the transport field than ever before. There have been years when many lovable characters have entered the scene and many firm friendships made. Years I can look back on, of opportunities taken and opportunities lost. Periods of frustration and periods of great satisfaction; and if the good Lord clapped me on the shoulder and said: 'If you were given another chance to live those years again, what would you do?', my reply would be, 'I'd do the same all over again!'.

My wife joined me on a permanent basis in September 1939 and has lived beside me through the last forty years of the Company's turbulent development, tempering my enthusiasm with caution, offering solace in periods of frustration, and sharing our moments of triumph; though in the background, she has been involved in no small way and shares much of the credit for what the Company is today. She hopes to join me in the years ahead in watching the prosperity of the Company from a detached distance, and in doing some of the things which we enjoy doing such as tennis, golf, skiing, fishing, and exploring the wilderness areas of New Zealand we both love so much on foot, by jeep and by jetboat.

We shall enjoy sitting back and watching others writing new chapters into the Company's history: new chapters which, when the opportunities are available, will be just as exciting and challenging as those of the past.

H.R.W.

APPENDIX I

The Southern Alps and Aorangi (Mt Cook)

SEVERAL MILLIONS OF YEARS AGO the earth's surface cooled and became cracked and wrinkled, like the skin of a withering apple. Some parts rose to become mountain ranges and some sank beneath the seas.

Water gradually covered the greater part of the Tasman Sea and the Pacific Ocean, leaving New Zealand with its three main islands isolated from the rest of the world by thousands of kilometres of watery wastes. The North Island's mountains are largely the product of erupting volcanoes, while the South is more a chunk of the earth's crust which has been thrust skywards to form a continuous chain of mountain ranges.

The softer parts of these mountain ranges have been whittled away by wind, frost and rain, until only the hard backbone remains, but this backbone, high, steep and rugged, stands defiantly facing the violent storms approaching from the Tasman Sea, and it determines the climate of the South Island.

The large expanses of empty ocean westward of New Zealand encourage the development of storms, which hurl their moisture-laden winds with some fury at the mountain barrier which obstructs their path, causing violent changes in the weather, deluging some areas with rain and snow while desiccating others.

The Southern Alps, as they are called, deflect the winds upwards into the icy cold atmosphere, causing them to deposit their moisture in the form of rain or snow. Westward of the mountains it is not uncommon for the rain to fall at the rate of three centimetres an hour, and to build up to a total of nearly nine metres a year; while eighty kilometres away, after the mountains have done their job of thrashing the last of the moisture out of the winds, the annual rainfall can be as low as twenty-five centimetres.

On the west coast there are subtropical forests with huge

trees; tree-ferns; trees covered with scarlet blossoms, such as the rata; vines; lianas; mosses and lichens, a growth so luxuriant and thick as to be almost impenetrable. To the east of the Alps, it is more like a desert, with predominantly clear skies and low rainfall, and a vegetation which has adapted to the semi-arid conditions.

In between, the high mountains are plastered heavily with ice and snow on any part of their surfaces which is not too steep to allow it to stick.

The depth of ice in many places is enormous. While the rain on the west coast may add up to nine metres a year, it will often fall in the mountains as snow, and on the assumption that three centimetres of rain will equal about thirty centimetres of snow, it will be seen that snowfall on the mountains can amount to some hundreds of metres a year. As more snow falls on top of it, it is compressed, and becomes denser and more icy in character. Its tremendous weight forces it to flow slowly down the mountainsides, where it gradually forms minor glaciers which flow into the larger ones, finally forming giants like the Tasman, which is thirty kilometres long, the best part of three kilometres wide, and often over 500 metres in thickness.

On the west coast these glaciers move rapidly down the mountainsides, twisting and turning over obstructions on their paths: in many places they become torn asunder into wide deep crevasses and, in others, forced skywards into huge pinnacles and séracs. They flow down to within 200 metres of sea-level, through the subtropical forests, the glistening of their white rugged surfaces contrasting with the dark green of the bush.

While the glaciers have smoothed out some parts of the mountains, they have in others accentuated their steepness and ruggedness. Glaciers such as the Tasman and the Murchison have gouged out kilometres-wide courses for themselves while, higher up, small snowfields near the crests of the ranges have, by a process of thawing, freezing and movement, eroded saucer-shape basins called cirques. This erosion, being faster than that of the surrounding peaks and ridges, has accentuated their steepness and ruggedness.

The whole 650-kilometre length of the Southern Alps is rugged, heavily forested in places, and glaciated in others, each in its own way exciting and attractive, but it was the area enclosing the highest peaks which first attracted the attention of the settlers. Aorangi — a beautiful name — was the one by which the highest peak in the area was known to the Maoris. Its height and massiveness so dominate its attendant peaks that it focuses attention on itself from wherever it is seen, whether north, east, south or west. Frequently it is capped by a streamlined lenticular cloud, like an inverted saucer; a standing wave, which indicates that a wind of some velocity is being deflected upwards. At other times its head is in the stratus cloud, hence the name Aorangi — the cloud-piercer.

Surprisingly, Captain Cook in his travels round the New Zealand coast made no mention of seeing Aorangi, probably because it was obscured in cloud when he was in its vicinity. It was not until 1846 that Charles Heaphy and Thomas Brunner, on an exploratory trip down the west coast, recorded its existence, about six years before Captain R. L. Stokes of HMS *Acheron* observed it from off the west coast and called it Mt Cook after the famous navigator and explorer.

Although Aorangi was well known to the Maoris, who often guided the first Europeans through the area, it is surprising that the first mentions of its existence were noted in the west, for here fast-flowing treacherous rivers, which could be swollen in a few hours to many times their normal volume by torrential rain in the Alps, contrasted with the much easier access from the eastern side, flat land extending right into the heart of the Alps.

John McKenzie, the notorious sheepstealer whose name (misspelt) was given to the Mackenzie Country, was probably the first white man to travel through it. He came from the Highlands of Scotland, which he was rumoured to have left rather precipitately after attracting undue attention to himself through certain cattle-stealing activities. He arrived in New Zealand after a period in Australia, where he had learned a lot about the handling of stock and the ways of the settlers in this part of the world. Land for settlement and farming was being taken up throughout the South Island and McKenzie, apparently working for settlers in various parts of the country and probably with a Maori friend, also made some exploration of the hitherto unknown inland areas.

He took up land in Southland and, being a thrifty Scot, decided to make the best use of his profession to stock it. He had a dog whose performances were legendary. This dog, it was said, could work out of sight of its master and, without barking, would silently round up mobs of sheep and bring them to him. When sufficient were gathered together, man, dog and sheep would head through the Mackenzie Pass into the Mackenzie Country, over the Lindis Pass and down the Clutha watershed to the coast. It's probable that he made this trip on three occasions — a tremendous performance when it is remembered that he had to drive his sheep across large, fast-flowing rivers, over high mountain passes and, in many places, through dense tussock and scrub, a trackless wasteland at that time.

In March 1855 he relieved the Rhodes brothers at The Levels station, not far from Timaru, of a thousand sheep, and proceeded to rustle them into the hinterland as quickly as possible; but, unfortunately for him, he was apprehended on the Mackenzie Pass by some of the Rhodes brothers' shepherds, thus ending his professional activities and his exploration of the country. There seems no doubt that he was the first white man to have travelled extensively through this area. A number of settlers took up land in the Mackenzie Country soon afterwards, but it was not until 1862 that Julius von Haast and Arthur Dudley Dobson surveyed the Mt Cook region and estimated the height of Mt Cook itself to be 12,349 feet (4,585 metres).

APPENDIX II

One Enterprise, Several Names

THE NAME OF THE COMPANY has undergone several changes over the years, sometimes to give it a better image when increases in capital have taken place, or when it was thought that it would give a better idea to the travelling public of the sphere of the Company's operations.

The original transport firm from which the later ones developed was the partnership of Wigley & Thornley. The name Mount Cook Motor Service was used when the first service by motor-car was operated from Fairlie to Pukaki in 1906. This firm went bung and RLW took over the assets and formed a new one to operate the routes in 1912 under the name of The Mount Cook Motor Co. Ltd.

In 1928 the capital was increased and the public were invited to buy shares and as it had been involved in buses, aeroplanes, lorries and hotels, it was called The Mount Cook Tourist Company of New Zealand Ltd. This name stayed with it until the mid 1930s when James Grant and other directors considered that the name should be enlarged to indicate more clearly the geographical ramifications of the Company when it was changed to The Mount Cook & Southern Lakes Tourist Company. This had a mixed reception from the public and particularly the staff, who resisted the efforts of the management to make them use it, and who kept up the pressure for many years to have it changed to something more simple. James Grant was proud of the fact that it was his idea and resisted any efforts to get it changed, and on one occasion when this was being debated he asked one member of the staff why he objected to the name so strongly. He said to Mr Grant, 'Have you ever tried to write "Mount Cook & Southern Lakes Tourist Company" with a Post Office pen?'.

Unhandy and all as it was, it did have the effect of discouraging other operators from calling their tours Mount Cook and Southern Lakes tours.

Finally in 1976 when the Company had extended its air and road operations from one end of New Zealand to the other, this name was quite inappropriate and it was reduced to The Mount Cook Group Ltd. This covered the wide range of the activities of the Company, while retaining the Mount Cook part which, complete with the Mt Cook lily symbol, had become so well known throughout New Zealand and overseas.

Now, nearly seventy five years after the first humble beginnings, the Mount Cook part of the name is so firmly established that it is not possible to see the need for further change; but, who knows, if the role of the Company changes, or if its structure changes, its present name could become outdated as well.

APPENDIX III

Family Interests

A NUMBER OF YEARS before she married my paternal grandfather and settled in South Canterbury, my grandmother travelled from Christchurch through the Mackenzie Country to Mt Cook, and her letter of 8 April 1877 to her father describes the trip.

My dear Father,

I dare say before you get this, you will have heard from home that we have got back safely from Mount Cook. We were not there very long as Mr Macfarlane was only able to spare a few days.

We left the Lake early on Wednesday morning and had rather a long ride. We stopped to eat our lunch at a hut on Braemar, which is Mr A. Cox's run, then went on to the nearest house to Mount Cook, which is on a run occupied by some people named Burnett, who came out some years ago. They gave us some tea.

No one else went except the three Macfarlanes and Francie. We started on Monday the 26th, and rode that day to the Kimbells', where we stayed the night. Mrs Meyer was staying there and a Mr Goodwin, who is a cadet there. On Tuesday we rode to Lake Tekapo and stayed the night at the inn there, having lunched at Mr Clulee's at Burke's Pass on our way.

Mr N. Macfarlane met us there. He had started with the gardener and the packhorses before we did and had got the tents ready. We got to the camp about dark. It seemed a very long ride as the last seven miles we did not go out of a walk as we were on the Tasman riverbed. We had fine weather all the way coming up, and the day from the Lake was very hot and clear and the views of the mountains were most grand.

We found our tent very comfortable, although a bit cold.

The next day we all walked on to the Hooker end of the Mueller Glacier. We saw a most wonderful ice cave where the Hooker River runs out from underneath the moraine . . . We went farther than any lady had been before. That day was fine and so was the next when we rode to the foot of the Tasman Glacier. I then climbed up the moraine, on the edge of which we came unexpectedly on four very pretty little lakes. We climbed about over the crevasses but could not get close to much clear ice as you can only get close to it by walking many miles over the moraine and then camping there, which of course we could not do as it would be too cold.

One thing that surprised me very much about the glaciers was that there was so little clear ice and so much broken stone . . . It certainly is very grand and wonderful. I can't think why more people don't go up there as there is a good road the whole way for riding and you can take a vehicle the whole way up.

When we got back to the camp in the evening we found some other people had arrived and pitched their tent. They were two 'globe trotters' of the name of Chamberlain. We found out that they come from Birmingham. They have something to do with the iron trade; their brother was or is an MP and Mayor of Birmingham. They came here on Saturday for the night and we came to the conclusion that they are the most free and easy people we have met for some time. They have a large amount of 'side on'. Do you know them by name or anything about them?

Now I must go back to my trip. The next day was Saturday. Unfortunately it began to rain when we finished breakfast but we were determined not to be stopped by the weather, so we put on our waterproofs and went for a great climb on the Mount Sefton end of the Mueller Glacier. We enjoyed the day very much and had a splendid near view though we could not see Mount Cook as it was lost in cloud.

The next day we left the camp and retraced our steps, only, instead of staying at the Kimbells', we went to Ashwick where Mr MacPherson lives now. Mr and Mrs J. Raine and a Mrs Howley from Timaru and a Mr Dennistoun were staying there. We came back to Albury on Wednesday.

We are going to stay at the Elworthys' next Saturday. We shall most likely stay there about a week and then go home. They live twenty-four miles from here so we are going to ride

over. Gloria is also going. Francie joins me in best wishes to
you,

I remain,
Your affectionate daughter,

Annie Lysaght.

Miss Lysaght of Hawera afterwards became the wife of the
Hon. Thomas H. Wigley, owner of Opuha Gorge station,
South Canterbury.

Notes on names mentioned
The Kimbells: Dr Frederick J. Kimbell owned Three Springs
station. The Kimbell district was named after him
Mrs Meyer: was probably the wife of Charles Meyer, the owner
of Blue Cliffs station. She died in 1878 and the Upper
Otaio church was built as a memorial to her.
Mr Goodwin: afterwards took up a large farm near Kimbell,
where his descendants still live,
Mr Clulee: was the county clerk and engineer of the Mount
Cook Road Board, which later became the Mackenzie
County Council.
Alfred Cox: owned Balmoral and Braemar stations until 1876.
N. Macfarlane: was probably Norman Macfarlane, who man-
aged a number of well-known Canterbury sheep stations.
Andrew Burnett: took up Mt Cook station in 1864. His descen-
dants still own it.
Joseph Chamberlain: father of British politicians Austen and
Neville, was elected Mayor of Birmingham in 1873.
Mr MacPherson: was probably Lachlan MacPherson, who
managed Four Peaks station.
John Raine: was in partnership with his brother, W. Sherwood
Raine, in the ownership of Sherwood Downs station.
Mrs Howley: was the wife of Thomas Howley, clerk of the
Magistrate's Court, Timaru.
J. Dennistoun: was in partnership with Smith and Wallace in the
ownership of Haldon station. Dennistoun afterwards
bought Peel Forest station, which his son still owns.
Edward Elworthy: owned Holme station, which was part of
Pareora station. Members of the Elworthy family still
own part of this station.

Among my grandmother's relics I have also located some
pieces of slate etched, in the script of the period, 'Slate from the

Tasman Glacier, March 30 1877'.

In this letter she claims to have been 'farther than any other lady', but Mrs Leonard Harper, who was probably there in 1873, may have gone as far. However, it is clear that when Annie Lysaght was there, there was no accommodation or other facilities.

I remember so vividly her descriptions of the various glaciers that they visited and the place where they camped, near the present Hermitage, that I was able to locate it exactly on a trip to Mt Cook soon after. The camp was beside a small spring where the fans of the Glencoe and Black Birch creeks meet, and not very far south of the present Mt Cook motels. Around the spring were flat grassy areas with a background of dwarf alpine pines, and not far away were stands of mountain ribbonwood and other shrubs. It was a rather delightful little oasis in the middle of a fairly harsh environment but, alas, it has all been covered by shingle, the result of erosion during the last forty-five years.

Although she states that 'there was a good road the whole way for riding, and you can take a vehicle the whole way up', I do not think that there was any formed road and in fact nothing more than a track made by the movements of stock and the horses and wagons of the local stations. They were certainly no more than tracks winding in and out among hills and creeks, so it was a fairly tough trip as far as these women were concerned.

APPENDIX IV

Directors of the Company

The Directors of the Company immediately before World War II were:

    Mr R.L. Wigley (Chairman)

    Messrs C.D. Elms, C.S. Elms, H. Coxhead,
    J. Campbell, J.G. Smith, A.G. Wigley and W.J. Sim,
    K.C. (Advisory Director), (later Sir Wilfrid Sim, Q.C.).

In 1946 the Directors were:

    Mr H.R. Wigley (Chairman)

    Messrs J.W. Grant, L.R. Jordan, Mrs R.L. Wigley,
    later joined by Messrs A.K. Rollinson, N.A. Keeley
    and later still by Mr R.A. McKenzie, Sir Leonard
    Wright, Mr R.W. Steele, Mr C.O. Marshall and Mr
    D.A. Patterson.

With the merger of the Hawkes Bay Motor Co. Ltd we were joined by Mr G.E. Bisson L.L.B. (now Mr Justice Bisson), Mr A.R. Giles and Mr R.C. Dockery.

    Today, the Board consists of:

    Sir Henry Wigley, KBE, FCIT, FRAeS (Chairman)
    Mr R.W. Steele, B.Com, FCA (Deputy Chairman)
    Mr C.O. Marshall, Mr D.A. Patterson, CBE, FCIT,
    FRAeS, Mr R.S. Odell, BA, Mr A.R. Giles, MCIT,
    Mr R.C. Dockery, Mr R.A. McKenzie, ACA, and Mr
    A.H. Gould.

Group General Manager is Mr P.S. Phillips, M.A.

General Manager Air Division is Mr M.L. Corner, B.Com, ACA.

Company Secretary and General Manager Finance & Tours is Mr T.K. Cherry, B.Com, ACA.

General Manager Land Division is Mr R.R. Forward, AIRTE.

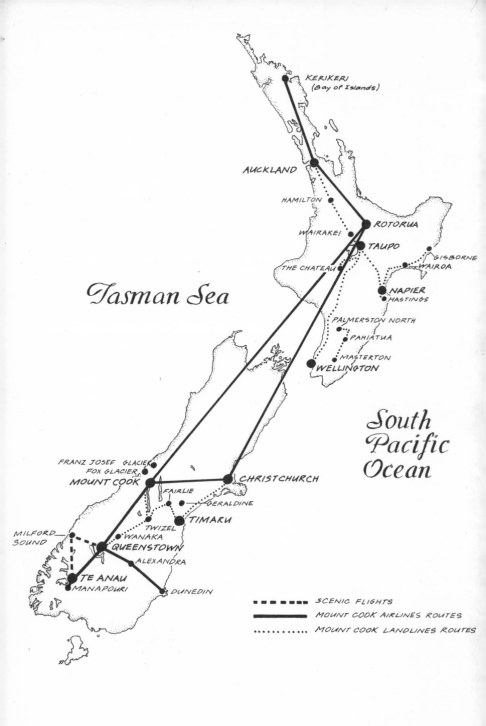